Pediatric Nursing:
Routine to Emergent Care

First Edition

WESTERN® SCHOOLS

By
Nancy J. Wallace, R.N., B.S.

P.O. Box 1930
Brockton, MA 02303
1-800-438-8888

ABOUT THE AUTHOR

Nancy J. Wallace, R.N., B.S., is a West Michigan-based medical writer with four years of medical writing experience and 16 years of clinical experience specializing in pediatric nursing. She is a certified medical writer through the American Medical Writer's Association and is currently pursuing a master's degree in communication at Western Michigan University.

Copy Editor: Jackie Bonham, RN, MSN

Indexer: Sylvia Coates

Typesetter: Kathy Johnson

ISBN: 1-57801-072-1

IMPORTANT: Read these instructions *BEFORE* proceeding!

Enclosed with your course book you will find the FasTrax® answer sheet. Use this form to answer all the final exam questions that appear in this course book. If you are completing more than one course, be sure to write your answers on the appropriate answer sheet. Full instructions and complete grading details are printed on the FasTrax instruction sheet, also enclosed with your order. Please review them before starting. *If you are mailing your answer sheet(s) to Western Schools, we recommend you make a copy as a backup.*

ABOUT THIS COURSE

A "Pretest" is provided with each course to test your current knowledge base regarding the subject matter contained within this course. Your "Final Exam" is a multiple choice examination. **You will find the exam questions at the end of each chapter.** Some smaller hour courses include the exam at the end of the book.

In the event the course has less than 100 questions, leave the remaining answer boxes on the FasTrax answer sheet blank. **Use a black pen to fill in your answer sheet.**

A PASSING SCORE

You must score 70% or better in order to pass this course and receive your Certificate of Completion. Should you fail to achieve the required score, we will send you an additional FasTrax answer sheet so that you may make a second attempt to pass the course. Western Schools will allow you three chances to pass the same course…*at no extra charge!* After three failed attempts to pass the same course, your file will be closed.

RECORDING YOUR HOURS

Please monitor the time it takes to complete this course using the handy log sheet on the other side of this page. See below for transferring study hours to the course evaluation.

COURSE EVALUATIONS

In this course book you will find a short evaluation about the course you are soon to complete. This information is vital to providing the school with feedback on this course. The course evaluation answer section is in the lower right hand corner of the FasTrax answer sheet marked "Evaluation" with answers marked 1–25. Your answers are important to us, please take five minutes to complete the evaluation.

On the back of the FasTrax instruction sheet there is additional space to make any comments about the course, the school, and suggested new curriculum. Please mail the FasTrax instruction sheet, with your comments, back to Western Schools in the envelope provided with your course order.

TRANSFERRING STUDY TIME

Upon completion of the course, transfer the total study time from your log sheet to question #25 in the Course Evaluation. The answers will be in ranges, please choose the proper hour range that best represents your study time. You MUST log your study time under question #25 on the course evaluation.

EXTENSIONS

You have 2 years from the date of enrollment to complete this course. A six (6) month extension may be purchased. If after 30 months from the original enrollment date you do not complete the course, *your file will be closed and no certificate can be issued.*

CHANGE OF ADDRESS?

In the event you have moved during the completion of this course please call our student services department at 1-800-618-1670 and we will update your file.

A GUARANTEE TO WHICH YOU'LL GIVE HIGH HONORS

If any continuing education course fails to meet your expectations or if you are not satisfied in any manner, for any reason, you may return it for an exchange or a refund (less shipping and handling) within 30 days. Software, video and audio courses must be returned unopened.

Thank you for enrolling at Western Schools!

WESTERN SCHOOLS
P.O. Box 1930
Brockton, MA 02303
(800) 438-8888
www.westernschools.com

Pediatric Nursing:
Routine to Emergent Care

WESTERN SCHOOLS
P.O. Box 1930
Brockton, MA 02303

Please use this log to total the number of hours you spend reading the text and taking the final examination (use 50-min hours).

Date	Hours Spent
_____	_____
_____	_____
_____	_____
_____	_____
_____	_____
_____	_____
_____	_____
_____	_____
_____	_____
_____	_____
_____	_____
_____	_____
_____	_____
_____	_____

TOTAL ☐

Please log your study hours with submission of your final exam. To log your study time, fill in the appropriate circle under question 25 of the FasTrax® answer sheet under the "Evaluation" section.

PLEASE LOG YOUR STUDY HOURS WITH SUBMISSION OF YOUR FINAL EXAM. Please choose the answer that represents the total study hours it took you to complete this 30 hour course.

A. less than 25 hours

B. 25–28 hours

C. 29–32 hours

D. greater than 32 hours

Pediatric Nursing: Routine to Emergent Care

WESTERN SCHOOLS
CONTINUING EDUCATION EVALUATION

Instructions: Mark your answers to the following questions with a black pen on the "Evaluation" section of your FasTrax® answer sheet provided with this course. You should not return this sheet. Please use the scale below to rate the following statements:

A Agree Strongly   **C Disagree Somewhat**
B Agree Somewhat   **D Disagree Strongly**

The course content met the following education objectives

1. Recognized the recent changes in pediatric specialty, specified the importance of family and community in Pediatric Nursing, identified the importance and controversy of pediatric ethics and chose appropriate health care promotion and prevention efforts.

2. Recognized the physical manifestations of seizure activity in the pediatric patient and identified appropriate assessment and treatment measures.

3. Recognized the symptoms of upper airway disorders and specified methods to treat them.

4. Recognized how the pathophysiology of asthma has changed over the past two decades and how this relates to the importance of long-term maintenance medications.

5. Recognized pediatric specific nursing considerations for a traumatic head or orthopedic injury and effective methods of pain assessment.

6. Identified harmful household substances and recognized symptoms, treatments and preventive measures of both inhalant and ingestion injuries.

7. Recognized the most common causes of pediatric burn injuries, the significant physiological effects and the potential psychological effects of severe burn injuries, and the important nursing implications of burn wound care and fluid resuscitation.

8. Indicated the prevalence and potentially devastating outcome for drowning and near-drowning victims, identified near-drowning specific pulmonary therapy and potential multisystem complications, and engaged in public education of drowning prevention by describing the prevalence, devastation, high risk factors and preventive measures of submersion accidents.

9. Recognized the significance of child abuse including the prevalence of abuse, consequences for victims, and their relevance to the nursing profession.

10. Recognized effective communication techniques, identified the importance of preventive sexual education and indicated the risks associated with a sexually active adolescent.

11. Identified the risk factors for developing abnormal adolescent psychological behaviors and their potential complications.

12. Identified the prevalence of adolescent violence and drug use and the potential long-term adverse drug effects on adolescents.

13. Recognized pediatric palliative care goals and the appropriate nursing interventions for the chronically ill child in relation to palliative care and gained comfort and instruction on dealing with the parents of the chronically ill child in relation to palliative care.

14. Recognized pediatric palliative care pain management goals and the appropriate nursing interventions for the dying child in relation to pain control and gained comfort and instruction on communicating about death with the dying patient.

15. The content of this course was relevant to the objectives.

16. This offering met my professional education needs.

17. The objectives met the overall purpose/goal of the course.

18. The course was generally well written and the subject matter explained thoroughly? (If no please explain on the back of the FasTrax instruction sheet.)

19. The content of this course was appropriate for home study.

20. The final examination was well written and at an appropriate level for the content of the course.

Please complete the following research questions in order to help us better meet your educational needs. Pick the ONE answer which is most appropriate.

21. What was the SINGLE most important reason you chose this course?
    A. Low price
    B. New or newly revised course
    C. High interest/Required course topic
    D. Number of contact hours needed

22. Where do you work? (If your place of employment is not listed below, please leave this question blank.)
    A. Hospital
    B. Medical clinic/Group practice/ HMO/Office setting
    C. Long term care/Rehabilitation facility/Nursing home
    D. Home health care agency

23. Which field do you specialize in?
    A. Medical/Surgical
    B. Geriatrics
    C. Pediatrics/Neonatal
    D. Other

24. For your last renewal, how many months BEFORE your license expiration date did you order your course materials?
    A. 1–3 months
    B. 4–6 months
    C. 7–12 months
    D. Greater than 12 months

25. **PLEASE LOG YOUR STUDY HOURS WITH SUBMISSION OF YOUR FINAL EXAM.** Please choose which best represents the total study hours it took to complete this 30 hour course.
    A. less than 25 hours
    B. 25–28 hours
    C. 29–32 hours
    D. greater than 32 hours

CONTENTS

PRETEST

Begin by taking the pretest. Compare your answers on the pretest to the answer key (located in the back of the book). Circle those test items that you missed. The pretest answer key indicates the course chapters where the content of that question is discussed. Circle the answers to the pretest questions. Do not log pretest questions on the Faxtrax answer sheet.

Next, read each chapter. Focus special attention on the chapters where you made incorrect answer choices. Exam questions are provided at the end of each chapter so that you can assess your progress and understanding of the material.

1. The most recent focus of pediatric research and treatment is on

    a. infectious disease.
    b. leukemia.
    c. Cystic Fibrosis.
    d. behavior.

2. What type of seizure is most at risk for continued or recurrent seizure activity?

    a. simple partial seizure
    b. prolonged complex seizure
    c. febrile seizure
    d. seizure associated with infection

3. Which of the following is a correct statement about SIDS?

    a. SIDS deaths usually involve children less than one-year-old.
    b. An autopsy usually determines the cause of a SIDS death.
    c. SIDS is a type of child abuse.
    d. SIDS is a type of infanticide.

4. Which of the following statements indicates the prevalence of asthma?

    a. Three million children in the U.S. have asthma.
    b. Preschoolers have the highest incidence of asthma.
    c. Asthma causes one million missed school days every year.
    d. The death rate from asthma has doubled in the last ten years.

5. Because asthma involves chronic inflammation, the maintenance medication of choice is

    a. inhaled glucocorticoids.
    b. oral theophylline.
    c. inhaled cromolyn.
    d. oral steroids.

6. What is the annual prevalence of head injuries?

    a. There are approximately 100,000 concussions each year and over 1,000 head injury victims die each year.

    b. There are approximately 200,000 concussions each year and over 2,000 head injury victims die each year.

    c. There are approximately 300,000 concussions each year and over 3,000 head injury victims die each year.

    d. There are approximately 500,000 concussions each year and over 5,000 head injury victims die each year.

7. Which of the following is an accurate statement regarding concussions?

    a. Concussion injuries are always mild and resolve within a few days.

    b. Concussions involve prolonged manifestation and lengthy recovery.

    c. Concussions can range from mild brief symptoms to prolonged dysfunctional injuries.

    d. A loss of consciousness always occurs with a concussion injury.

8. The most lethal form of salicylate poisoning is

    a. a single dose of 100 mg/kg of adult aspirin.

    b. seven days of dosing at 200 mg/kg of children's aspirin.

    c. a single dose of children's aspirin of 250 mg/kg.

    d. one teaspoonful of an aspirin based liniment.

9. An important diagnostic tool for both inhalation and ingestion injuries is a(n)

    a. colonoscopy.

    b. upper GI.

    c. barium enema.

    d. endoscopy.

10. The primary reason that carbon monoxide causes injury is because carbon monoxide

    a. causes burning of tissues.

    b. replaces oxygen on hemoglobin.

    c. attaches to WBCs.

    d. destroys the immune system.

11. Which activity will protect viable tissues from further injuries for the burn patient?

    a. shearing forces with repositioning

    b. bacterial growth

    c. hypoxia

    d. adequate perfusion

12. Which of the following statements about drowning prevalence is accurate?

    a. About 50% of all pediatric submersion victims are declared dead at the scene.

    b. Caucasians drown more often than African Americans do.

    c. About 40% of submersion victims are more than 4 years old.

    d. Submersion accidents in lakes account for 50% of all submersion accidents.

13. Children with which of the following Glasgow Coma Scale score after submersion typically have good outcomes?

    a. >0

    b. >2

    c. >4

    d. >6

14. Two characteristics of children who are at increased risk of child abuse are

    a. children under the age of five or children with a chronic illness.

    b. an only child or a child born at full term.

    c. an unusually quiet child or a child that plays well alone.

    d. a child raised in a two-parent home or a child with one sibling.

15. Aside from sexual abuse, the percentage of abuse inflicted by parents is

    a. about 25%.

    b. about 50%.

    c. about 75%.

    d. nearly 100%.

16. Emergency contraception

    a. is taken after intercourse to provide one full month of protection.

    b. involves one dose taken less that 24 hours after intercourse.

    c. involves two doses, with the first taken within 72 hours after intercourse.

    d. involves one dose that is taken immediately prior to intercourse.

17. Which of the following is a correct statement about the incidence of eating disorders?

    a. An overweight fifteen year-old who begins to diet in a healthy way is not at high risk for an eating disorder.

    b. Most adolescent females with eating disorders are problem students who have low grades.

    c. About 75% of eating disorders develop during adolescence.

    d. There has been no genetic link associated with eating disorders.

18. Which of the following is a correct statement regarding alcohol in the U.S.?

    a. Legal intoxication in most states is an alcohol level of 0.05%.

    b. There are less than 4,000 deaths related to alcohol every year.

    c. Alcohol levels over 200 mg/dL are potentially fatal.

    d. Alcohol is involved in about 2,000 suicides and homicides each year.

19. What are some communication factors that are appropriate when talking to a dying pediatric patient?

    a. Wait for the child to ask about death, never initiate that kind of conversation.

    b. There may never be a perfect time to talk about death, look for clues that the child is interested in talking about death.

    c. Reassure the child by telling him that he is not really that sick and new treatments may be available soon.

    d. If a child asks if he is dying, change the subject and later tell the mother about the question.

20. The age at which children understand that everyone will die and that death is irreversible is

    a. before the age of 5.

    b. after the age of 6.

    c. age 12.

    d. 15-years-old.

INTRODUCTION

There are many physiological differences between pediatric and adult nursing. This course will focus on those differences and will present the latest information regarding pediatric nursing. Like all areas of nursing, pediatrics is a dynamic specialty with ongoing research and technology that nurses need to learn. This course includes journal reviews for up-to-date information.

Course participants are encouraged to refer to the American Heart Association's Pediatric Advanced Life Support (PALS) for up-to-date information on resuscitation of the pediatric patient. Although some disease specific information is provided, pediatric advanced cardiac life support (ACLS) is not covered in this course.

The goal of this continuing education course is to provide the novice pediatric nurse with an overview of pediatric issues while providing the seasoned pediatric nurse with updated information on disease physiology, treatment measures, and the changing focus of pediatric nursing.

CHAPTER 1

THE CHANGING AND GROWING ROLE OF PEDIATRIC NURSING

CHAPTER OBJECTIVE

After completing this chapter, the reader will be able to recognize the recent changes in the pediatric specialty, specify the importance of family and community in Pediatric Nursing, identify the importance and controversy of pediatric ethics, and choose appropriate health care promotion and prevention efforts.

LEARNING OBJECTIVES

After studying this chapter, the learner will be able to

1. recognize the dynamic process of Pediatric Nursing and recent health care changes.

2. identify the goals of health supervision visits and the inclusion of family, education and community in children's health care.

3. select examples of pediatric ethical issues, competence and paternalism.

4. choose examples of nursing participation in health care promotion and prevention.

THE DYNAMIC PROCESS OF PEDIATRICS

Pediatrics is a dynamic process concerned with the physical, emotional and educational well-being of infants, children and adolescents. Pediatric practitioners have a vested interest in social and environmental issues that have an impact on the health and well-being of children and their families. Children are vulnerable, and their needs are best met through the coordinated efforts of parents and health care providers.

Over 100 years ago, the recognition of illness and treatment differences between children and adults led to the development of pediatrics as a medical specialty (Behrman, 2000). Perinatology and adolescent medicine also became new areas of pediatrics since the 1900s (*The Merck Manual,* 2001a). The scope of pediatrics is dynamic and changes frequently with the introduction of new disease processes and the scientific development of new treatments.

In the late 1900s, 200 children out of every 1,000 were expected to die before the age of one year (Behrman, 2000). Thanks to advancements from pediatricians, scientists and public health officials infant mortality rates have dropped. In the U.S. infant mortality rates have dropped from 75 per 1,000 births in 1925 to 7.2 per 1,000 births in 1996 (Behrman, 2000). Since 1970, the decline in infant mortality rates is in part related to improved treatment of low-birth weight infants.

In 1967, the first pediatric intensive care unit (PICU) in the U.S. was opened in the Children's Hospital of Philadelphia. It consisted of six monitored beds, a procedure room and a small laboratory (Curley & Moloney-Harmon, 2001). Medical training for pediatric intensivists began near the end of the 1970s. In 1985, the American Board of Pediatrics recognized Pediatric Critical Care Medicine as a subspecialty. In 1992, there were 328 PICUs in the U.S., and in 1998, that number rose to 411 (Curley & Moloney-Harmon, 2001).

The introduction of antibacterial and antibiotic agents in the mid-twentieth century profoundly improved control of infectious diseases. Scientific pediatric medicine was then able to focus on other serious or chronic conditions such as leukemia and cystic fibrosis. Recently, there has been a greater focus on behavioral and social aspects of pediatric health such as child rearing, abuse and neglect (Behrman, 2000). In 1996, 26.4% of children under the age of 18 lived with only one parent, and in 1995, 20% of U.S. children lived in poverty. Family income is an important factor in good health maintenance of children. Children from poor families are at a higher risk for poor health, low academic achievement, and violent behavior (Behrman, 2000). Important pediatric goals are the provision of adequate health care for all families, continuity of care from prenatal to adolescence, reduction of accidents and environmental risk, improved health education, and an increase in behavioral science research (Behrman, 2000).

Currently, the leading medical diagnoses for children are asthma, pneumonia, bronchiolitis, fever, gastroenteritis, seizures, croup, apnea and cellulitis (Ponitz, Mortimer & Behrman, 2000). The most common causes of death vary depending on age *(see Table 1-1).*

Hospitalized and critically ill children are just one aspect of the health care continuum (Curley, 2001). Caring for children without regard to their home or their future may interrupt long-term care goals. Nurses need to find a balance that equally values preventive, maintenance, educational, primary, acute and chronic care.

HEALTH CARE PREVENTION AND PROMOTION

Health care cost is one of the motivating factors for improved health care prevention. In 1970, 4% of the gross national product (GNP) was spent on health care (Ponitz et al., 2000). By the 1990s, health care costs had increased to 14% of the GNP. This was caused by unrestricted demand and new expensive technology. The result of these uncontrolled costs was the development of managed care. Managed care led to reduced revenues for hospitals and less support for research. Preventive medicine is an important factor in controlling or reducing health care cost for Americans.

In a period of rapid social change, health care and social services are undergoing profound changes also. Among the rapid changes, promoting health and well being of children is as important as ever (American Academy of Pediatrics [AAP] Committee on Community Health Services, 1999). Pediatric nurses should extend their focus from the children in their practice or on their unit to those in the local community. Family, educational, social, spiritual, economic, environmental and political factors all play a role in the good health of children in the community. Nurses can collaborate with other professionals, agencies and parents to provide optimal health services, especially to those who have limited access to health care. Children's needs are best met in the context of their family and community (AAP, 1999). The focus of some recent health promotion efforts include seat belts, bike helmets, fire prevention, and DARE for drug prevention. Immunizations continue to be an important factor of health prevention. Nurses need to keep updated on changes in immunization schedules and continue parent teaching on the importance of local preventive care. (See Appendix A for a current immunization list.)

TABLE 1-1
Causes of Death at Various Ages

Rank*	Causes	Sub-rank	Rate
	Under 1 Year: All Causes		*875* †
1	Perinatal conditions		
	Intrauterine growth retardation/low birth weight	1	
	Respiratory distress syndrome	2	
	Newborn affected by maternal complications of pregnancy	3	
	Newborn affected by complications of placenta, cord, and membranes	4	
	Infections, perinatal	5	
	Intrauterine hypoxia/birth asphyxia	6	
2	Congenital anomalies		
3	Sudden infant death syndrome		
4	Accidents and adverse events		
5	Infections (respiratory)		
	1–4 Years: All Causes		*38* †
1	Injuries		
2	Congenital anomalies		
3	Malignant neoplasms		
4	Homicide and legal intervention		
5	Diseases of the heart ‡		
6	Respiratory infections		
	5–14 Years: All Causes		*22* †
1	Injuries		
2	Malignant neoplasms		
3	Homicide and legal interventions		
4	Congenital anomalies		
5	Diseases of the heart ‡		
6	Suicide		
	15–24 Years: All Causes		*90* †
1	Injuries		
2	Homicide		
3	Suicide		
4	Malignant neoplasms		
5	Diseases of the heart ‡		

* Adapted from Monthly Vital Statistics Report 46:2, 1997. Rates and rankings are for 1996 (Provisional). Source U.S. National Center for Health Statistics.
† Rate per 100,000 population.
‡ Excludes congenital heart anomalies.

Source: Behrman, R. (2000). *Nelsons textbook of pediatrics* (16th ed.). [Available online: http://home.medconsult.com/das/book/body/18153049/view/873]. Accessed September 18, 2001.

The challenge of preventive pediatric nursing is the integration of effective educational programs into all aspects of nursing care. There will never be an immunization or therapeutic agent that will eradicate the behavioral issues that put children at the greatest risk for injury. Changes in smoking, alcohol, drugs, sexually transmitted diseases (STDs), pregnancy, violence, abuse, unhealthy diets, and lack of exercise will only occur with proactive educational public programs. Cigarette smoking is the most preventable cause of illness in the U.S. Obstetric and pediatric office nurses can reinforce smoking cessation education to new parents. New parents who quit smoking are protecting their child from years of passive smoke exposure and are dramatically reducing their child's risk of starting to smoke as an adolescent. Nurses need to teach parents that 80% of smokers begin smoking before the age of 18. Each reminder of the tobacco related effects of lung cancer, emphysema and heart disease can take a smoker one step closer to quitting.

THE GROWING ROLE OF PEDIATRIC NURSING

Pediatric health care supervision visit guidelines have been issued by the American Academy of Pediatrics (AAP). These supervision visits expand on pediatric health care to include childhood injuries, educational failure, child abuse and neglect, family violence, teen pregnancy, environmental health concerns and substance abuse (Behrman, 2000). Pediatric nurses need to have an increased awareness and skills related to cognitive development, social competence and the family life of pediatric patients. The AAP recommends establishing a therapeutic alliance and collaboration with parents to achieve the optimal health of each patient (Behrman, 2000). Nurses need to understand the individuality of each child within the context of their family, culture, ethnicity, language, socioeconomic status, special health care needs, and educational background.

Empowering families with knowledge provides a greater opportunity for prevention and early disease detection. Parents' participation should include shared responsibility for health care, development of self-esteem, confidence, and competence for each child. Although the role of the nurse has always included a focus on psychosocial aspects of health care, the role of health care providers is changing from healing to the incorporation of education and counseling at even greater levels than in the past. The positive impact of health care becomes evident over a period of years; yet, the positive health care outcome would not occur without the accumulation of multiple brief educational health care encounters. Health supervision visits focus on developmental milestones, parent-child interactions and anticipatory guidance. Nurses should always consider the family perspective when creating a plan of care. Effective nurse-patient communication is an important factor in accomplishing health care goals. Effective communication principles are essential in improving education and counseling of patients and their families.

Effective communication techniques for nurses:

- Show respect and empathy, which will help to create a trusting relationship.

- Engage in active listening with both patients and their parents;

- Remain nonjudgmental in all responses to patient questions;

- Use open-ended questions to increase patient participation;

- Use positive reinforcements to improve patient self-esteem and self-confidence; and

- Engage children in conversations independently from their parents (Behrman, 2000).

Group well-child-care sessions are 45-minute sessions that are held for parents with the goal of improving parental education. Age appropriate topics are discussed. Sessions for new parents would cover newborn care; parents of toddlers could learn toilet-training tips; and parents and adolescents could learn practical ways to avoid substance abuse. These sessions allow observation of parent/child interactions and allow time for child-rearing questions. Handouts, brochures, and web site addresses are helpful supplements to office visits. (See Appendix B for a helpful web site list.)

PEDIATRIC ETHICS

There are many issues in medical ethics, but the ethical issues that frequently involve children are competence, paternalism, trust and confidentiality (Behrman, 2000). Changes in scientific research and improved technology create new and more complex ethical issues.

Competence

Competent patients have the right to make their own health care decisions including the refusal of life prolonging treatments (Behrman, 2000). Adolescents and sometimes even younger children are capable of such decisions. The definition of competence is when the patient is able to understand the possible consequences of their decisions and is aware of all alternative treatment options. Pediatric issues of competence are complicated when the patient and parental treatment preferences are different.

Complications may also occur if a patient chooses withdrawal of life prolonging treatments or chooses to refuse life saving treatment against the physician's advice. For example, a 17-year-old girl was diagnosed with sarcoma of her left ankle and lower leg. She was a beautiful girl, and her appearance was a very important factor in her life. Her self-esteem and self-confidence revolved around her physical appearance. When her physician told her that the only curative treatment for her condition was amputation, she immediately and adamantly refused the treatment. The benefits and risks were thoroughly explained to both the patient and her mother. It was clear that this was the only treatment course available and that refusing treatment would almost surely mean disease progression and death. The mother chose to support her daughter's decision and also refused the amputation. It was not long before this patient developed metastasis and died (Stafford, 2001). It seems incredulous that anyone would risk their life over their appearance or the loss of a leg, but this scenario surely demonstrates the reality that end-of-life wishes are so completely subjective that others cannot possibly predict the desires of another person.

Paternalism

Paternalism is the interference of another person's preferences for his or her own benefit (Behrman, 2000). This has been considered standard practice for parents, although it is questioned with regard to competent children and adolescents. Paternalism is typically justified when there is a high risk of serious harm without treatment, and it is assumed that the patient would appreciate the treatment later on. Many treatments for children are based on this view of paternalism. This area of ethics becomes more complicated as children become sicker, older and more knowledgeable about their disease process.

In the preceding case report, the physician would certainly have supported the mother if she had chosen to go against her daughter's decision and request the amputation. Although the patient and parents have a right to choose to receive or hold treatments, if a parent's decision to withhold treatment appears negligent or not in the child's best interest, legal intervention may be required. Enactment of child abuse laws dictates that society has a responsibility to protect children from harm.

The Baby Doe dilemma in 1982 initiated a change in laws regarding medical treatment of handicapped children (Behrman, 2000). In the case of Baby Doe, the parents of a Down Syndrome baby with esophageal atresia allowed their baby to die at six days old (Behrman, 2000). There were several similar cases that involved Down Syndrome babies or babies with spina bifida. These children had a good prognosis for a long happy life, and the courts ruled that the parents were not acting in the child's best interest. Regulations were made under the child abuse laws that prohibited the withholding of treatment just because a child may suffer a handicap regardless of the severity (Behrman, 2000). Following this ruling there was a shift toward over-treatment. Hospitals have developed ethics committees to provide guidance in decision making when complex cases arise. Physicians have never been found liable for withholding or withdrawing treatment for any reason (Behrman, 2000).

Truth and Confidentiality

Telling the truth is a requisite of good patient care. Lying or an intentional omission of information is a failure to follow this ethical principle (Behrman, 2000). Omissions should never be used to manipulate a patient's acceptance of treatment. Confidentiality is another ethical issue, and it is based on trust. Without the patient's trust in confidentiality, there would be a lack of disclosure by the patient that could hinder health care delivery (Behrman, 2000). For example, a pregnant teen may not admit her pregnancy if she felt threatened by her parents finding out. Exceptions to confidentiality involve circumstances that may cause serious physical harm to others and that harm is likely to be prevented by disclosure of information.

CONCLUSION

Pediatric nurses are challenged to keep up, not only with new scientific research and technology, but they are also expected to expand beyond bed baths, pain medication and dressing changes to address the emotional, behavioral and family needs of every patient. In addition to assessing for stable family environments and making referrals for psychiatric or financial needs, nurses are asked to become proactive within their community and support political issues to promote pediatric health for both living children and for those who are dying. It may seem overwhelming to consider all the potential responsibilities while dealing with managed care, early discharges, nursing shortages and mandatory overtime (Curley & Moloney-Harmon, 2001). Looking at the big picture the goals can certainly seem insurmountable; however, nurses will not only persevere but will rise to meet the growing challenges just as they always have — one patient and one crisis at a time.

EXAM QUESTIONS

CHAPTER 1
Questions 1–3

1. The expanded role of pediatric health care means

   a. collaboration with parents is only necessary for chronically ill children.

   b. pediatric nurses should focus on illness and wellness, not social issues.

   c. pediatric nurses should consider each patient in the context of their family.

   d. only parents should be concerned with discipline and behavioral issues.

2. Which of the following is accurate regarding pediatric ethical issues of competence and paternalism?

   a. A 17-year-old girl and her mother do not have the right to refuse life saving treatments.

   b. Parents have the right to seek life saving treatment for their child against the child's wishes.

   c. The legal system is never involved in the issues of refused life-prolonging treatments.

   d. No one under the age of 18 has any rights with regard to treatment decisions.

3. Which of the following statements represents nurses' involvement in health care promotion and prevention?

   a. Nursing preventive health is limited to office or hospital patients.

   b. Nurses have no political voice and need not get involved in political issues.

   c. Nurses can initiate parent education about smoking cessation.

   d. Providing families with health care information only exacerbates their stress.

CHAPTER 2

SEIZURES

CHAPTER OBJECTIVE

After completing this chapter, the reader will be able to recognize the physical manifestations of seizure activity in the pediatric patient and identify appropriate assessment and treatment measures.

LEARNING OBJECTIVES

After studying this chapter, the learner will be able to

1. specify the time period when a child is at the greatest risk for seizure recurrence.

2. identify treatment methods for new onset pediatric seizures.

3. indicate the factors that put a pediatric patient at increased risk for developing epilepsy or recurrent seizures.

4. differentiate between a partial, complex and absence seizure.

INTRODUCTION

There are many classifications of seizures and many syndromes with seizures. The focus of this section is to review the most common physical manifestations of seizure activity that nurses will need to be able to recognize in the pediatric patient. Although the topic of epilepsy is

not fully covered in this course, the definition and risk factors for developing epilepsy are discussed.

Seizures or convulsions are a sudden involuntary disturbance of brain function manifested as a change in consciousness, abnormal motor activity, behavioral abnormalities, sensory disturbances or autonomic dysfunction. The type of seizure activity that occurs is related to the part of the brain that has malfunctioned (Whaley & Wong, 1999). Seizure is not a diagnosis; it is a symptom of a central nervous system (CNS) disorder (Behrman, 2000). Some types of seizure may be inherited.

Epilepsy involves recurrent seizures that are not related to a fever or an acute cerebral insult (Behrman, 2000). Both epilepsy and seizures may develop initially in association with a viral illness. Seizures frequently occur in the early morning hours and are associated with drowsiness. Epileptic seizures are often preceded by auras that can be described as mood swings, headaches or personality changes. These auras may begin as early as several days before the seizure occurs. Sometimes parents can predict an epileptic seizure based on their child's behavioral changes.

There are 150,000 new onset seizures every year. Approximately 30,000 of these will be diagnosed as epilepsy (McAbee & Wark, 2000). Seizures occur most often in children under two years old. Most seizures in this age group are from known causes at birth such as trauma, hemorrhage, anoxia, congenital defects, or infection. When seizures occur over the age of three, the cause is most often epilepsy.

It is important to determine the type of seizure in order to initiate the appropriate treatment and to help learn the cause of the seizure. Determining the type of seizure can be difficult because the clinical manifestations of different types of seizures are so similar. The majority of seizures are idiopathic (Whaley & Wong, 1999). Although the cause is often not known, some possible causes are related to genetic factors, congenital defects, or a familial tendency toward febrile seizures. If the cause of a seizure is not known, it is often referred to as idiopathic epilepsy. Some causes of seizure activity are known. Seizures can occur following traumatic brain injury, hypoxia, infections, toxins, hypoglycemia or hypocalcemia.

SIMPLE PARTIAL SEIZURES (SPS)

Partial seizures are the most common type of childhood seizures, comprising 40% of childhood seizures. Partial seizures may be simple or complex. In a simple seizure consciousness remains intact, whereas with a complex seizure consciousness is impaired. Movements in SPS are asynchronous, clonic or tonic. Movements involve the neck and extremities. These seizures may include head turning and eye movements. There may be an aura such as chest pain, headache or a "funny" feeling. The average SPS lasts for 10 to 20 seconds. Patients are conscious and may even verbalize during the seizure. No postictal state follows the seizure. SPS may be confused with tics; however, tics can be briefly suppressed whereas partial seizures cannot (Behrman, 2000).

COMPLEX PARTIAL SEIZURES (CPS)

Complex seizures are prolonged, repetitive, focal or a combination of these. CPS may occur with or without an aura. An aura may involve a vague unpleasant feeling, epigastric pain, or fear. The presence of an aura indicates a focal onset of the seizure. A change in consciousness may occur at the onset or during the seizure. A decrease in consciousness in infants and young children may be difficult to determine. Signs of a change in consciousness can vary from a blank stare to a sudden pause in activity or lack of responsiveness. Automatisms are repetitious behaviors that are seen in 50–75% of CPS (Behrman, 2000). Automatisms are seen more often in older children. In an older child, movements of automatism appear semi-purposeful or uncoordinated. Some examples are picking and pulling at clothing or sheets, rubbing or caressing objects, or running or walking without direction in a repetitive and fearful way. Tonic-clonic activity may also be seen in the extremities or face. An example of facial tonic-clonic activity is eye blinking. Automatisms in infancy are similar to normal infant behavior, so they may not always be recognized as seizure activity. Typical automatisms in infancy include lip smacking, chewing, swallowing and excessive salivation. Nursing documentation of all repetitive or suspicious movements can help determine a diagnosis. The average duration of CPS is one to two minutes. CPS is significantly longer than SPS (Behrman, 2000) (*see Table 2-1*).

GENERALIZED SEIZURES

Absence Seizures

Absence or petite mal seizures involve a sudden stop of motor activity or speech, followed by a blank expression and flickering of the eyelids. This type of seizure is more

TABLE 2-1
Comparison of Simple Partial, Complex Partial and Absence Seizures

Clinical Manifestations	Simple Partial	Complex Partial	Absence
Age of onset	Any age	Uncommon before age 3 years	Uncommon before age 3 years
Frequency (per day)	Variable	Rarely over 1–2 times	Multiple
Duration	Usually less than 30 seconds	Usually over 60 seconds, rarely less than 10 seconds	Usually less than 15 seconds rarely more than 30 seconds
Aura	May be sole manifestation of seizure	Frequently	Never
Impaired consciousness	Never	Always	Always, brief loss of consciousness
Automatisms	No	Frequently	Frequently
Clonic movements	Frequently	Occasionally	Occasionally
Postictal impairment	Rare	Frequently	Never
Mental disorientation	Rare	Common	Unusual

Source: Whaley L. & Wong, D. (1999). *Nursing care of infants and children.* St. Louis: The Mosby Company.

common after the age of five and is seen more often in girls than in boys (Behrman, 2000). There is rarely an aura, and the absence seizure lasts only 30 seconds. There is no postictal state. There may be several seizures in one day. There is no loss of muscle tone; however, the head may fall forward. Immediately after the seizure patients resume their previous activity. Automatic behaviors may be seen. Hyperventilation can elicit an absence seizure. A more complex version of an absence seizure can include myoclonic movements of the face, fingers, or extremities and a loss of body tone (Behrman, 2000).

Tonic-Clonic Seizures

Tonic-clonic seizures are very common and may follow a partial seizure. Tonic-clonic seizures may be associated with an aura. A description of the aura may assist in determining the cause of the seizure. Loss of consciousness occurs suddenly. There may be a shrill piercing cry, and the eyes often roll back. Tonic-clonic contractions occur, and apnea and cyanosis may be seen. The seizure will last for a few minutes, and there is often a sigh as it ends abruptly. Children may inadvertently bite

their tongue during a seizure, but they rarely vomit. There may be incontinence of urine. Anything tight around the neck should be loosened. Slight hyperextension of the neck and jaw will prevent airway obstruction. Nurses should not try to remove anything from the mouth of a seizing child. Postictal status is often a semicomatose state. There may be vomiting or headache after the seizure ends. The child may sleep for a period of 30 minutes or up to two hours. Possible causes of tonic-clonic seizures are low-grade fever, infections, fatigue, stress, or medications (Behrman, 2000).

Febrile Seizures

Febrile convulsions and febrile seizures are the same thing. Febrile seizures occur in neurologically healthy children between the ages of six-months and five-years-old. There may be a genetic predisposition for febrile seizures. Seizures usually develop with a fever over 39°C (102.2°F). Most febrile seizures are tonic-clonic, tonic or clonic, or, rarely, atonic. Febrile seizures usually last from a few seconds up to ten minutes. They do not reoccur within 24-hours, and there is no postictal neurological abnormalities. Febrile seizures rarely lead to epilepsy. They usually resolve without treatment and typically have a good outcome. Febrile seizures are common in pediatric patients. Approximately 3% of young children experience ferbile seizures, and of those 50% will recur (Behrman, 2000).

Febrile seizures occur without intracranial infection or a defined cause. They usually occur without a prior history of afebrile seizures. A seizure and a fever may coexist and lead to a diagnosis of an acute infectious disease such as sepsis or bacterial meningitis. However, a febrile seizure is distinguished as a seizure with a fever, not a seizure with meningitis, encephalitis, cerebral malaria, neurological disorders, or mental retardation. In other words, a febrile seizure has no known cause for the fever and no known cause for the seizure (Knudsen, 2000). A lumbar puncture may be done to rule out meningitis. Viral upper airway infections, Roseola, and Otitis Media are the most common causes of seizures with fevers (Behrman, 2000).

Complex febrile seizures are focal, prolonged, recur within 24-hours, or are associated with postictal neurological abnormalities such as Todd's paresis (Knudsen, 2000). A complex seizure may last more than 30 minutes, either as one long seizure or several short ones, without regaining consciousness between seizures (Knudsen, 2000).

Neonatal Seizures

Neonates have a higher risk of seizure than any other age group. Seizure incidence for neonates is between one and five per 1,000 births. A ten-year study at the West Virginia University Children's Hospital showed that neonates between 30 to 34 weeks gestation have the lowest neonatal risk of seizures. Neonates of 30 weeks gestation or less have a 11.9% risk of seizure, and neonates over 36 weeks gestation have a risk of 14.1% (Sheth, Hobbs & Mulett, 1999). Fifty-one percent of all neonatal seizures are associated with a coexisting

neurological disorder. Infants who experience a seizure and have a history of a neurological problem are two times more likely to die. In the West Virginia University Children's Hospital study the overall mortality rate for infants with seizures was 19% (Sheth et al., 1999). The most common etiology for early neonatal seizures in this study was intracranial hemorrhage. For neonates close to term, the cause of seizure was often hypoxic ischemic encephalopathy (Sheth et al., 1999).

Neonates are at a greater risk of seizure because they are more prone to metabolic, toxic and infectious diseases than any other age groups. Because of incomplete neurological development, tonic-clonic seizures do not occur in the first month of life. Neonatal seizures are manifested in five different ways: Focal, multifocal, tonic, myoclonic and subtle. Seizures may be difficult to detect in the neonate. Tachycardia and increased blood pressure are often seen with seizures. Another distinguishing factor is that true seizures can not be suppressed by gentle restraint. The most common cause of seizures is hypoxic-ischemic encephalopathy. Other possible causes include metabolic, infectious, traumatic, structural, hemorrhagic, embolic or maternal disturbances in the neonate (Behrman, 2000).

STATUS EPILEPTICUS

Status Epilepticus is a continuous seizure that lasts for more than 30 minutes or a series of seizures without regained consciousness in between them. Nursing priorities include maintaining an adequate airway, administering oxygen, providing IV hydration, and IV diazepam, phenobarbital or Ativan®. (Rectal diazepam is safe, simple and effective.) A loading dose of phenytoin will be needed. Seizure medications may cause respiratory depression. Close observation is necessary to determine the need for intubation and ventilation (Whaley & Wong, 1999). If seizure activity persists, paralytic agents such as curare may be considered. Although paralytics stop the physical seizure activity, seizure activity may still be evident on an EEG.

Status epilepticus is a medical emergency and requires immediate intervention in order to prevent brain injury or death. Accurately diagnosing the cause of the seizure will assist in providing the appropriate treatment.

DIAGNOSIS

Nurses can assist with diagnosing by obtaining a complete history including behaviors that were observed before the seizure began. The most common auras for children are epigastric pain or fear. A detailed description of the seizure is helpful in making a diagnosis. Nurses can ask parents if the seizure was focal or generalized. Parents can often describe the seizure in great detail and may even act out the seizure with accuracy. A description of the postictal state, such as sleep or headache, can also be helpful. Nurses are also responsible for documenting the duration of the seizure, the status of consciousness, the presence of cyanosis and the occurrence of incontinence. The child's blood pressure, head circumference and weight are obtained. The weight and head circumference can be plotted on a growth chart. A neurological examination is a very important diagnostic tool. Blood work following a seizure is not routinely done. However, blood work may be done to determine the cause of a fever, especially if there are symptoms that suggest otitis media or gastrointeritis (Duffner & Baumann, 1999). Possible lab work may include fasting glucose, calcium, magnesium, electrolytes and blood urea nitrogen (Behrman, 2000).

Lumbar Puncture (LP)

A child less than 18-months-old with a febrile seizure should have a lumbar puncture to rule out

meningitis. Children in this age group are at a higher risk of meningeal infection, and they may exhibit subtle meningeal symptoms or no symptoms at all (Duffner & Baumann, 1999). Children older than 18-months should have a lumbar puncture if their history suggests infection or if there are clinical symptoms of meningitis such as a stiff neck, or a positive Kernig or Brudzinski sign (Duffner & Baumann, 1999). If the seizure is related to an infectious process, subarachnoid hemorrhage, or a demyelinating disorder, cerebral spinal fluid should always be tested.

Electroencephalogram (EEG)

In a retrospective study of children with seizures, it was noted that only 8.6% of seizures were caused by an abnormality. Therefore, the use of routine EEGs for all new onset simple febrile seizures or complex febrile seizures in healthy children is not recommended (Maytal, Steele, Eviatar & Novak, 2000; Duffner & Baumann, 1999). The American Academy of Pediatrics agrees that EEGs should not be done routinely for simple febrile seizures in healthy children.

A postictal EEG should be considered for suspicion of cerebral pathology, developmental delay, prior neurological impairment; or prolonged or focal seizures followed by residual neurological symptoms (Maytal et al., 2000). A follow-up EEG should be done for all children with complex febrile seizures who return with nonfebrile seizures; with febrile seizures and developmental delay; or abnormal neurological exam (Maytal et al., 2000).

Computed Tomography (CT SCAN)

Another study looked at the need for routine CT scans for new onset seizures. A one-year retrospective study showed that for new onset febrile seizures 78.8% of patients have a normal CT scan. Therefore, the routine use of CT scan is not recommended for the first febrile seizure in a healthy child. The risk of sedation, radiation and adverse events from contrast dye are greater than the potential benefits (Maytal et al., 2000; Duffner & Baumann, 1999). Computed tomography and magnetic resonance imaging should be done for the following conditions:

- Suspected intracranial lesions;
- Complex partial seizures;
- Focal neurologic signs associated with a seizure;
- A change in seizure patterns;
- A change in mental status;
- Signs of increased intracranial pressure;
- Trauma; or
- The first seizure in any adolescent patient (Behrman, 2000).

TREATMENT

Seizures should always be considered a pediatric emergency (see *Table 2-2*). There are four possible treatment strategies. In some cases there is a clear need for immediate treatment of an ongoing seizure. In the past long-term prophylactic anticonvulsants were given routinely. For nonepileptic seizures, long-term treatment was replaced with intermittent prophylaxis. Recent studies show that the benefits of intermittent and long-term treatment for febrile seizures in healthy children frequently do not outweigh the risks. Several sources recommend no treatment for a febrile seizure in a healthy child.

Nursing Assessment

Although witnessing a seizure momentarily paralyzes most nurses, nurses need to think fast in order to respond appropriately. While assessing for an open airway and preventing injury to the patient, nurses need to make a mental note of the physical activity that is occurring (Whaley & Wong, 1999). Remember what body parts are involved, what type of movements occurred, check for changes in

the face or eyes, note what time it started and stopped, watch for apnea and cyanosis, then observe the postictal activity when the seizure ends (see *Table 2-3*). Although all these observations are important, airway and oxygenation remain the top priority.

Immediate Treatment

Treatment with anticonvulsants should be given for infants with seizures caused by hypoxic-ischemic encephalopathy or acute intracranial bleed (Behrman, 2000). Focal seizures, prolonged seizures, or seizure activity under one year old may require immediate medication (Whaley & Wong, 1999). Rectal diazepam (DZP) is recommended for an ongoing pediatric seizure. A rectal tube with liquid DZP is safe, and absorption is rapid. The drug reaches the brain within minutes (Knudsen, 2000). Rectal dosing is almost as effective as intravenous medication and is a safe, simple and cost effective method of treatment. DZP rectal gel is available in the U.S. and is a good choice for children. This method is practical for both professional and non-professional use, in the home or in the hospital, and can help to decrease doctor visits. When treated with rectal DZP, most seizures will stop within two minutes.

Another choice is short-term treatment of ongoing febrile seizures with benzodiazepenes. An intravenous route is the first choice in immediate situations; although this route is often not effective in small children.

Long-Term Treatment

Daily phenobarbital prophylaxis is universally considered a poor choice. This treatment may not be effective, and there is a significant risk of adverse effects. The benefits do not usually outweigh the risks. Adverse events include drowsiness, aggression, hyperactivity, inattention or hepatotoxicity. These effects could be a large price to pay for a benign condition (Knudsen, 2000; Camfield & Camfield, 2000).

TABLE 2-2
Emergency Treatment

TONIC-CLONIC SEIZURE
During the Seizure
Time seizure episode.
Approach calmly.
If child is standing or seated, ease child down to the floor. Place pillow or folded blanket under child's head. If no bedding is available, place own hands under child's head.
Loosen restrictive clothing.
Remove eye glasses.
Clear area of any hazards or hard objects.
Allow seizure to end without interference.
If vomiting occurs, try to turn child to one side as a unit.
Do not:
    Attempt to restrain child or use force.
    Put anything in child's mouth
    Give any food or liquids
After the Seizure
Time postictal period.
Check for breathing. Check position of head and tongue.
    Reposition if head is hyperextended. If breathing is not present, give rescue breathing and call EMS.
Check around mouth for evidence of burns or suspicious substances that might indicate poisoning.
Keep child on side.
Remain with child until full recovery.
Do not give food or liquids until fully alert and swallowing reflex has returned.
Call EMS when necessary.
Look for medical identification and determine what factors occurred before onset of seizure and which may have been triggering factors.
Check head and body for possible injuries and fractures.
    Check inside of mouth to see if tongue or lips have been bitten.
COMPLEX PARTIAL SEIZURE
During the Seizure
Do not restrain unless in danger.
Remove harmful objects from path.
Redirect to safe area.
Do not agitate; instead, talk in calm, reassuring manner.
Do not expect child to follow instructions.
Watch to see if seizure generalizes.
After the Seizure
Stay with child and reassure until fully conscious.
CALL EMERGENCY MEDICAL SERVICE IF:
Child stops breathing.
There is evidence of injury or youngster is diabetic or pregnant.
Seizure lasts for more than 5 minutes (unless duration of seizure is typically longer than 5 minutes) and written medical order is present.
Status epilepticus occurs.
Pupils are not equal after seizure.
Child vomits continuously 30 minutes after seizure has ended (sign of possible acute problem).
Child cannot be awakened and is unresponsive to pain after seizure has ended.
Seizure occurs in water (shock and aspiration may be delayed).
This is child's first seizure.

Modified from *Seizure recognition and first aid,* Landover, MD, 1989, Epilepsy Foundation of America.

Source: Whaley L. & Wong, D. (1999). *Nursing care of infants and children.* St. Louis: The Mosby Company.

TABLE 2-3
General Observations: The Child During a Seizure

OBSERVE SEIZURE

Describe

Only what is actually observed

Order of events (before, during and after)

Duration of seizure

  Tonic-clonic—from first signs of event until jerking
    stops

  Absence—from loss of consciousness until regains con-
    sciousness

  Complex partial—from first sign of unresponsiveness,
    motor activity, automatisms until there are signs of
    responsiveness to environment

Onset

Time of onset

Significant preseizure precipitating events—bright lights,
  noise, excitement, emotional outbursts

Behavior

  Change in facial expression, such as for fear

  Cry or other sound

  Stereotypic or automatous movements

  Random activity (wandering)

Position of eyes, head, body, extremities

  Unilateral or bilateral posturing of one or more
    extremities

  Body deviation to side

Movement

Change of position, if any

Site of commencement—head, thumb, mouth, generalized

Tonic phase, if present—length, parts of body involved

Clonic phase—twitching or jerking movements, parts of
  body involved, sequence of parts involved, generalized,
  change in character of movements

Lack of movement or muscle tone of body part or entire
  body

Face

Color change—pallor, cyanosis, flushing

Perspiration

Mouth—position, deviating to one side, teeth clenched,
  tongue bitten, frothing at mouth, flecks of blood or
  bleeding

Lack of expression

Eyes

Position—straight ahead, deviation upward, deviation
  outward, conjugate or divergent

Pupils (if able to assess)—change in size, equality, reaction to light and accommodation

Respiratory Effort

Presence and length of apnea

Presence of stertor

Other

Involuntary urination

Involuntary defecation

OBSERVE POSTICTALLY

Duration of postictal period

Method of termination

State of consciousness—unresponsiveness, drowsiness,
  confusion

Orientation to time, persons, etc.

Sleeping but able to be aroused

Motor ability

  Any change in motor power

  Ability to move all extremities

  Any paresis or weakness

  Ability to whistle (if appropriate to age)

Speech—changes, peculiarities, type and extent of any
  difficulties

Sensations

  Complaint of discomfort or pain

  Any sensory impairment of hearing, vision

  Recollection of preseizure sensations, warning of attack

  Awareness that attack was beginning

Recall of words spoken to child by observer during
  seizure

Source: Whaley L. & Wong, D. (1999). *Nursing care of infants and children.* St. Louis: The Mosby Company.

Intermittent Prophylactic Treatment

Intermittent prophylactic diazepam can be given orally at the start of a fever before a seizure occurs. This is a safe and effective treatment for febrile seizures. Diazepam has been used extensively in Europe and Japan for over 20 years. In Denmark, only two patients out of 30,000 who were treated with this method were found to have benign respiratory problems. There were no long-term sequelae or fatalities reported (Knudsen, 2000). If sufficient doses are given, this seems to be effective in decreasing the recurrence rate. Adverse effects of diazepam may include lethargy, irritability and ataxia. These adverse effects may subside with dose reduction (Behrman, 2000). Low risk children should be left untreated.

Studies show that antipyretic treatment for febrile episodes does not decrease the recurrence rate of seizures. However, antipyretic agents may be given as a comfort measure (Knudsen, 2000; Duffner & Baumann, 1999).

No Treatment

From 4–10% of all children have an unprovoked seizure without recurrence (McAbee & Wark, 2000). Most seizures stop spontaneously within two minutes and do not require treatment (Knudsen, 2000). Anticonvulsants are not effective for febrile seizures and have potential adverse effects (Behrman, 2000). Duffner and Baumann (1999) note that neither continuous nor intermittent treatment with anticonvulsants are recommended for a child with simple febrile seizures. Nurses can provide support and education to reduce parental anxiety. Parents may not understand that the risks of seizure treatment often outweigh the benefits (Duffner & Baumann, 1999).

Parent Education

Parental attitudes regarding seizure activity varies. Many parents feel guilty or anxious. Some may feel humiliated. Often parents are concerned about cognitive development. Parents always need reassurance about what remains normal about their child. Supportive nurses may need to explain more than one time that seizures will not shorten the life span of a child. Children with seizures can resume most normal activities. Children with epilepsy may need vocational guidance, and parents may need to become familiar with local laws about limitations regarding seizure disorders.

Nurses need to encourage parents to maintain a positive attitude toward the child. There should be no special treatment or overprotection. Parents should try not to make the child feel different from other children. Nurses should encourage parents to talk honestly and openly about the disorder with their child. Some parents may try to conceal the illness because they feel ashamed. There are support groups available in most areas. The Epilepsy Foundation of America is a national program that provides assistance with legal, educational and employment issues.

RISK FACTORS

The outcome for the vast majority of children with febrile seizures is benign. Children with simple, complex and recurrent febrile seizures have the same benign prognosis (Knudsen, 2000). From 1–9% of children who experience a febrile seizure have the potential to develop epilepsy (Behrman, 2000; Sheth et al., 1999). For those with a complex febrile seizure, the risk of developing epilepsy is greater at 27% (Sapir, Yael, Harel & Kramer, 2000). Patients with recurrent partial febrile convulsions are at a higher risk for afebrile seizures. (Sheth et al., 1999). Determining the risk of recurrence is important when deciding whether or not to initiate long-term treatment. The greatest risk of recurrence is during the first weeks or months after the initial seizure, and the risk gradually decreases over the next two years. The risk of recurrence of a symptomatic seizure is much greater at 96% compared to an idiopathic seizure at 46% (Lizana et al., 2000).

Risk factors for epilepsy or recurrent seizures include:

*   Prolonged seizures;

*   Partial seizures;

*   Complex febrile seizures;

*   Multiple seizures in the same day;

*   Abnormal neurological development prior to seizure onset;

*   Onset at an early age (<3-years-old);

*   Epileptiform activity or other abnormality on EEG;

*   Family history of epilepsy;

*   Seizures during sleep;

*   Symptomatic seizures; or

*   Genetic predisposition (Sheth et al., 1999; Knudsen, 2000; Lizana et al., 2000).

SUMMARY

Even though most seizure activity is benign, the possibility of a serious cause makes every seizure a pediatric emergency. Accurate detailed documentation may help determine the diagnosis and treatment method for seizures. Many sources recommend no treatment at all for new onset simple febrile seizures in a healthy child. The lack of treatment may make parents very anxious; therefore, nurses assume an important role of educating parents regarding the risks and benefits of anticonvulsants.

EXAM QUESTIONS

CHAPTER 2
Questions 4–7

4. Children at the greatest risk of febrile seizures when they are

   a. over 15 years of age.

   b. between 10 and 15 years of age.

   c. between 5 and 10 years of age.

   d. under 5 years of age.

5. The recommended treatment for a new onset simple febrile seizure in a two-year-old is

   a. no treatment.

   b. Phenobarbital.

   c. Dilantin.

   d. Curare.

6. The type of seizure most at risk for continued or recurrent seizure activity is a

   a. simple partial seizure.

   b. prolonged complex seizure.

   c. febrile seizure.

   d. seizure associated with infection.

7. The nurse's top priority when a seizure is witnessed is to

   a. write a description of seizure activity.

   b. hold the child's arms and legs to stop the seizure.

   c. maintain an open airway and give oxygen.

   d. provide reassurance to the parents.

CHAPTER 3

UPPER AIRWAY DISORDERS

CHAPTER OBJECTIVE

After completing this chapter, the reader will be able to recognize the symptoms of upper airway disorders and specify methods to treat them.

LEARNING OBJECTIVES

After studying this chapter, the learner will be able to

1. identify symptoms of mild to severe viral croup.

2. recognize the first two signs that indicate impending respiratory failure in a pediatric patient with a severe case of viral croup.

3. choose the two most effective medications used to treat moderate to severe cases of viral croup.

4. specify the emergent factor related to epiglottitis.

5. indicate the appropriate treatment measures for epiglottitis.

6. recognize the potential causes of a SIDS death.

7. select important diagnostic information needed to make a SIDS diagnosis.

CROUP

Introduction

Croup is the most common type of upper airway obstruction in children. More than 15% of pediatric respiratory tract illnesses are caused by croup. Currently, 6% of U.S. children with croup are hospitalized. Before the use of glucocorticoids, 31% of children with croup were hospitalized, and 1.7% required intubation (Klassen, 1999). United States' health care costs for croup are estimated at $56 million (Klassen, 1999).

Croup syndrome refers to a group of diseases including laryngotracheitis, spasmodic croup, bacterial tracheitis, laryngotracheobronchitis, and laryngotracheobronchopneumonitis. Laryngotracheitis is also known as viral croup. Viral croup involves progressive obstruction of the upper airway. Croup is caused by the parainfluenza type 1 and type 2 viruses. Laryngotracheobronchitis and laryngotracheobronchopneumonitis are caused by a viral infection, which has been complicated by a secondary bacterial superinfection. Aspiration of a foreign body presents with symptoms similar to viral croup and should be ruled out.

Viral croup usually occurs between the ages of one and six. Croup may reoccur often for children between three and six years old. Croup is less severe as children grow older, and their airways grow larger. Although croup may occur any time of the year, it is most prevalent during the late fall and winter months. Croup occurs more often in boys than in girls.

Pathophysiology

Croup begins with inflammation, erythema and edema in the tracheal walls. Vocal cord mobility becomes impaired. The area of the trachea below the larynx is the narrowest part of the child's airway, and swelling here can significantly restrict airflow. Narrowing of the airway leads to an audible inspiratory stridor. Vocal cord swelling causes a hoarse voice, and there is a characteristic barking cough. As the disease progresses, the tracheal lumen becomes even more obstructed with exudate. If the illness is complicated by a secondary bacterial infection, it moves from the trachea into the bronchi and alveoli and becomes laryngotracheobronchitis or laryngotracheobronchopneumonitis.

SYMPTOMS

Mild to Moderate

Croup can range from a mild virus lasting two to three days to a severe illness lasting up to two weeks. Most patients with croup develop stridor and dyspnea. Some patients with croup develop severe obstruction. Croup is preceded by an upper respiratory tract infection. It usually starts with a runny nose, sore throat and a few days of low-grade fever. There is a mild cough and occasional stridor. As inflammation increases, the inspiratory stridor occurs more often until it is continuous. The voice becomes hoarse, and a dry barking cough develops. The obstructive upper airway symptoms develop over 12 to 24 hours. The characteristic barking cough, hoarseness and inspiratory stridor can occur with or without fever. Gas exchange is normal unless symptoms progress to a more severe case. Pulse oximetry is typically normal. Nasal flaring, suprasternal, substernal and intercostal retractions are all indications of inflammatory progression.

Severe

In a severe case of croup, tachypnea and tachycardia are the first signs of progressive airway obstruction. Hypoxia becomes evident by increased restlessness, anxiousness, nasal flaring, retractions and cyanosis. Crying and agitation can make the symptoms worse. The child usually prefers to sit up or be held upright. Nurses should allow the child to stay on the parent's lap. Death from hypoventilation can occur if treatment is not sought. If the lower respiratory tract becomes involved, there will be a slight increase in temperature, although the temperature rarely reaches 102°F (39°C).

Diagnosis

The diagnosis of viral croup is made clinically. Lab values are not very helpful. In 50% of croup cases, there will be a "steeple sign" on x-ray of the nasopharynx and upper airway. This indicates a narrowing of the airway in the subglottic area. Decreased breath sounds, rhonchi, and scattered rales may be noted upon auscultation of the lungs.

In more severe cases, there will be hypoxemia and hypercapnia. The child will become weak from the increased work of breathing. Air exchange will be diminished, and tachycardia will occur. If a child is hypoxemic, cyanotic or obtunded, oral exam of the airway may result in sudden cardiorespiratory arrest. An airway exam should be postponed until the child is in an emergency room setting where resuscitation equipment is available.

Treatment

In mild to moderate cases, the symptoms usually resolve in three to seven days. In severe cases, the illness may last from seven to fourteen days. The primary goal of treatment is to maintain adequate oxygen exchange. Close monitoring for progressive hypoxia is important in severe cases.

A cool mist or hot steam will decrease the viscosity of secretions, and a cool mist may help to reduce edema. Cool night air has the same effect of reducing swelling and laryngeal spasms. If wheezing continues or worsens, nurses should discontinue the mist. If there is lower airway involvement, the wheezing may worsen during mist treatments.

Children with croup should be hospitalized for progressive stridor, severe stridor at rest, cyanosis, high fever or changes in mental status. In the hospital, nurses will frequently or continuously monitor respirations while administering supplemental oxygen. Intravenous fluids may be given to replace respiratory water loss. Sedatives should not be given because they may depress respiration, dry secretions and mask increasing restlessness. Antibiotics are only indicated for patients with a secondary bacterial infection. With treatment most patients with croup recover completely; however, nurses should be aware that a rare incidence of severe croup might require intubation or tracheotomy.

Epinephrine

Since its use began almost 30 years ago, epinephrine has significantly reduced the need for intubation in children with severe croup. Epinephrine improves croup by constricting the capillaries and arterioles, decreasing mucous and reducing edema in the larynx. The effects of epinephrine only last for two hours and may need to be repeated. Rebound symptoms may occur after the epinephrine wears off. For this reason nurses should observe patients for three to four hours after treatment with epinephrine. After administration of epinephrine, nurses should also watch for tachycardia and hypertension. Nurses should use caution in administering epinephrine to patients who already have an increased heart rate. Epinephrine should only be used in severe cases of croup.

Corticosteroids

By the 1980s, the use of glucocorticoids to treat croup was well established. Glucocorticoids (dexamethasone and budesonide) quickly reduce the symptoms of croup and decrease the incidence of intubation. It has also been noted that when glucocorticoids are administered at the same time as epinephrine, there is no rebound effect after the epinephrine wears off (Klassen, 1999). Treatment with corticosteroids and observation in the emergency room (ER) may significantly reduce the number of hospital admissions for croup. Studies do not show any significant difference in effectiveness between budesonide and dexamethasone.

Dexamethasone is a long acting corticosteroid. Oral or intramuscular administration has been proven to be safe and effective treatment for croup (Malhotra & Krilov, 2001). There are no significant adverse effects with the use of dexamethasone (Klassen, 1999; Behrman, 2000). Symptoms will improve about six hours after the administration of oral dexamethasone. Oral preparations are the least expensive and easy to administer.

Budesonide is a synthetic glucocorticoid. It is administered via nebulizer and has twice the potency of belcomethasone. It is effective within one to two hours after administration and lasts up to 24 hours (Klassen, 1999).

Helium

A mixture of helium and oxygen has been used to treat viral croup. The helium has low density and viscosity. It moves through the airway easier and provides increased gas flow. Administration of helium reduces the work of breathing and improves oxygenation. The use of helium may reduce the need for intubation in patients with progressive airway obstruction.

Complications

Approximately 15% of patients with viral croup develop complications. Spread of the infection to other parts of the respiratory tract is one potential complication. Infection may also spread to the middle ear or to the terminal bronchioles. Nurses should assess the patient frequently for signs of bacterial infection.

From five to seven days after the onset, viral croup may progress with bacterial superinfection to laryngotracheobronchitis or laryngotracheobronchopneumonitis. If this occurs, pulmonary infiltrates will be evident upon chest x-ray. Bacterial superinfection usually presents with a fever, wheezing, rales and increasing respiratory distress. Symptoms may progress to tachypnea, tachycardia, retractions, cyanosis, hypercarbia and changes in mental status. These symptoms of respiratory failure should be treated promptly with endotracheal intubation or tracheotomy. Intubation is rarely needed for more than a few days. Complications from viral croup have occasionally been associated with toxic shock syndrome.

Prognosis

The outcome for patients with croup and its complications is usually excellent. The length of hospital stay for croup patients varies, depending on the degree of respiratory involvement. Complications from a tracheotomy or complete airway obstruction are the two most common causes of death for patients with croup.

Spasmodic Croup

Spasmodic croup involves noninflammatory edema with no direct viral infection. Obstruction is caused by a sudden occurrence of edema. It is thought that spasmodic croup is caused by an allergic reaction to a viral antigen. Spasmodic croup occurs at night in children between the ages of three months and three-years-old. The child will wake at night with sudden dyspnea, a croupy cough and inspiratory stridor. There is no fever. Nurses should warn parents that sudden subglottic edema can reoccur the first night and again for the next three to four nights. The diagnosis for spas-

modic croup can be differentiated from viral croup by an endoscopic exam. With spasmodic croup, the laryngeal mucosa will appear pale and boggy. With viral croup, the mucosa will appear erythematous and inflamed. This exam should only be performed in a hospital setting where emergency intubation is available if needed. Treatment for spasmodic croup consists only of moist air.

EPIGLOTTITIS

The H flu type B vaccine, developed in 1990, has resulted in a sharp decline in the incidence of epiglottitis. Other organisms may also cause epiglottitis, and there are some children who do not receive immunizations; so, health care professionals should not forget about this potentially fatal illness (Chameides & Hazinski, 1999). Acute epiglottitis occurs in children from ages two to seven-years-old. The average age of occurrence is three-years-old. The progression is rapid, and there is a high risk for death if not treated promptly. Air hunger and restlessness may lead rapidly to cyanosis, coma and death. If it is less severe, the child may have only mild hoarseness and a large, shiny, cherry-red epiglottis.

Symptoms

Acute epiglottitis requires emergency treatment. A child with epiglottitis should be taken to the nearest emergency room. The child often goes to bed well and wakes up later in the night with a high fever, sore throat, aphonia, drooling, moderate to severe respiratory distress and stridor (Chameides & Hazinski, 1999). The child will not be able to rest supine. The child will sit up and lean forward with labored breathing. Nasal flaring and suprasternal, supraclavicular, intercostal and subcostal retractions may be seen. The epiglottis can swell rapidly in a pediatric airway, and there is a greater risk of obstruction (*see Figure 3-1*). The respiratory distress caused by airway obstruction

FIGURE 3-1
Effects of Edema on Airways Resistance in the Infant Versus the Adult

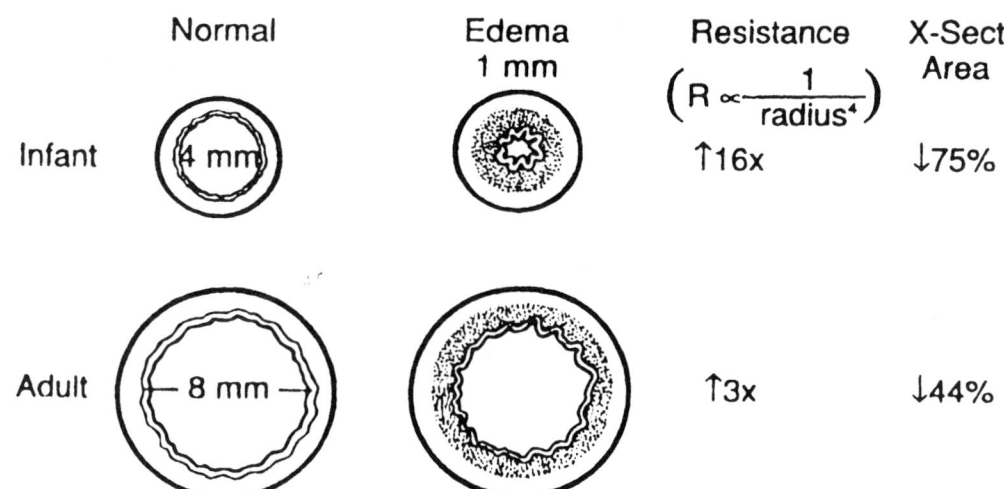

Normal airways are represented on the left and edematous airways (1 mm circumferential edema) on the right. Resistance to flow is inversely proportional to the radius of the lumen to the fourth power for laminar flow and the fifth power for turbulent flow. The net result is a 75% decrease in cross-sectional area and a sixteenfold increase in resistance in the infant versus 44% and threefold, respectively, in the adult.

Source: Curley, M. & Moloney-Harmon, P. (2001). *Critical care nursing of infants and children* (2nd ed.). Philadelphia: W.B. Saunders.

progresses rapidly within minutes or hours. There will be increased stridor, large amounts of mucus and saliva, hoarseness, cough and rhonchi. Hypoxemia may progress causing pallor, cyanosis and impaired consciousness or shock. Complete airway obstruction and death will occur unless treatment is sought.

Diagnosis

Diagnosis is made by a laryngoscopic exam, which will show a red inflamed epiglottis. Complications of this exam may include reflex laryngospasm, an acute complete obstruction, aspiration of secretions and cardiorespiratory arrest. Cardiorespiratory arrest may occur during or after an exam of the pharynx with a tongue blade. This exam should be delayed until the child is in an emergency room where proper intubation and resuscitation equipment are available. An X-ray of the nasopharynx and upper airway will show a "thumb sign," which indicates a swollen epiglottis. This may be done prior to a physical exam.

Treatment

If this diagnosis is suspected, immediate exam and control of the airway with intubation should be done. This is often done in the operating room and may require a tracheotomy. Intubation or tracheotomy is indicated for all epiglottitis patients regardless of the degree of respiratory distress. As many as 6% of these patients will die without a secured airway. Routine intubation for epiglottitis has significantly decreased the mortality rate (Behrman, 2000). Intubation may be required for two to three days, but this time frame may vary.

A child with suspected epiglottitis should have a physician and intubation equipment available at all times. Nurses should keep the child in an upright position to prevent airway obstruction caused by the swollen epiglottis. The child should be disturbed as little as possible. Nursing responsibilities will include administration of supplemental oxygen, drawing blood cultures and obtaining cultures of the epiglottis. Bacteremia is common and should be treated with appropriate antibiotics for seven to ten days. With treatment, epiglottitis usually lasts only two to three days. Usually, the child is the only family member who is ill. Prompt diagnosis and treatment will ensure an excellent prognosis.

Complications

Potential complications of epiglottitis are pneumonia, cervical lymphadenitis, otitis media or rarely meningitis or septic arthritis. Potential complications of a tracheotomy include mediastinal emphysema and pneumothorax.

SUDDEN INFANT DEATH SYNDROME (SIDS)

Definition

When a healthy infant younger than one-year-old dies suddenly and unexpectedly, the cause is often sudden infant death syndrome (SIDS) (Kairys, Committee on Child Abuse and Neglect & American Academy of Pediatrics, 2001). This was previously known as "crib death." SIDS involves a death that remains unexplained even after an autopsy, a thorough investigation, a review of medical history and evaluation by a child abuse professional. In order to make a diagnosis of SIDS, child abuse injuries must be ruled out as a cause of death (Kairys et al., 2001).

SIDS Facts

SIDS is more common than infanticide. It usually occurs between the ages of one and six-months-old. Despite research, there is no clear understanding of what causes SIDS. Research has shown that SIDS rates are higher in African American and some American Indian populations

(Kairys et al., 2001). Studies also support the hypothesis that upper airway obstruction is the final event in SIDS. The diagnosis of SIDS requires the exclusion of all other possible causes of death. A postmortem examination and death scene investigation are necessary in order to determine a diagnosis of SIDS. If an autopsy is not done, a diagnosis of SIDS should not be made (Kairys et al., 2001). A SIDS death is not diagnosed by the presence of certain symptoms, but rather by the lack of any diagnostic symptoms at all. Even mild suspicious symptoms will preclude SIDS as a possible cause of death, and the cause of death may be left as unknown.

There has been a link between SIDS and a prone sleeping position, sleeping on a soft surface, maternal smoking during and after pregnancy, overheating, late or no prenatal care, young maternal age, prematurity, low birth weight, and male gender (Kairys et al., 2001). There has been no correlation between SIDS and cyanotic or apneic episodes or immunizations.

History of Events

The history of the events prior to the infant's death and a description of the death scene are important. Following the death, a skeletal survey of the infant should be done (Kairys et al., 2001). This may reveal previous traumatic skeletal injury or skeletal abnormalities. An autopsy is done to rule out other causes of death. Often, the infant is fed just before being put to bed. The infant is often found in the same position in which it was placed at bedtime. The position of the infant, marks on the body, body temperature, rigor, type of bed or crib, any defects, amount and position of clothing and bedding, room temperature, ventilation, and reaction of the infant's caregivers are all important factors that may help with the diagnosis (Kairys et al., 2001). There may be evidence of terminal motor activity, such as a clenched fist. There may be a serosanguineous, watery, frothy or mucous discharge from the nose or mouth. Intrathoracic petechiae are seen in 80% of SIDS cases (Kairys et al., 2001). Skin mottling, postmortem lividity in dependent parts and anal dilation are commonly seen (Kairys et al., 2001).

A death review committee will ideally include protective services, a social worker, a law enforcement officer, a public health officer, the medical examiner, a pediatrician (with child abuse expertise), a forensic and pediatric pathologist and the local prosecutor (Kairys et al., 2001). Proceedings should always remain confidential. A SIDS diagnosis is made only when there is a negative skeletal survey and a complete autopsy reveals no other possible cause of death, such as trauma or disease (Kairys et al., 2001). There must be no evidence of alcohol, drug, or toxic exposure. Both the scene investigation and medical history must be negative for other possible causes of death.

CHILD ABUSE VERSUS SIDS

About 50 years ago, the medical community began a search to understand and prevent SIDS. About that same time, there was increased awareness of child abuse. Recently, there have been reports of child abuse and infanticide by suffocation masquerading as SIDS. The distinction between SIDS and fatal child abuse can usually be diagnosed if the death is approached properly (Kairys et al., 2001).

Intentional suffocation is impossible to distinguish from SIDS at autopsy. There is a possibility of intentional suffocation if there have been previous incidents of cyanosis or apnea while under the care of the same person. If the infant's death occurred after the age of six months, intentional suffocation is more likely. The previous unexplained death of one or more siblings, including a twin, is suspicious of suffocation. The previous death of other infants under the care of the same unrelated person is also suspicious. Blood on the infant's nose or mouth may also indicate suffocation (Kairys et al., 2001).

Occult cocaine exposure is widespread and potentially lethal. In one study 17 out of 43 infants who died before they were two-days-old, without an obvious cause of death, had toxicological evidence of cocaine exposure (Kairys et al., 2001).

Parents

Nurses may not have frequent contact with a SIDS infant; however, distinguishing the difference between SIDS and child abuse is important. Parents of a SIDS death deserve to be approached in a nonaccusatory way. If a diagnosis of SIDS has been made, it is because child abuse has been ruled out as a cause of death. Parents of SIDS victims are usually anxious to provide an unlimited amount of information to professionals involved in the investigation of the death (Kairys et al., 2001).

Nurses who do have contact with parents following a SIDS death should offer the parents the opportunity to hold the infant after the death has been pronounced and can assist the family in making baptism and funeral arrangements. Information about grief counseling and SIDS support groups should be provided. Nurses need to assist with cessation of breast-feeding if needed. Parents should be encouraged to grieve for their loss, share their grief with siblings and allow siblings to express their grief also.

Nurses need to explain to the parents that the procedures after an infant death are necessary in order to understand why the infant died. An accurate cause of death may help prevent future deaths of siblings or other infants. The discovery of a congenital anomaly or syndrome on autopsy may be significant if there are siblings. If the diagnosis was SIDS, parents need to be informed that there is no increased risk of SIDS in subsequent children (Kairys et al., 2001).

If careful examination of the death is not done, abuse may be missed, genetic diseases may not be identified, public health threats may not be reported, inadequate medical care may not be detected, and product safety issues may not be revealed (Kairys et al., 2001).

Thanks to SIDS investigations, the potential hazards of defective infant furniture, water beds, and beanbag mattresses have been uncovered (Kairys et al., 2001). National campaigns to reducing prone sleeping during infancy have dramatically reduced the incidence of SIDS in the United States and in other countries.

CONCLUSION

The American Academy of Pediatrics endorses universal performance of autopsies on sudden, unexpected infant deaths. Postmortem findings in cases of fatal child abuse often reveal cranial injuries, abdominal trauma, burns, drowning or exposure as the cause of death (Kairys et al., 2001).

EXAM QUESTIONS

CHAPTER 3
Questions 8–14

8. The symptoms of mild to severe viral croup include

    a. stridor, dyspnea and cyanosis.
    b. fever over 104°F, stomach cramps and flushing.
    c. two months of sinusitis, rhinorrhea and cough.
    d. hematuria, afebrile and dizziness.

9. The first two signs of airway obstruction in a pediatric patient with a severe case of viral croup are

    a. crying and agitation.
    b. coughing and fever.
    c. tachypnea and tachycardia.
    d. bradycardia and hypothermia.

10. The medication that is most effective in reducing the need for intubation in the patient with severe viral croup is

    a. antihistamines.
    b. antibiotics.
    c. epinephrine.
    d. anticholinergics.

11. Which of the following factors, related to epiglottitis, causes the need for emergency treatment?

    a. There is rapid progression of airway obstruction.
    b. A six-month-old may not be able to communicate symptoms.
    c. Older children may not have received the H flu type B vaccine.
    d. Treatment may be needed if the swelling is still present after one week.

12. An appropriate treatment measure for epiglottitis is

    a. an airway examination at the doctors office.
    b. airway examination by the parents.
    c. airway examination in the operating room.
    d. no exam of the airway unless the patient is unconscious.

13. A potential cause of SIDS death is

    a. an abusive injury.
    b. asphyxiation while sleeping in a prone position.
    c. aspiration while sleeping supine.
    d. following an infectious respiratory illness.

14. What important diagnostic information is needed to make a SIDS diagnosis?

    a. An autopsy always provides the correct diagnosis of SIDS.

    b. A positive skeletal survey is diagnostic of SIDS.

    c. Toxins in the blood are indicative of SIDS.

    d. SIDS can only be diagnosed if there is no other possible cause of death.

CHAPTER 4

LOWER AIRWAY DISEASE: ASTHMA

CHAPTER OBJECTIVE

After completing this chapter, the reader will be able to recognize how the pathophysiology of asthma has changed over the past two decades and how this relates to the importance of long-term maintenance medications.

LEARNING OBJECTIVES

After studying this chapter, the learner will be able to

1. identify the pathology of asthma that requires long-term medication.

2. recognize the problems involved in maintaining long-term management of asthma.

3. specify the most important medications used in treatment of acute and chronic asthma.

EPIDEMIOLOGY

Asthma is the most common chronic childhood disease in the United States (Smith & Strunk, 1999; Werner, 2001; Behrman, 2000; Martinez, 1999). Five million children in the U.S. have asthma (Kemp & Kemp, 2001; Smith & Strunk, 1999; Szefler, 2001). The highest incidence of asthma occurs in preschoolers (Larsen, 2000). The childhood death rate from asthma has almost doubled from 1980 to 1993 (Kemp & Kemp, 2001; Werner, 2001). Asthma causes 10 million missed school days every year (Kemp & Kemp, 2001). Despite all of the increased knowledge and research about asthma, the incidence, morbidity and mortality from asthma are increasing (Werner, 2001).

There is no cure for asthma. Recent research regarding the physiology of asthma indicates that asthma involves chronic airway inflammation, which varies in severity based on a variety of triggers (Szefler, 2000). This research indicates the need for long-term therapy. Because of the chronic aspect of asthma, long-term medications are necessary in order to maintain control of symptoms and reduce the incidence of exacerbations.

HISTORY

In 1960, epinephrine was the first line therapy to relieve bronchospasms. In the 1970s isoproterenol, metaproterenol, albuterol and pirbuterol were found to have longer half-lives than epinephrine. In the 1980s, theophylline extended-release was the preferred treatment and measuring serum concentrations allowed accurate dosing. Theophylline use declined with the introduction of cromolyn. Cromolyn was found to reduce the pulmonary response to allergens, thus reducing asthma exacerbations.

New diagnostic tools such as the bronchoscopy, bronchoalveolar lavage and biopsy provided a method to learn more about the pathology of asthma. In the 1990s, it was proven that asthma involves chronic inflammation not intermittent inflammation (Szefler, 2000). Inhaled glucocorticoids replaced theophylline and cromolyn as the asthma maintenance medication. Glucocorticoids improve asthma control because they significantly resolve chronic inflammation.

In 1996, leukotriene modifiers were approved for use in the United States. Zileuton and zafirlukast have been used to treat asthma. Montelukast, approved in 1998, is also being prescribed for asthma (Szefler, 2000). New research has found that leukotrienes are potent mediators of inflammation (Szefler, 2000). Leukotrienes are released in response to allergic stimuli and contribute to airway edema. Montelukast has been used in clinical studies involving children from two to six-years-old. There is a general consensus that allergy avoidance is a major factor in long-term asthma control. Although environmental control of allergies can be a focus of home treatment, environmental control throughout the day is not a viable option. Antileukotriene agents inhibit the effects of leukotrienes. This class of drugs is the first new approach to asthma therapy in 25 years.

In 1998, The FDA supported the use of inhaled steroids as the preferred medication for long-term control of asthma.

PHYSIOLOGY

During the last couple of decades research has shown that asthma symptoms are caused not only by bronchial smooth muscle spasms but also from chronic airway inflammation. There is both an acute and chronic inflammatory process. Both large and small airways are involved. Mast cells, eosinophils, T lymphocytes, macrophages and neutrophils are involved in the inflammatory process. Bronchial and tracheal biopsies of asthmatics have shown the presence of lymphocytic and eosinophilic infil-

trates. The prevalence of these cells appears to correlate directly with disease severity. Histamine and leukotriene mediators are released in response to the inflammatory cells. Increased concentrations of these mediators can be found in the blood as well as in the airway. Chronic inflammation causes smooth muscle hyperplasia, bronchial hyper-responsiveness and increased collagen deposits, which narrows the airway.

The irritable, inflamed airway of an asthmatic child is hyper-responsive to triggers such as allergens, infections, tobacco smoke, fumes, cold air, exercise and stress. All of these triggers can cause an exacerbation of the chronic inflammation to create an acute inflammatory airway with increased secretions, mucous and edema. This acute inflammation puts the asthmatic child at risk of airway obstruction. Acute bronchial spasms, bronchial constriction, airway edema and mucous plugs all play a role in reducing airflow.

A reduction in airflow causes inspiratory muscle activity to increase. Inspiratory muscles contract in an effort to hold the airways open even during expiration. This results in hyperinflation. The increased work of breathing under hypoxic conditions causes an accumulation of lactic acid and acidosis. Respiratory alkalosis initially compensates for this acidosis, but if respiratory failure occurs, there will be a rapid and drastic drop in pH. Pulmonary pressure changes affect the function of both the right and left ventricles. These pulmonary and cardiac changes result in an increased risk of pulmonary edema. Progressive respiratory failure in an asthmatic child is called status asthmaticus.

The chronic infiltration of inflammatory cells in the airway of an asthmatic can have long-term irreversible effects on the airway (Martinez, 1999). Airway smooth muscle, vessels, nerves and tissues of the airway may be altered or injured. The airway wall can thicken, and smooth muscle may hypertrophy (Larsen, 2000). Studies have shown that the rise in inflammatory cells causes not only thickening of the airway epithelium but also collagen deposits in the airway walls (Martinez, 1999). These airway changes may contribute to the airway hyper-responsiveness seen in asthmatics.

SYMPTOMS

Symptoms vary from one asthmatic patient to another. Symptoms are often worse in the early morning hours and are often associated with triggers such as exercise or allergen exposure. Preschoolers are more likely to experience seasonal symptoms of asthma, whereas older children are more likely to have chronic or persistent asthma symptoms (Martinez, 1999).

Wheezing can be caused by obstruction of both small and large airways. Wheezing usually begins as expiratory wheezing then progresses to a combination of inspiratory and expiratory wheezing. As air passage is reduced, wheezing may progress further from audible wheezing to no wheezing at all. Nurses should be reassured by wheezing upon auscultation, this means that there is sufficient airflow to cause respiratory sounds. Distant or absent breath sounds indicate impending respiratory failure and are far more ominous. A decreased level of consciousness, inability to speak, diminished breath sounds, cyanosis and diaphoresis are all signs of progressing respiratory failure. Frequent causes of respiratory failure are severe obstruction and muscle fatigue (Smith & Strunk, 1999).

An asthmatic cough is an intermittent, dry cough, or a cough with clear mucous. A persistent cough with purulent sputum is more likely caused by bronchiectasis or cystic fibrosis.

Symptoms of Asthma

- Wheezing
- Cough
- Chest tightness

- Shortness of breath
- Increased work of breathing
- Anxiety
- Mouth breathing

DIAGNOSIS

Because asthma is not the only disease process that involves wheezing, it is important to rule out other potential diagnoses such as respiratory infections, vocal cord problems, foreign body aspiration and cystic fibrosis. It is difficult for health care professionals to distinguish between transient wheezing and early onset of asthma, especially in infants. However, children develop asthma symptoms before the age of five in 50–80% of the cases. In infancy, the first episode of wheezing is often diagnosed as bronchiolitis, especially when triggered by a viral infection. There is a reluctance to diagnose a chronic illness in the first year of life, and the diagnosis of bronchiolitis may be made more than once. Asthma is more prevalent in African American children (Kemp & Kemp, 2001) and in those with a low economic status (Smith & Strunk, 1999). Many specialist believe that asthma is underdiagnosed and undertreated (Szefler, 2001). Misdiagnosis and delayed treatment of chronic asthma could cause a loss of pulmonary function later in life.

Diagnosis is difficult for several reasons. It is very difficult to obtain an objective measurement of symptoms from young children. Children are not able to verbalize their symptoms, and their parents are not objective reporters. Objective measurements for older children are possible with the use of peak flow meters and spirometry. These tools are not very useful in the young patient. Many diagnostic tests are difficult to perform and are not reliable in infants and preschool age children. Therefore, the primary diagnostic tool for young children is clinical assessment. Pulmonary function tests, spirometry before and after inhaled bronchodilators and allergy tests may confirm the diagnosis for older children. Studies indicate that wheezing six-year-olds who tested positive for asthma-related allergens were more likely than those who tested negative for allergens to have persistent asthma symptoms after school-age years (Martinez, 1999).

Bronchoalveolar lavage and biopsy have shown that bronchial inflammation is present in chronic asthma as well as during acute episodes. Biopsy and identification of inflammatory cells has been done primarily in older children and adults. However, basal membrane thickening and high eosinophil levels in airway mucosa have been found in bronchial biopsies of wheezing infants who were later diagnosed with asthma (Naspitz & Tinkelman, 2001). Also, bronchial biopsies done during mild episodes of asthma or during asthma remission have shown evidence of inflammatory changes (Martinez, 1999). Chest x-rays are not done routinely for acute exacerbations of asthma. A chest x-ray is indicated if barotrauma, foreign-body aspiration or congestive heart failure is suspected. Atelectasis on x-ray is difficult to distinguish from pneumonia because they both appear as increased density. A focal infiltrate and high fever are suggestive of an infection.

Nurses must learn to ask key questions in order to obtain differential diagnostic information from parents and care givers. Specific questions about risk factors, triggers, preceding events and family history can assist in accurate diagnosing. It is helpful for nurses to list a child's risk factors along with their symptoms *(see Table 4-1)*. Along with making note of risk factors, nurses can make note of other associated diagnosis that may help support the diagnosis of asthma. Atopic dermatitis, rhinitis and bilateral wheezing are often seen in association with asthma. An increase in the chest diameter may indicate a chronic asthmatic change; although this

is not a very exact diagnostic tool. There may be an association between symptoms and certain activities, which can help to confirm the diagnosis. Triggers or preceding events may initiate asthma symptoms. Symptoms may occur after the lawn is mowed, while the house is dusted, during physical activity or while exposed to tobacco smoke.

Obtaining a complete medical history is important in establishing a diagnosis of asthma. Nurses should obtain a thorough patient history from the child or the child's parent by asking very specific asthma related questions (see *Table 4-2).*

There have been several scoring systems established to assist health care professionals in determining the severity of an acute asthma attack. Small portable pulmonary function test machines may provide a quick evaluation for older children. Peak expiratory flow rate meters may also be available as hand-held models. Nonmechanical scoring systems include the Pulmonary Index Score and Wood-Downes Score. These systems lack either ease of use or accuracy. A preferred scoring system is the Pulmonary Score (PS) (see *Table 4-3).* The Pulmonary Score involves assessment of the respiratory rate, wheezing and use of accessory muscles. A PS of less than 3 is a mild exacerbation. A PS of 4 to 6 is moderate. A PS of more than 6 is severe. The Clinical Asthma Score is another scoring system that indicates disease severity (see *Table 4-4).* A score of more than 5 indicates impending respiratory failure and a score greater than 7 indicates existing respiratory failure.

TREATMENT

Acute respiratory distress requires immediate attention to airway, breathing and circulation. Children who have a decreased level of consciousness or cyanosis should be treated for impending respiratory failure. Cardiorespiratory monitoring is important for any child in status asthmaticus. Sedatives are con-

---

TABLE 4-1
Risk Factors for Potentially Fatal Asthma

Medical factors

    Previous attack with:

        Severe, unexpected, rapid deterioration

        Respiratory failure

        Seizure or loss of consciousness

    Attacks precipitated by food

Psychosocial factors

    Denial or failure to perceive severity of illness

    Associated depression or other psychiatric disorder

    Noncompliance

    Dysfunctional family unit

    Inner-city residents

Ethnic factors

    Nonwhite children (African American, Hispanic, other)

Source: Werner, H. (2001). Status asthmaticus in children, a review. *The American College of Chest Physicians, 119.* [Available online: http://home.mdconsult.com/das/article/bod...&sp=11859322&sid=58198870/N/226998/1.html]. Accessed September 8, 2001.

---

traindicated because they may depress respirations. Nurses can assist an acutely asthmatic child by maintaining a calm relaxed atmosphere to help reduce the child's anxiety.

Many asthmatic children are dehydrated by the time they receive treatment. Hydration is needed to thin secretions; however, overhydration may increase the risk of pulmonary edema and should be avoided. Careful monitoring of intake and output is an important nursing responsibility. Often asthma attacks are triggered by viral pathogens; therefore, antibiotics are not routinely administered.

Long-term asthma management includes regular assessments, control of triggers, acute and chronic medications and patient and family education. Emergency action plans are made to provide families with specific medical instructions for asthma exacerbations. These detailed instructions will ensure prompt treatment and may eliminate the need for hospitalization.

Oxygenation

High-flow humidified oxygen via a partial or non-rebreather mask is the most effective method of delivering supplemental oxygen to children. Supplemental oxygen should be administered to keep pulse oximeter readings greater than 90% (Smith & Strunk, 1999). PaO_2 levels from arterial blood gases (ABGs) are the most accurate, but pulse oximeters provide a good estimation of PaO_2 levels. An oxygen saturation of 90% is comparable to a PaO_2 of 60 mmHg, and an oxygen saturation of 75% is comparable to a PaO_2 of 40 mmHg. ABGs should be checked for children receiving supplemental oxygen at 100% concentration when their oxygen saturation drops below 90% (Smith & Strunk, 1999).

TABLE 4-2
Obtaining a Patient History

- How long have the asthma symptoms been present?

- Were there any triggers prior to the exacerbation?

- Are there any infectious symptoms?

- What type and amount of medications did the patient receive prior to arrival to the ER?

- Obtain peak flow rates if possible.

- What are the patient's chronic medications?

- Describe previous and most recent exacerbations and their severity.

- How many attacks have there been in the last year?

- How many previous hospital admissions have there been for asthma?

- Is there a history of ICU admissions?

- Is there a history of previous intubation for asthma exacerbations?

Nurses should assess respiratory effort, pulse oximetry and level of consciousness frequently for signs of disease progression and the need for intubation and artificial ventilation. Tachypnea must be related to the normal values for each age group To determine severity see Appendix D for normal vital signs by age. A normal or decreased respiratory rate may be a sign of fatigue. Sternocleidomastoid muscle retractions are an indicator of significant airway obstruction.

Intubation and Mechanical Ventilation

Hypoxemia and hypocarbia are typical in the early phase of severe asthma. With continued deterioration, hypercarbia will develop indicating impending respiratory failure. Even a mild elevation in PaCO2 can cause tachypnea. A PaCO2 >60 mmHg is a sign of respiratory failure. Aggressive high-dose nebulization of beta-agonists and anticholinergics with IV corticosteroids should precede the decision to intubate, unless a cardiorespiratory arrest is imminent (Werner, 2001). Positive-pressure ventilation can be effective without intubation. Positive pressure will decrease the work of breathing, reduce muscle fatigue and allow spontaneous respirations. The decision to intubate a child is not easy. Intubation should be avoided if possible because there are risks involved. Intubation may aggravate bronchospasms and the increased pressures put the child at risk for barotrauma. Cardiac arrest, respiratory arrest, severe hypoxia and rapid mental status deterioration are indications for intubation and mechanical ventilation. Sedation given to a ventilated child will increase comfort and decrease oxygen consumption. In some cases, paralysis may be needed for successful mechanical ventilation.

Along with bronchospasms and inflammation, mucous plugging also effects a small number of asthmatics in acute respiratory distress. Bronchoscopy and bronchial lavage have been used along with mechanical ventilation in severely ill children (Werner, 2001).

Drug Therapy

The primary goal of pharmaceutical treatment is decreasing inflammation. Medications should be given aggressively to gain control over acute symptoms, then tapered to the minimum dose needed to maintain control of symptoms (Kemp & Kemp, 2001). Long-term medications should be taken regularly to maintain control of persistent

TABLE 4-3
Pulmonary Score

Score	Respiratory Rate <6 Years	>6 Years	Wheezing*	Accessory Muscle Use (Sternocleidomastoid Activity)
0	<30	<20	None	No apparent activity
1	31–45	21–35	Terminal expiration, with stethoscope	Questionable increase
2	46–60	36–50	Entire expiration, with stethoscope	Increase apparent
3	>60	>50	Inspiration and expiration without stethoscope	Maximal activity

* If no wheezing due to minimal air exchange, score 3.

Source: Smith S. & Strunk, R. (1999). Acute asthma in the pediatric emergency department. *Pediatric Clinics of North America, 46,* 1145–1165. [Available online: http://home.mdconsult.com/das/article/bod...&sp=11158354&sid=58198870/N/158861/1.html]. Accessed September 8, 2001.

symptoms (see *Table 4-5).* There is a limited amount of information regarding adverse effects of asthma medications in young children. Most information is obtained from studies involving adults or older children.

Although nebulization is the preferred route, inhaled medications are difficult in young children because there is no way to measure the exact amount that will reach their lungs (Naspitz & Tinkelman, 2001). Less than 10% of nebulized medication will reach the lungs in most pediatric cases (Werner, 2001). Face masks may be needed along with nebulizers for children less than five-years-old. Spacers, although they are not perfect, provide the best option of inhaled delivery for young children. Metered dose inhalers (MDI) are also very difficult for young children to use.

Many children, who receive treatment for exacerbations in an emergency room, do not receive follow-up or long-term therapy, which predisposes them to exacerbations and repeat ER visits. The lack of continuity in their care contributes to their families' lack of knowledge about appropriate asthma therapies. The need for long-term care and crisis planning are important for all children with asthma. The cycle of repeat ER visits without proper follow-up increases the morbidity and mortality of asthmatic children.

Beta-agonists

Beta-agonists are bronchodilators. They rapidly relax smooth muscles and improve mucous clearance. These medications can relieve acute symptoms and prevent exercise-induced bronchospasms. Common beta-agonists are epinephrine, isoproterenol, terbutaline and albuterol. Budesonide is a new inhalation medication that was recently approved by the Food and Drug Administration (FDA). Albuterol is the most common choice of beta-agonists in the U.S. Beta-agonists can be given via inhalation, intravenous, subcutaneous or oral routes. Oral administration is not effective in severe asthma. Nebulized administration is the preferred route because there is a reduced incidence of adverse reactions with this route. Continuous nebulization is more effective than intermittent doses. Nebulized doses should always be given with oxygen at 10 to 12 L/min flow rate.

Intravenous beta-agonists should be given for patients who are not responsive to continuous nebulizer treatments. Terbutaline is the most common choice of IV beta-agonists in the U.S. Nurses should watch for cardiovascular adverse effects

TABLE 4-4
Clinical Asthma Score

	Score		
Variables	**0**	**1**	**2**
Cyanosis or PaO2, mm Hg	None	In 21% O2	In 40% O2
	70–100 in 21% O2	<70 in 21% O2	<70 in 40% O2
Inspiratory breath sounds	Normal	Unequal or absent	Decreased
Accessory muscles used	None	Moderate	Maximal
Expiratory wheezing	None	Moderate	Marked
Cerebral function	Normal	Depressed or agitated	Coma

*From Wood et al. A score of ≥5 indicates impending respiratory failure: a score of ≥7 is consistent with respiratory failure.

Source: Werner, H. (2001). Status asthmaticus in children, a review. *The American College of Chest Physicians, 119.* [Available online: http://home.mdconsult.com/das/article/bod...&sp=11859322&sid=58198870/N/226998/1.html]. Accessed September 8, 2001.

when administering beta-agonists. Tachycardia, dysrhythmia, hypertension or hypotension may be seen. Myocardial ischemia has been related to IV isoproterenol given to asthmatic children. Hypokalemia and tremors are also potential adverse reactions.

Although these medications are very effective, they are frequently overused. Overuse can cause bronchial hyper-reactivity, central nervous system overstimulation, worsening of asthma and death. Overuse of acute medications indicates that the asthma is not well controlled and additional long-term anti-inflammatory medication is needed. In well-controlled asthma an inhaler can last for one year.

Steroids

Corticoids are a first-line treatment for status asthmaticus. Inhaled corticosteroids are the most effective long-term anti-inflammatory medications (Kemp & Kemp, 2001). Studies have shown that glucocorticoids improve asthma symptoms and reduce airway inflammation (Szefler, 2000; Smith & Strunk, 1999). Glucocorticoids are effective in reducing airway inflammation, lymphocytes, eosinophils and decreasing mucous secretions. Inhaled steroids may help to prevent the progression of asthma and may decrease the risk of irreversible airway changes that result from persistent symptoms. Similar to long-term effects of chronic obstructive pulmonary disease (COPD), undertreating asthma may cause a loss of pulmonary function over time. It is possible that early anti-inflammatory treatment of asthma will improve lung growth and prevent morbidity (Szefler, 2001).

Short courses of oral corticoids are used for acute episodes. Glucocorticoid dosing should be repeated every 6 to 12 hours until the child is clinically improved or until follow-up with the child's primary physician within three days (Smith & Strunk, 1999). If treatment continues after five to ten days, the dosage should be tapered instead of discontinued abruptly. Short-term use of high-dose steroids does not usually cause any significant adverse reactions.

Hyperglycemia, hypertension and acute psychosis have been associated with steroid use. Long-

TABLE 4-5
Medications

Medication	Route	Dose	Contraindications
Albuterol	MDI/DPI, nebulizer (short) nebulizer (continuous)	2–4 puffs with spacer 2.5 mg in 2.0–3.0 mL NS 10 mg in 6.0–7.0 mL NS	H/O hypersensitivity
Epinephrine	SC	0.01 mg/kg of 1:1000 (max. 0.03 mg)	
Etomidate	IV	0.2–0.4 mg/kg	H/O hypersensitivity
Fentanyl	IV or IM	1–3 mcg/kg	H/O hypersensitivity
Ipratropium bromide (Atrovent®)	MDI, nebulizer	2–4 puffs with spacer 250–500 micrograms WITH albuterol*	H/O hypersensitivity to soya lecithin, soybean, peanut, atropine, or related products
Ketamine	IV IM	1–3 mg/kg 3–5 mg/kg	H/O hypersensitivity, elevated ICP, hypertension, aneurysms, thyrotoxicosis, CHF, angina, psychotic disorders
Methylprednisolone	IV or IM	2 mg/kg (max, 80 mg)	
Midazolam (Versed®)	IV	0.05 mg/kg (max, 2.5 mg)	H/O hypersensitivity, acute narrow-angle glaucoma
Prednisone	PO	2 mg/kg (max, 80 mg)	Systemic fungal infection
Succinylcholine	IV or IM	2–4 mg/kg	H/O hypersensitivity, H/O or family H/O malignant hyperthermia, skeletal myopathies, after acute phase of major burns, multiple trauma, extensive denervation of skeletal muscle, or upper motor neuron injury

MDI = metered-dose inhaler, DPI = dry powder inhaler, H/O = history of, SC = subcutaneously, NS = normal saline, IV = intravenously, IM = intramuscularly, PO = by mouth, ICP = intracranial pressure, CHF = congestive heart failure.
* Should only be added to short albuterol treatments; no studies prove the safety or efficacy of ipratropium with continuous albuterol.

Source: Smith S. & Strunk, R. (1999). Acute asthma in the pediatric emergency department. *Pediatric Clinics of North America, 46,* 1145–1165. [Available online: http://home.mdconsult.com/das/article/bod...&sp=11158354&sid=58198870/N/158861/1.html]. Accessed September 8, 2001.

term use of inhaled glucocorticoids have shown adverse effects on children's growth and bone density and have also been shown to cause ocular disorders. Although Martinez (1999) suggests that it is poorly controlled asthma that delays a child's growth, not only the use of steroids. Steroids also have immunosuppressant effects that may increase the risk of unusual or severe infections. Children with a recent exposure to chickenpox should not receive steroids. Nurses should also be aware of potential allergic reactions. Rash, anaphylaxis and death have been seen with the use of methylprednisolone, hydrocortisone and oral prednisone in asthmatic patients.

Anticholinergics

Anticholinergics are given for bronchodilation. They have become an important part of asthma therapy. The most common route is inhalation, and the most common agent is ipratropium. Ipratropium is not absorbed into the bloodstream; therefore, there are minimal cardiovascular adverse effects.

Theophylline

Theophylline is not recommended as routine treatment for children with asthma (Werner, 2001; Smith & Strunk, 1999). The therapeutic range (10 to 20 mcg/mL) overlaps the toxic range (>15 mcg/mL). Nausea and vomiting, tachycardia and agitation may be seen with the administration of theophylline. Serum concentrations >35 mcg/mL may cause arrhythmias, hypotension, seizures and death.

Magnesium

Magnesium relaxes smooth muscles by reducing calcium uptake. Magnesium is most effective in bronchodilation when airway inflammation is not prevalent. It is not considered a first line drug for asthma. An infusion of magnesium may cause flushing and nausea. Serum concentrations >12 mg/dL cause toxic effects of weakness, areflexia, respiratory depression and arrhythmia.

Heliox

Heliox is a combination of helium and oxygen. This mixture has a reduced density and can improve oxygen delivery. However, high concentrations of oxygen cannot be delivered when mixed with helium. Heliox has not been proven to be an effective treatment in asthmatic pediatric patients (Werner, 2001).

NURSING INTERVENTIONS

Poor compliance is a major problem of asthmatics (Kemp & Kemp, 2001). A determining factor in patient compliance is the patient's or parents' perception of asthma severity (Naspite & Tinkelman, 2001). Underestimating asthma severity and noncompliance are two major risk factors that can be prevented with appropriate patient and parent education. Nurses should allow extra time for education. Nurses should provide detailed instructions and stress the importance of follow-up care. All emergency room visits for asthma should be followed up by the primary physician within 72 hours. The National Heart, Lung and Blood Institute (NHLBI) recommends that asthmatic children see their primary physician four times every year to establish and maintain effective long-term asthma therapy (Smith & Strunk, 999). Nurses can play an important role in reinforcing the importance of long-term medications. Nurses can help patients and families to prepare an emergency plan and stress the importance of following the plan. An asthma action plan for an acute exacerbation may prevent progression to a more severe asthma attack (Smith & Strunk, 1999).

Patient education includes teaching or reinforcing the families' knowledge about triggers, environmental controls, risk factors, importance of long-term medication and regular check-ups and follow-up visits with the primary physician. A consult with an allergist may help to isolate specific allergens that need to be avoided. Trigger avoidance is an important part of patient education (see *Table 4-6*). Families need to understand the use of medications, importance of compliance and proper technique for inhalation devices. Environmental control includes removing carpet, keeping pets outdoors, washing bed linen weekly, using plastic mattress and pillow covers and removing stuffed animals. A standard home air filter captures only 15% of allergen particles; however, an electrostatic or hepafilter can remove up to 98% of allergen particles from the air.

TABLE 4-6
Potential Allergens or Triggers

- Dust mites
- Cleaning agents
- Mold spores
- Aspirin
- Animal dander
- Exercise
- Cockroaches
- Hyperventilation
- Pollen
- Cold air
- Tobacco smoke
- Stress
- Fireplace smoke
- Gastroesophageal reflux
- Perfumes
- Respiratory infection

EXAM QUESTIONS

CHAPTER 4
Questions 15–23

15. Which of the following statements is accurate regarding the long-term treatment and management of asthma?

    a. Non compliance and misunderstanding of asthma severity interferes with long-term management of asthma.

    b. Treatment of acute exacerbations prevents progressive airway changes and chronic inflammation.

    c. Control of asthma triggers is not necessary if there is compliance with regular medication.

    d. Emergency action plans are designed to direct the patient to the nearest emergency room for treatment.

16. The chronic inflammation of asthma causes

    a. decreased collagen deposits.

    b. smooth muscle hypoplasia.

    c. bronchial hyperresponsiveness.

    d. laryngospasms.

17. Leukotrienes contribute to airway edema and are released in the body in response to

    a. emotional upset.

    b. inhaling cold air.

    c. allergic stimuli.

    d. environmental irritants such as dirt.

18. Impending respiratory failure in an untreated child with asthma is indicated by

    a. inspiratory and expiratory wheezing.

    b. distant or absent breath sounds.

    c. increased activity or hyperexcitability.

    d. coughing with talking.

19 The most effective mode of beta-agonist administration is

    a. oral administration.

    b. intravenous administration.

    c. intermittent nebulizer treatments every 4 hours.

    d. continuous nebulization.

20. Positive pressure ventilation

    a. can be effective without intubation.

    b. increases the work of breathing.

    c. does not allow spontaneous respirations.

    d. decreases formation of mucous plugs.

21. The best option for delivery of inhaled medications for young children is by

    a. metered dose inhaler.

    b. spacer.

    c. facemask.

    d. mouthpiece.

22. Maintaining long-term management of asthma is difficult

    a. because long-term medications are used regularly.

    b. physician office visits are frequent.

    c. there is poor patient/parent understanding of asthma.

    d. emergency action plans are used.

23. In spite of asthma research, changes in asthma morbidity and mortality are described as

    a. decreased mortality.

    b. no change in morbidity or mortality.

    c. increased morbidity and mortality.

    d. decreased morbidity.

CHAPTER 5

TRAUMA

CHAPTER OBJECTIVE

After completing this chapter, the reader will be able to recognize pediatric specific nursing considerations for a traumatic head or orthopedic injury and effective methods of pain assessment.

LEARNING OBJECTIVES

After studying this chapter, the learner will be able to

1. recognize the physiological and anatomical differences of the pediatric trauma patient and their implications in nursing care.

2. identify the significance of a concussion in relation to second impact syndrome.

3. select the most age appropriate pain assessment techniques for the pediatric patient.

4. specify the significance of infection following a cat bite.

5. choose the nursing responsibilities during conscious sedation.

INTRODUCTION

Injury is the most common cause of death and disability of children and adolescents (*The Merck Manual*, 2001b; Agran, Winn, Anderson, Trent & Walton-Haynes, 2001; Roback,

2000). About 1,000 children under one-year-old die each year from falls, burns, drowning or suffocation (*The Merck Manual*, 2001b). For every one pediatric death, there are another 1,000 children injured. A significant number of these preventable accidents will result in disability (*The Merck Manual*, 2001b). In 1997, in California alone there were 35,277 children from ages 0 to19 hospitalized for injuries. Of those Californian children hospitalized in 1997, 1,934 of them died.

Eighteen-year-olds are at the highest risk for traumatic injury, the second highest risk age group is 1-year-olds (Agran et al., 2001). Motor vehicle accidents (MVAs) are the leading cause of death for children from ages 5 to 14 years old. Boys are injured more often than girls (*The Merck Manual*, 2001b). The estimated cost for unintentional injuries in the U.S. is 347 billion dollars annually (Agran et al., 2001).

Most childhood injuries are preventable. Accidents often occur as a result of a child's natural curiosity. Childhood injuries are more likely to occur when the child is tired or hungry (*The Merck Manual*, 2001b). New surroundings, busy parents or a new daycare provider can all attribute to increased risk of injury.

PEDIATRIC TRAUMA ASSESSMENT

For complete instructions on advanced pediatric life support refer to the American Academy of Pediatrics guidelines.

Airway and Oxygenation

As always, airway management is the top priority. Intubation and stabilization of the cervical spine may be the first interventions needed. Anatomy differences in pediatrics involve a large head and small face, short neck and large tongue compared to the mouth (*The Merck Manual,* 2001b). The pediatric larynx is smaller and more anterior, making intubation more difficult. The narrowest part of the pediatric airway is below the cords at the cricoid ring; therefore, the cuffed endotracheal tubes (ETTs) are not necessary for children less than 8-years-old (Roback, 2000; *The Merck Manual,* 2001b). A pediatric airway is only about 4 cm in diameter, which is half the adult size. A quick reference for a pediatric ETT selection is the size of the child's smallest finger. Primary respiratory responsibilities are to check for obstruction, suction, ventilate and give oxygen. If an obstruction is present, intervene only if stridor and respiratory distress are present or if there is a loss of consciousness (*The Merck Manual,* 2001b). While maintaining oxygenation, the possibility of a pneumothorax or hemothorax should be considered.

There is a higher risk of cervical injuries in children because the child's head is larger and the neck muscles are less developed (Roback, 2000). There is no cervical traction needed for intubation of pediatric patients. The prominent occiput of children requires a shoulder roll to prevent flexion of the neck and ensure immobilization of the cervical spine (Roback, 2000).

Circulation

Children have a large physiologic reserve. Pediatric patients will show little change in vital signs in response to blood loss until the blood loss is severe (Roback, 2000). The initial response is tachycardia. Hypotension will not be evident until 25–30% of blood volume is lost. Early signs of blood loss are prolonged capillary refill and mottled, pale and cool extremities. Weak peripheral pulses, altered mental status and decreased urine output are also early signs of compromise (Roback, 2000). Bradycardia is an ominous sign of impending arrest in children (*The Merck Manual,* 2001b). In newborns, a heart rate less than 80 beats per minute requires cardiac compressions (see *Table 5-1* and *Appendix D).*

Circulation assessment is required while controlling bleeding and during fluid resuscitation. Careful attention to fluid resuscitation will avoid fluid overload. Fluid overload occurs easily in children because they have a smaller blood volume than adults (*The Merck Manual,* 2001b). The first choice of vascular access in the pediatric patient is a central venous catheter. If this is not possible, two peripheral IVs should be started. The third choice for access is a cut down in the femoral, jugular, or subclavian veins. The last resort for emergent situations in children less than six-years-old is an intraosseous access (*The Merck Manual,* 2001b).

Mortality for infants and children with cardiac arrest is about 90–97%. Mortality for respiratory arrest only is 50%, but results in frequent neurological sequelae (*The Merck Manual,* 2001b). The manifestation of cardiac arrest in children is usually from a primary cause such as drowning, MVA, burns, respiratory problems or congenital heart disease. The most frequent cause is hypoxemia or compromised airway.

Thoracic Injuries

Thoracic and abdominal injuries should be assessed next. The elasticity of the pediatric skeleton results in greater risk of internal organ injury (Roback, 2000). The most common type of trauma in pediatrics is blunt trauma. The nurse needs to

TABLE 5-1
Normal Heart, Respiratory Rates, and Blood Pressure in Children

Age	*Normal Heart Rates in Children*		Normal Respiratory Rates in Children (breaths/min)	*Normal Blood Pressures in Children*	
	Awake HR (beats/min)	Sleeping HR (beats/min)		Systolic Pressure (mmHg)	Diastolic Pressure (mmHg)
Neonate	100–180	80–160	30–60	60–90	20–60
Infant	100–160	75–160	30–60	87–105	53–66
Toddler	80–110	60–90	24–40	95–105	53°66
Preschooler	70–110	60–90	22–34	95–110	56–70
School-age child	65–110	60–90	18–30	97–112	57–71
Adolescent	60–90	50–90	12–16	112–128	66–80

Estimated systolic blood pressure norms (for infants and children beyond 1 year of age): 50th percentile systolic blood pressure = 90 mmHg - (2 x age in years): 5th percentile systolic blood pressure = 70 mmHg + (2 x age in years)

Source: Curley, M. & Moloney-Harmon, P. (2001). *Critical care nursing of infants and children.* Philadelphia: W.B. Saunders.

watch for symptoms of blood loss. Injuries to the spleen and liver may cause internal bleeding. There may also be renal contusions, pulmonary contusion, hemothorax or duodenal hematoma. The nurse should assess for urine output, but should not insert a foley if there is blood at the meatus. An orogastric tube may be needed for decompression.

Serious injuries usually occur from large amounts of force (Roback, 2000). Nurses should obtain as much information as possible about the incident that caused the trauma. If the trauma causing incident was a MVA, the speed of the vehicle, extent of damage to the vehicle, death of other victims and the position of the child in the vehicle should be recorded (Roback, 2000). This information is an important assessment tool. The conditions causing the injuries can indicate the need for extensive evaluation for internal injuries.

Hypothermia

Children are more susceptible to hypothermia because they have less subcutaneous tissue and increased surface area (*The Merck Manual,* 2001b; Roback, 2000). Temperatures below 35°C cause increased oxygen consumption and increased cardiac output, which increases morbidity. Eventually, oxygen consumption decreases and severe bradycardia occurs. Asystole will result with in 10 to 15 minutes of profound hypothermia (*The Merck Manual,* 2001b).

Although induced hypothermia has been used to reduce CNS damage in adult head injuries, there is not enough research to document its effectiveness in children (Bernardo, Henker & O'Connor, 2000). If hypothermia is induced for pediatric head injuries, it should be done early, within the first six hours of the injury. Unless hypothermia is a planned treatment, nurses should prevent heat loss for all pediatric trauma patients (Bernardo et al., 2000). The passive warming methods of a warm room, dry blankets and removal of wet clothing are not usually sufficient in preventing heat loss in children (Bernardo et al., 2000). Active warming methods of forced warm air or a warm water circulating mattress are more effective, but these methods are not always practical for patients who are frequently moved for tests or treatments (Bernardo et al., 2000). Core warming methods involve the infusion of warm IV fluids. This is an effective treatment for adults who require large amounts of fluids, but the small amount of fluids given to children prevents this method from having a significant effect (Bernardo et al., 2000). Additional research is needed to discover optimal warming methods for pediatric patients (Bernardo et al., 2000).

TABLE 5-2
Pediatric Trauma Score

Component	+2	+1	-1
		Category	
Size	>20 kg	10–20 kg	<10 kg
Airway	Normal	Maintainable	Unmaintainable
Systolic BP	>90 mmHg	50–90 mmHg	<50 mmHg
CNS	Awake	Obtunded/LOC	Comatose
Skeletal	None	Closed fracture	Open/multiple fractures
Cutancous	None	Minor	Major

Sum_____

BP = blood pressure; CNS = central nervous system; LOC = loss of consciousness

Reprinted with permission from: Tepas, J., Ramenofsky, M., Mollitt, D. et al. (1988). The pediatric trauma score as a predictor of injury severity: An objective assessment. *J Trauma, 28,* 427, http://lww.com.

Once the airway, breathing and circulation have been stabilized, rapid stabilization of the precipitating problem is essential (*The Merck Manual,* 2001b). Orthopedic injuries are assessed last; however, femur and pelvic fractures can cause complications and poor outcomes if not treated promptly (*The Merck Manual,* 2001b). Improper pediatric resuscitation can cause preventable death. Common errors are inappropriate airway management, inaccurate fluid resuscitation or mistreatment of internal hemorrhaging. Pediatric patients with a pediatric trauma score of eight or less should be transferred to a pediatric trauma center (see *Table 5-2).*

HEAD INJURIES

There are as many as five million pediatric head injuries each year. About 4,000 head injury victims will die and approximately 15,000 victims will require prolonged hospitalization. The mortality rate for children with a Glasgow Coma Scale (GCS) <5 is <10% (see *Table 5-3).* Prolonged rehabilitation may be needed for many victims of head injuries (*The Merck Manual,* 2001b). There is an increased incidence of head injuries for children less than one year of age and for adolescents over 15-years-old. Boys are more likely than girls to sustain a head injury (*The Merck Manual,* 2001b).

Both individual and team sports are common causes for adolescent head injuries (Proctor & Cantu, 2000). Approximately 300,000 concussions occur each year (Poirier & Wadsworth, 2000). In 1991, there were an estimated 1.5 million head injuries that occurred during sporting events (Poirier & Wadsworth 2000).

Common Head Injury Sequelae

- Retrograde amnesia;

- Behavioral changes;

- Emotional liability;

- Sleep disturbance;

- Decreased intellectual ability; and

- Residual seizures (*The Merck Manual,* 2001b).

Definitions

Although most head injuries are minor without a loss of consciousness, concussion, contusion or fracture, a head injury should never be considered insignificant (Poirier & Wadsworth, 2000). Serious head injuries are less common but can be fatal from an epidural, subdural, intraparenchymal or intraventricular hematoma (*The Merck Manual,* 2001b).

- **Contusions** are focal bruising or tearing of cerebral tissue and parenchymatous hemorrhage and/or local edema. Neurological signs and symptoms depend on the precise location of the contusion. There may be disturbances of strength and sensation, altered sensorium and possible increased intracranial pressure with large injuries (*The Merck Manual,* 2001b).

- A **diffuse axonal injury** is caused from acceleration-deceleration forces with shearing and tearing of axons (white matter) and disruption of myelin sheaths. Cerebral edema often results without bleeding. This is one of the most common severe brain injuries in childhood, occurring more often than intracranial hematomas (*The Merck Manual,* 2001b).

- An **epidural hematoma** is a collection of blood between the dura mater and the skull resulting from arterial or venous injury (*The Merck Manual,* 2001b). An epidural hematoma progresses rapidly. It may reach a fatal size within 30 to 60 minutes (Proctor & Cantu, 2000). There may be an increasing headache and a progressive decline in the level of consciousness as the intracranial pressure increases. If the clot is removed promptly, there is usually a complete recovery. If the hematoma is missed it can be fatal (Proctor & Cantu, 2000).

- A **subdural hematoma** is a collection of blood beneath the dura mater, usually associated with significant contusion of the brain (*The Merck Manual,* 2001b). If the symptoms are so severe that surgery is required, the mortality is very high (Proctor & Cantu, 2000). The victim of a subdural hematoma does not usually regain

consciousness, and the need for treatment is obvious.

- An **intraventricular hemorrhage** is caused by a collection of blood in the brain's ventricular system. An intraparenchymal hemorrhage involves bleeding in the brain tissue (*The Merck Manual,* 2001b).

- **Subarachnoid hemorrhages** are in the subarachnoid or cerebral spinal fluid space along the surface of the brain (*The Merck Manual,* 2001b; Proctor & Cantu, 2000). A subarachnoid hemorrhage causes headaches, neurological deficits and possibly seizures.

Concussions

A concussion injury can range from a brief period of neurological dysfunction to a prolonged period of unconsciousness and amnesia (Poirier & Wadsworth, 2000). According to Poirier & Wadsworth (2000), a concussion is a traumatically induced alteration in mental status which may or may not involve a loss of consciousness. It is also described as a diffuse brain injury (Poirier & Wadsworth, 2000). If present, a loss of consciousness usually occurs immediately after the injury. There are often no neurologic signs, but there may be amnesia of both the event and the time just before the event (*The Merck Manual,* 2001b). The primary method of injury is a rotational accelerated force (Poirier & Wadsworth, 2000). Falls greater than 20 feet can result in significant injury (Roback, 2000).

Pathophysiology of a Concussion

A coup injury is a forceful blow to a resting movable head. The injury occurs beneath the point of impact. A contra-coup injury is caused from a moving head that collides with a nonmoving object, such as running into a wall. In a contra-coup injury, the brain is injured on the opposite side of cranial impact. Skull fractures cause a direct injury to brain tissue (Poirier & Wadsworth, 2000). Compressive factors are tolerated fairly well, but shearing forces are not well tolerated by brain tissues (Poirier & Wadsworth, 2000). A child's head can sustain a greater force if the neck muscles are tensed, like when the child sees the collision coming. There is an increased risk of injury when a child does not see a blow coming and cannot maintain neck muscle rigidity (Poirier & Wadsworth, 2000).

Second Impact Syndrome (SIS) is injury caused by two or more traumatic impacts to the head. If a second impact occurs before there is complete recovery from the first impact, there can be an uncontrollable increase in intracranial pressure and secondary diffuse brain swelling. A second blow to an already injured head can even cause death (Poirier & Wadsworth, 2000). SIS has significant implications for competitive contact sports, such as football, where there is significant risk of repeat head injuries. Perhaps the stereotypical term "dumb jock" originated from past incidence of misdiagnosed SIS or post concussion syndrome.

Post concussion syndrome can last for up to six months. There may be a persistent headache, light-headedness, fatiguability, irritability, ataxia, memory loss, poor concentration or sleep disturbances. Symptoms should be completely resolved for two weeks before the child is allowed to return to physical activities. If symptoms are present after one week, a CT or MRI should be done. An abnormal CT or MRI means no more sports or other high-risk activities for one season. Parents should also consider permanent withdrawal from contact sports. Once a concussion occurs, there is an increased risk of secondary impact syndrome (Poirier & Wadsworth, 2000).

Concussion Symptoms

- Headache;
- Dizziness;
- Unsteadiness;
- Nausea;

- Blurred vision;
- Double vision;
- Unequal pupils;
- Brief confusion;
- Altered mental status;
- Poor concentration;
- Inability to perform sequential task;
- Retrograde amnesia;
- Unconsciousness;
- May be easily distracted;
- Cannot maintain coherent thought; and
- Poor coordination (Poirier & Wadsworth, 2000).

Treatment

After a head injury has occurred, the child should be removed from the activity. If there is unconsciousness, immobilize the cervical spine and take the victim to the nearest emergency room immediately. If consciousness in not lost, examine the child immediately, then again every five minutes. Frequent checks will reveal changes in mental status. Assess orientation to person, place and time, three digit recall and memory tests. Before the child returns to play or participates in a sport, assess for symptoms by engaging the child in a physical activity such as sprinting or sit ups, and watch for symptoms of head injury.

In the emergency room airway, breathing and circulation (ABCs) come first. When the patient is stable, a complete history should be obtained. The nurse needs to ask the patient or visitor if there was a loss of consciousness, determine the duration of amnesia and ask whether vomiting occurred. The nurse should also ask if there were other recent incidents of head trauma. Neuro checks and GCS are important assessment tools. The nurse needs to report focal neurological symptoms or a GCS of <14, as a CT scan may be indicated to check for treatable lesions or hematomas that may need evacuation. (Poirier & Wadsworth, 2000).

Children may require hospitalization if there is a loss of consciousness, depressed skull fracture, neurological changes or signs of child abuse (*The Merck Manual*, 2001b). Nurses need to monitor for changes in neuro status, vital signs, pupil changes or seizure onset (*The Merck Manual*, 2001b). A treatment goal is to prevent further dysfunction by avoiding hypoxia, hypercarbia, hypotension and increased intracranial pressure. Increased intracranial pressure (ICP) requires urgent treatment to maintain oxygen delivery to the brain. Fixed and dilated pupils and decerebrate posturing are not necessarily irreversible. Aggressive early treatment of increased ICP can reduce the risks of complications (*The Merck Manual*, 2001b). Prevention is important because brain tissue cannot regenerate. A conservative approach is recommended (Poirier & Wadsworth, 2000).

Children with a GCS of <8 will require intubation with the use of a sedative or lidocaine and a paralytic. Hyperventilation to a PCO2 of 34 to 36 mmHg is recommended for best cerebral perfusion. Arterial blood gases, pulse oximetry, and end tidal PCO2 will indicate the adequacy of ventilation. ICP monitoring may be done to keep the ICP <15 mmHg. The head of the bed (HOB) needs to be elevated to 30°. Mannitol may be given to decrease ICP, and IV Lasix® is used to treat hypervolemia. Dexamethasone is not effective and is not recommended. A phenobarbital coma, hypothermia and treatment of seizures may be needed.

Discharge instructions should include teaching the symptoms of increased intracranial pressure, post concussion syndrome symptoms, when to follow-up with the physician and when to resume activity (Poirier & Wadsworth, 2000). In many areas, there are brain injury support groups for families.

TABLE 5-3
Modified Coma Scale for Infants

	Score
Eye Opening	
Spontaneous	4
To speech	3
To pain	2
None	1
Best Verbal Response	
Coos and babbles	5
Irritable cries	4
Cries to pain	3
Moans to pain	2
None	1
Best Motor Response	
Normal spontaneous movements	6
Withdraws to touch	5
Withdraws to pain	4
Abnormal flexion	3
Abnormal extension	2
None	1
Total Score	3–15

Source: Rogers, M. (1992). *Textbook of pediatric intensive care.* Baltimore: Lippincott Williams & Wilkins. Reprinted with permission of Elsevier Science (*The Lancet*, 1972, Vol. 2, p. 81).

ORTHOPEDIC INJURIES

Children are susceptible to fractures because they have an immature skeleton. Torn ligaments and dislocations are not often seen in children because the ligaments are often stronger than the relatively immature bones (Curley & Moloney-Harmon, 2001). The most problematic fractures are those that involve the epiphyseal plate, because fractures in this location can disrupt bone growth and can cause permanent disability (Curley & Moloney-Harmon, 2001).

Skull and clavicle fractures may occur at birth; however, other fracture injuries are rarely seen in children under two years of age. Fractures in children under two may be suspicious of child abuse, skeletal problems or bone disease. Children from two-years-old to adolescents commonly sustain fractures. The most common location is the upper extremities. Children under six typically sustain fractures from fall accidents. Children ages six to nine are more likely to be involved in auto-pedestrian accidents, and adolescents are more likely to sustain injuries from motor vehicle accidents.

Scooter injuries have presented a new source of orthopedic injury for children. During one summer, one orthopedic office saw eleven children with fractures sustained while riding a scooter (Abott, Hoffinger, Nguyen & Weintraub, 2001). Five of the eleven had more than one fracture, and one child sustained a skull fracture. Causative factors included going too fast, inability to stop, striking an object and tipping the scooter over (Abott et al., 2001).

Assessment

Orthopedic assessment begins with observation of spontaneous movements. Nurses look at and feel each bone and joint to assess for abnormalities. There may be visible deformity, bruising, swelling or crepitus. Nurses need to document the location and appearance of all injuries. Nurses must also assess below the level of injury for circulation, sensitivity and motion (Curley & Moloney-Harmon, 2001).

Circulation checks include color, temperature, capillary refill, edema and pulse. Sensation changes such as numbness, tingling or pain should be noted. Movement of the injured part should be assessed for coordination, symmetrical motion and strength. These circulation, sensation and movement (CSM) checks should be done frequently for the first 24 hours after the injury occurs, after surgery or after the application of a cast, splint or traction (Curley & Moloney-Harmon, 2001).

Nurses must always assess for compartment syndrome with fractures, especially those in the lower leg. Compartment syndrome causes pressure

on blood vessels, which reduces circulation and injures tissues. Bleeding or inflammation can cause compartment syndrome. Swelling beneath a cast or splint may also cause compartment syndrome. Symptoms of compartment syndrome are severe pain, paresthesia, paralysis and eventually pallor and pulselessness (Curley & Moloney-Harmon, 2001).

Types of Fractures

Greenstick fractures are incomplete fractures that usually occur before age 10. Transverse fractures are caused by direct trauma. Spiral fractures are caused from torsion injuries and are often a sign of child abuse. Comminuted (crushed) fractures are frequently from falls or motor vehicle accidents (Curley & Moloney-Harmon, 2001). Long bone fractures at the epiphysis or metaphysis are often associated with child abuse (Hopkins, 2000).

Pelvic fractures may also occur following a MVA. A stable pelvic fracture does not interfere with weight bearing. An unstable pelvic fracture involves a separated symphysis pubis or an opened pelvic ring. If unstable, a portion of the pelvis is displaced which interferes with function. A pelvic fracture may be complicated by bleeding, ruptured bladder or urethral injury.

Treatment

Treatment of orthopedic injuries begins with control of bleeding. CSM checks are done frequently for 24 hours. The application of a splint, cast or traction may be required. If crutches are indicated, nurses will review crutch walking prior to discharge. Nurses should monitor patients for infection and compartment syndrome. Discharge teaching may include symptoms of infection, symptoms of compartment syndrome, CSM checks and cast care. Childhood fractures heal rapidly in comparison to adults; however, children are more prone to osteomyelitis (Curley & Moloney-Harmon, 2001).

Prevention

The number one way to reduce mortality and morbidity of childhood injury is prevention and safety education. Safety education for parents and children is an important nursing function. Distribution of safety information is an effective method of reducing pediatric injuries (*The Merck Manual,* 2001b).

Nurses can help by reminding parents that the safety examples they set are more effective than any verbal teaching (*The Merck Manual,* 2001b). Parents can set good safety examples for children by wearing seat belts and bike helmets. Children must be taught about potential hazards from a young age. Nurses and physicians can also help by anticipating risk factors in families with a sick child. For instance, nurses can encourage parents to seek extra help caring for other children when they have a hospitalized child (*The Merck Manual,* 2001b).

Protection of children from MVAs and pedestrian accidents remains a challenge despite recent advancements. Airbags have decreased the risk of injury; however, when small children are struck in the face or neck with an airbag at 200 mph, severe injury can result (Rivara, 1999). Activated airbags have caused death in infants and children (z 2001b). Children are at the greatest risk if they are unrestrained or improperly restrained during a rollover or ejection accident, as these injuries are the most severe (Roback, 2000). The American Academy of Pediatrics (AAP) recommends that all children under four years of age or 40 pounds be secured in a car seat in a back seat. Children under one-year-old or 20 pounds should be in a rear-facing car seat to reduce the risk of cervical spine injury (Roback, 2000). Children over four years of age should sit in a booster seat to ensure a proper fit of the shoulder harness. Teenagers' lack of seat belt use puts them at a higher risk for injury (Rivara, 1999).

An unrestrained child may be the only casualty of a sudden stop that results in no property damage. All occupants should be restrained. It is extremely unsafe for an adult to hold a child. An adult cannot maintain hold of a child who will be thrown with tremendous force even at minimal speeds. An adult holding a ten-pound child during an accident at 30 mph requires the strength equal to lifting 300 pounds one foot off the ground. The use of seat belts has reduced fatalities and serious injuries by about 50%.

Studies showed that when only one child is riding with one adult, the child frequently rides in the front seat regardless of the increased risk of injury (Wittenberg, Goldie & Graham, 2001). Parents and families may need to be reminded to avoid high-risk seating for children.

Pedestrian/auto collisions are another major cause of traumatic brain injury and disability in children. Males between the ages of five and nine are at the greatest risk of pedestrian injury. Brain and spinal cord injuries are not capable of regeneration, which makes them particularly disabling (Proctor & Cantu, 2000).

ANIMAL AND HUMAN BITES

Introduction

Animal bite injuries can be terrifying for children. Aggressive dog stories have been a topical issue that has prompted stricter laws regarding dog-related injuries. In the U.S., between 1979 and 1996, there were 304 dog bite related deaths (Behrman, 2000). Approximately 70% of these deaths involved children under 11-years-old. Rottweilers, pit bulls and German shepherds were responsible for more than 50% of these dog bite related deaths (Behrman, 2000).

The severity of bite wounds depends on several factors. The location of the bite and the source of the bite will determine the type of treatment needed and the potential complications (Hopkins, 2000). Bite injuries can range from scratches, abrasions, crush injuries and contusions to punctures, tears and lacerations. Complications of superinfection can be caused by oral aerobic and anaerobic bacteria. Dog bite injuries are prone to infection from staphylococcus aureus and pasteurella multocida (Hopkins, 2000). It is important to identify and isolate the animal whenever possible to assess for rabies (Hopkins, 2000).

Case Report

A three-year-old was admitted to a pediatric intensive care unit (PICU) at a children's hospital after being attacked by the family pet. The family's pit bull attacked the three-year-old for no known reason. The dog jumped up and grabbed the child by the neck with its teeth. Upon arrival to the PICU the child was in respiratory distress. She was intubated, sedated and her neck wounds were cleansed. Assessment of the wounds revealed crepitus in the neck tissues that extended to the upper chest. The puncture wounds of the neck had pierced the trachea. Mechanical ventilation, antibiotics and wound care led to a complete recovery. As severe as the wounds were, they could have been much worse. The puncture wounds were only centimeters away from the carotid arteries.

The parents were appropriately concerned for their child but insisted that the dog was a wonderful pet. They were certain that this was a "freak" accident that would not occur again. After several days of conversations with physicians, nurses and police officers, the parents relented and had their dog put to sleep.

This case illustrates the devastating wounds that can be caused by animal bites as well as the need for public awareness regarding the dangers of keeping aggressive dogs as pets.

Dog Bites

Dog bite injuries often involve children between the ages of 6 and 11. Boys are slightly more affected than girls are. Approximately one-half of the attacks are reported as unprovoked attacks. About two-thirds of the attacks occur around the home, and the dog is known by the child.

Cat Bites

There are 450,000 cat bites reported every year, and most of them involve a household pet (Behrman, 2000). Cat bites are more common in girls than in boys. Cat bite wounds are usually deep puncture wounds, which makes cleaning the wounds difficult, increasing the risk of infection (Hopkins, 2000). Cat bites may present in a fulminant manner with rapid development of redness swelling and pain within 12 to 24 hours. Cat bite infections are slow to respond to drainage and antibiotics. Cat scratches are common and have a risk of superinfection.

There are approximately 24,000 incidents of cat scratch disease every year in the U.S. Cat scratch disease can be transmitted through a cat scratch or bite. Kittens less than six-months-old are most likely to carry the infectious bacteria. There is an incubation period of 7 to 12 days. One or more 3 to 5 mm red papules develop near the scratch or bite. These lesions are very small and may not be noticed. The disease may present with lymphadenitis, fever, anorexia, fatigue, headache and malaise (Hopkins, 2000; Behrman, 2000). Occasionally, a rash will also be present. Lymph involvement is seen between one to four weeks after exposure. The lymph nodes will be enlarged, tender and erythematous for one to two months, and there may be a prolonged period of fever. Treatment involves systematic care and observation. The symptoms resolve over several months, and the prognosis is generally excellent.

Potential complications are osteomyelitis or an abscess of the liver or spleen (Behrman, 2000). Encephalopathy occurs in approximately 5% of patients with cat scratch disease. Encephalopathy occurs suddenly with seizures, bizarre behavior or altered consciousness. Recovery occurs slowly over many months but usually without sequelae.

Human Bites

Preschoolers are at the greatest risk for human bite wounds. These injuries often occur at child care centers. Human bites in adolescents are often caused from fist-to-mouth contact. In younger children, a bite to the face or trunk is more common. Nurses should consider child abuse when human bites are involved. Many organisms can infect a human bite including hepatitis B, herpes simplex and syphilis (Hopkins, 2000).

Wound Care

Wound care is based on the type, size and depth of a bite injury. Nursing assessment of bite wounds should include assessment for damage to underlying structures. Tendons, bones, vessels and nerves can be injured with a severe bite injury (Hopkins, 2000). For deep bite wounds, x-rays should be taken to check for bone involvement.

If indicated, wound care should begin with a culture of the wound. An anesthetic prior to wound cleansing is important for the pediatric patient (Behrman, 2000). Only 1% providone-iodine should be used for cleansing because stronger antiseptics can damage the wound surface and delay healing (Hopkins, 2000). Peroxide should not be used on bite wounds because it prevents migration of white blood cells. After cleansing, the wound should be irrigated with copious amounts of normal saline. Puncture wounds can be irrigated gently using a blunt tipped needle. Debridement of tissue, foreign bodies and contaminants is essential (Hopkins, 2000).

Wounds that involve tendons, joints, deep fascial layers or major vasculature should be evaluated by a plastic surgeon or hand surgeon and closed in the operating room if needed (Hopkins, 2000). Deep sutures should be avoided. Head and neck bite wounds require copious amounts of irrigation and debridement. Facial bites require closure for cosmetic reasons. These wounds are at lower risk for infection because there is a good vascular supply in the face (Hopkins, 2000).

All hand wounds need to be immobilized in a position of function for three to five days (Behrman, 2000; Hopkins, 2000). Extremity wounds should be kept elevated for 24–36 hours or until edema subsides. Follow-up should be done for all bite wounds within 24–48 hours (Hopkins, 2000). Wound care is very important. Wounds should be kept clean and dry. Parents should be taught to watch for symptoms of infection.

Complications

Infections

Infection is the most common complication of bite injuries (Behrman, 2000). Infection rates after dog bites that received early treatment are 20%, whereas cat bite infections following early treatment occur at a rate of 50% (Behrman, 2000). Because of the increased risk of infection with cat bites, all cat bite wounds should be cultured. Human bites are also at a greater risk of infection and should always be cultured (Behrman, 2000). All other wounds should be cultured if symptoms of an infection are present. Hand bites are prone to infection because tendons, vessels and bones all occupy a small compact area (Hopkins, 2000). Wounds that are at a higher risk of infection include puncture wounds, minor hand or foot wounds, cat bites or human bite wounds. Wounds that have not received treatment within 12 hours or wounds in an immunosupressed patient are also at a greater risk of infection (Hopkins, 2000). Wounds that are high risk for infection should not be sutured closed. Osteomyelitis is the most common complication in hand bite injuries that become infected (Hopkins, 2000).

Prophylactic antibiotics are recommended for all but very low risk wounds. The number of microbes that could be present in a bite wound ranges from none to 16 (Behrman, 2000). Cultures of infected dog and cat bite wounds have an average of five types of bacteria present. Severe infected bite wounds with systemic symptoms may require intravenous antibiotics (Hopkins, 2000). If a wound does become infected, drainage and debridement will be necessary. Cultures should always be obtained before antibiotics are started or changed. Although tetanus after human or animal bites is rare, a tetanus toxoid should be given to any bite victim who has not had a tetanus injection in the last ten years.

Rabies

An infectious rabies exposure can occur from a domestic or wild animal. Rabies can occur from bites, scratches or from the contact of animal saliva with a person's open wound (Hopkins, 2000). All rabies exposures must be reported to a public health authority. A rabies vaccine may be needed if there has been a local problem with rabid animals. A rabies injection is not needed if the animal was vaccinated against rabies. If it is unknown rather or not the animal had a vaccine, then the animal should be quarantined to observe for symptoms of rabies.

Wound management for suspected or known rabies exposure begins with immediately cleaning the wound with soap and water. Suturing should be avoided, and antibiotics are given if needed. If needed, a rabies vaccine is given in the deltoid or gluteal muscle, depending on the age of the patient. There are two parts to the rabies vaccine. One injection is a vaccine using inactivated rabies virus, and the second contains rabies immune globulin (RIG). If there has been no previous exposure to

rabies, then both injections are given on days 0, 3, 7, 14 and 28. If the patient has received previous rabies prophylaxis, then one vaccine is given on day 0 and one on day 3. The rabies immune globulin is not given for repeat exposures.

Prevention

Parents should be counseled about having harmful breeds of dogs as pets. Newborns are especially at risk for attack because they are new to the home (Behrman, 2000). Nurses should teach parents the importance of close observation of children and their pets. Parents should also teach children respect for animals and teach them to be cautious of injury.

PEDIATRIC PAIN MANAGEMENT

Children are frequently under-medicated. Pain control in children is difficult because pain is so subjective, and there are often communication barriers, especially with young children (Franck, Greenberg & Stevens, 2000). Untreated pain can cause short and long-term complications. When children are in pain they do not eat (Franck et al., 2000). A decrease in nutrition can cause delayed wound healing. Pain can also impair mobility, interrupt sleep and cause developmental regression (Franck et al., 2000). Mortality and morbidity can increase when pain is not controlled (American Academy of Pediatrics [APA]; American Pain Society Task Force on Pain in Infants, Children and Adolescents, 2001).

Methods of Pain Assessment

Nurses assess pain routinely with all patients, and documentation of pain is standard practice. Some institutions refer to pain as the 5th vital sign. There are three effective methods of pediatric pain assessment. Verbal reports of pain are the most effective method. However, behavioral and physi-

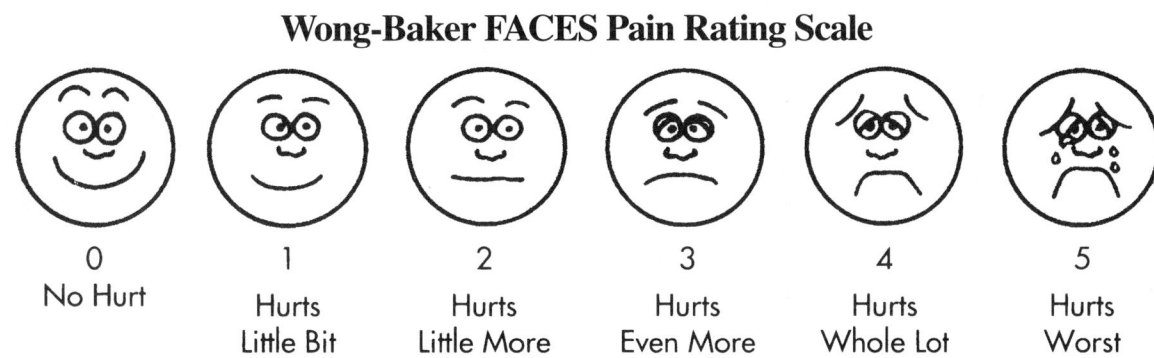

FIGURE 5-1
Wong-Baker FACES Pain Rating Scale

Explain to the person that each face is for a person who feels happy because he has no pain (hurt) or sad because he has some or a lot of pain. Face 0 is very happy because he doesn't hurt at all. Face 1 hurts just a little bit. Face 2 hurts a little more. Face 3 hurts even more. Face 4 hurts a whole lot. Face 5 hurts as much as you can imagine, although you don't have to cry to feel this bad. Ask the person to choose the face that best describes how he is feeling. Rating scale is recommended for persons age 3 years and older.

From Wong, D., Hockenberry-Eaton, M., Wilson, D., Winkelstein, M. & Schwartz, P. *Wong's Essentials of Pediatric Nursing,* 6/e, St. Louis, 2001, P. 1301. Copyrighted by Mosby, Inc. Reprinted with permission.

cal observations are also useful at all ages (Franck et al., 2000).

Verbal

Self-reporting of pain is the most effective pain assessment because more information can be communicated. Older children can explain in detail the location, intensity and duration of pain. They can also describe patterns or changes in pain. School age children can rate their pain on a scale of one to ten, which allows nurses to assess changes in intensity (Franck et al., 2000). By age three or four children are able to provide some type of rating. A picture scale of six facial expressions helps a three-year-old rate the intensity by pointing to the picture that correlates best with the intensity of pain (see *Figure 5-1).* Children as young as 18-months-old often have one or two words, such as "boo boo" or "owie," to indicate that they are having pain (Franck et al., 2000).

Behavioral

Behavioral indicators are not as black and white as verbal statements, but close observation of behavior can help nurses determine location and intensity of pain. Some behavioral characteristics

of pain include withdrawal, irritability, fear, anxiety and agitation. Facial expressions and body movements are good indicators of distress. Muscle tension or rigidity signifies discomfort. Crying and the inability to sleep are often caused by pain (Franck et al., 2000). Nurses might observe how easily the child is consoled or how the child responds to touch to assess the level of discomfort. Parents are a great resource for behavioral assessment. Studies show that parents' assessment of their child's pain is usually more accurate than nurses' observations, and parents typically do not over estimate pain level (Franck et al., 2000).

Physical

Physical indications of pain include increased heart rate, increased respiratory rate and increased blood pressure. Diaphoresis and pupil dilation may also demonstrate the presence or intensity of pain (Franck et al., 2000). Considering the physical symptoms of pain alone, it may be difficult to distinguish pain from other sources of anxiety or fear; however, when assessed in combination with behavioral characteristics, physical symptoms can help to guide pain control measures of a young child who cannot communicate verbally (Franck et al., 2000).

Pain Control Options

There are several pain control options used in pediatrics today. Nurses may be responsible for the administration of pain medication or for continuous monitoring and assessment throughout the duration of sedation. Improved methods of pain control are accompanied by increased risk of drug reactions or overdose.

Narcotics

The most common narcotic drugs used for analgesia and sedation in pediatrics are morphine, demerol, fentanyl, codeine and oxycodone. Nurses should refer to their unit drug book for a detailed description, adverse events and dosing (Cameron, Sponseller & Rossberg, 2000).

- Morphine is the most common narcotic used. Its peak effect is in 20 minutes. Morphine can be given IV, and the adverse events are nausea and vomiting, itching and respiratory depression.

- Demerol causes less sedation than morphine and is primarily used for analgesia. Demerol should not be used with MAO inhibitors. This combination can cause seizures and death. There is also an increased risk of addiction with demerol.

- Fentanyl has a rapid onset of 10 minutes. It has a short half-life and will last for 30 to 45 minutes. It can be given IV or sublingual. Rapid administration may cause chest wall rigidity, glottic rigidity and respiratory depression for several hours.

- Codeine, for post procedural pain, has an increased incidence of nausea and vomiting.

- Oxycodone is for post procedural pain, and it causes less nausea and vomiting than codeine. It is available in tablet or elixir.

Conscious Sedation

Conscious sedation use is increasing in management of pediatric pain and anxiety (Cameron et al., 2000). Cameron et al's definition of conscious sedation is "A controlled lessening of a patient's awareness of the environment and/or pain perception while maintaining stable vital signs, an independent airway and adequate spontaneous respirations." During conscious sedation, cardiac monitoring, pulse oximeter readings and respiratory assessment are nursing responsibilities. A reversal agent and dose should always be available. Flumazenil and naloxone are the most commonly used reversal agents (Cameron et al., 2000). Infants and children with the afflictions listed below are at a greater risk of complications with the use of conscious sedation (Cameron et al., 2000).

- Sleep apnea

- Obesity

- Craniofacial abnormalities

- Heart or lung disease

- Neuro-muscular disorders

- Neurological disorders

- Cerebral palsy

- Trauma patients

- Hemodynamically unstable

- Reflux or swallowing dysfunction

- History of anesthesia complications

According to Cameron et al. (2000), discharge criteria after conscious sedation includes:

- Stable cardiovascular function;

- Stable airway;

- Child is easily arousable;

- Protective reflexes are intact;

- Age appropriate mentation;

- Child can sit up; and

- Child is adequately hydrated.

TABLE 5-4

The Recommended Fasting Criteria for Conscious Sedation

Less than six-months-old	No liquids for 2 hours and no solids for 4 hours.
Under three-years-old	No liquids for three hours and no solids for six hours.
Over three-years-old	No clear liquids for 3 hours and no solids for 6 to 8 hours.

Source: Cameron, M., Sponseller, P. & Rossberg, M. (2000). Pediatric analgesia and sedation for the management of orthopedic conditions. *The American Journal of Orthopedics*, September, 665–672.

Deep Sedation

Deep sedation is a profound depression of consciousness and involves possible loss of protective reflexes. A patient who fails to move or respond to verbal or noxious stimuli is in deep sedation. Deep sedation is required for painful orthopedic procedures and requires assessment of the airway, ventilation and blood pressure.

General Anesthesia

General anesthesia is a medically controlled state of unconsciousness with a loss of protective reflexes, the inability to maintain an open airway and the inability to respond to stimuli. Nurses need to be prepared for complications of general anesthesia. The distinction between adequate and excessive sedation is much narrower in children (Cameron et al., 2000). Important nursing steps include checking the child's current medications, allergies, time of the child's last meal and a brief review of the child's physical exam. Fasting before general anesthesia is always best.

SUMMARY

Untreated pain can prolong hospitalization and convalescence (Franck et al., 2000). Nurses can anticipate painful procedures and request premedication before they begin. Nurses can also utilize parents for suggestions, distraction and assistance. Nurses must always remain calm around children, this will lessen the anxiety levels of both the parents and the child. Pediatric pain control has improved in recent years, and with careful verbal, behavioral and physical assessments nurses can continue to provide optimal pain free care for children.

EXAM QUESTIONS

CHAPTER 5
Questions 24–33

24. Which statement about the prevalence of pediatric trauma in the U.S. is accurate?

    a. Less than 500 children under the age of one die each year from traumatic events.

    b. Children between the ages of 6 and 12 are the age group at the greatest risk of traumatic injury.

    c. The majority of childhood traumatic injuries cannot be prevented.

    d. Injury is the most common cause of death and disability of pediatric patients.

25. The pediatric airway is

    a. the same size as an adult's airway.

    b. one-half the size of an adult's airway.

    c. larger than the adult airway.

    d. about 8 cm in diameter.

26. Which of the following statements most accurately describes the pediatric circulatory systems?

    a. Pediatric heart rate and blood pressure will drop dramatically with a blood loss of only 5%.

    b. Hypotension is evident after a pediatric patient has lost about 25% of their blood volume.

    c. Tachycardia will not occur in the pediatric patient until there is a 75% blood loss.

    d. Blood pressure and heart rate fluctuations are the same in children as in adults.

27. Which is an accurate statement about second impact syndrome (SIS)?

    a. A second impact syndrome injury results from a second impact that occurs before the first has completely recovered.

    b. Second impact syndrome is always a very mild injury.

    c. Second impact syndrome should not prevent a child from returning quickly to participation in competitive sports.

    d. There are no closed head injury symptoms associated with second impact syndrome.

28. Compartment syndrome may cause

    a. pulselessness.

    b. rapid pulse.

    c. bounding pulse.

    d. irregular pulse.

29. What is the most age appropriate pain assessment technique for the pediatric patient?

    a. Verbal reports of pain are the most useful method of assessment in a five-year-old.

    b. The best assessment of pain intensity in a 12-year-old comes from a change in vital signs.

    c. Pain assessment for older children should be done first using behavioral indicators.

    d. The six face picture scale should be used on children over age 9.

30. Cat bite wounds

    a.   are usually large open wounds.

    b.   may develop infection within 12 hours.

    c.   are easy to clean and low-risk for infection.

    d.   will respond rapidly to antibiotics.

31. What is the correct statement about pediatric dog bite wounds?

    a.   About 30% of dog bite wounds involve children under 11 years old.

    b.   About 2/3 of all dog bite injuries occur at home by dogs known to the child.

    c.   About 90% of dog attacks are provoked by the child.

    d.   About 2/3 of all dog bite wounds occur away from home by strange dogs.

32. Which of the following statements describes rabies?

    a.   Only animal bites can transmit rabies, scratches are not a concern.

    b.   Rabies cases do not need to be reported to public health.

    c.   Rabies can only be transmitted from wild animals.

    d.   Rabies vaccines are given in a series of five injections.

33. What is the appropriate nursing responsibility during conscious sedation?

    a.   Keep visitors occupied so that they will not disturb the patient.

    b.   Assist the physician with the procedure or treatment being given.

    c.   Assess the patient's respirations and pain level.

    d.   Closely monitor peripheral pulses.

CHAPTER 6

HOUSEHOLD TOXINS AND POISONS

CHAPTER OBJECTIVE

After completing this chapter, the reader will be able to identify harmful household substances and recognize symptoms, treatments and preventive measures of both inhalation and ingestion injuries.

LEARNING OBJECTIVES

After studying this chapter, the learner will be able to

1. select two examples of toxicity caused by salicylate poisoning.

2. identify symptoms of inhalation and ingestion toxicity.

3. recognize treatment measures for both inhalation and ingestion injuries.

4. specify complications that can occur as a result of toxic ingestions or inhalations.

5. choose two preventive measures that should be included in parent teaching after an ingestion accident.

INTRODUCTION

Poison exposure is the most common nonfatal accident in the home (*The Merck Manual,* 2001b). Poisoning can occur through ingestion, inhalation or by skin or eye exposures. Harmful household toxins, based on their chemical content, fall into four categories. There are medications, acidic agents, alkaline agents and hydrocarbons. Acetaminophen and aspirin are often readily available and are commonly ingested medications. Toilet bowl cleaners, swimming pool products and battery fluids are common acid exposures. Alkaline agents include drain openers, lye, hair permanent products and oven cleaners. Hydrocarbons are organic compounds some of which can cause systemic toxicity (Curley & Moloney-Harmon, 2001).

Many common caustic household substances can cause functional and cellular damage on contact with body surfaces (Curley & Moloney-Harmon, 2001). Some tissue damage is caused by thermal energy that is released upon contact causing tissues to burn. Many accidental ingestions occur when caustic substances are stored in familiar containers such as milk cartons and soda cans (Curley & Moloney-Harmon, 2001).

MEDICATIONS

Acetaminophen

The use of acetaminophen dramatically increased following the occurrence of Reye Syndrome in connection with the use of aspirin. There are over 100 products on the market that contain acetaminophen (*The Merck Manual,*

2001). An acute acetaminophen overdose causes necrosis of the liver. Children under 12-years-old usually tolerate liver toxicity fairly well and rarely die from acetaminophen overdose. However, symptoms and prolonged liver function test abnormalities are more severe in adolescents. The reason for this age difference is unknown. There are typically no residual effects seen in previously healthy children under the age of 12 (*The Merck Manual,* 2001b). A dose greater than 150 mg/kg is considered toxic for children under 12-years-old. For children over the age of 12, a dose of 7.5 g in a single ingestion is toxic.

There are four phases of symptoms following toxic ingestion of acetaminophen (Behrman, 2000). Symptoms of acetaminophen toxicity are usually mild for the first 48 hours. There may be nausea, vomiting, anorexia, malaise, pallor and diaphoresis. If the ingestion was not witnessed, this can easily be misdiagnosed. From 24 to 48 hours there is less nausea and vomiting, but right upper quadrant pain and oliguria are seen. Labs will show an increase in bilirubin, prothrombin time and liver enzymes. The third stage of symptoms occur from 72 to 96 hours when there is a peak in liver enzymes, and the anorexia, nausea and vomiting may return. The last phase of symptoms continues for four days to two weeks. During this phase, there is either resolution of liver dysfunction or complete liver failure (Behrman, 2000).

Serum levels of acetaminophen are not useful until four hours after ingestion because there is incomplete absorption before that time. Liver enzymes, bilirubin and prothrombin time are drawn after four hours. Acetaminophen ingestion is treated first by the induction of emesis with syrup of ipecac. Gastric lavage may also be done, followed by the use of activated charcoal (Behrman, 2000). Charcoal is useful for up to two hours after the ingestion. The administration of other medications that may exacerbate liver toxicity such as

antihistamines, corticosteroids and phenobarbital should be avoided.

For overdoses greater than 150 mg/kg, acetylcysteine may be needed. Acetylcysteine (Mucomyst®) is the antidote for acetaminophen toxicity (Behrman, 2000). Acetylcysteine can reduce or prevent hepatic cellular damage. If at four or more hours after the ingestion the serum blood level of acetaminophen is 990 mmol/L or more, then acetylcysteine is needed. Acetylcysteine is started with a loading dose of 140 mg/kg either orally or via nasogastric tube. This loading dose is followed by 17 more doses at 70 mg/kg every four hours (*The Merck Manual,* 2001b). If there is emesis less than one hour after any dose, that dose should be repeated. Acetylcysteine must be diluted in a carbonated beverage or juice before administration. This drug has a noxious odor and is best tolerated cold, covered with a lid, and taken through a straw. An intravenous preparation of acetylcysteine is used in other countries and will be available in the U.S. soon (Behrman, 2000).

For severe liver effects where clotting is affected, vitamin K, plasma or clotting factors may be needed (*The Merck Manual,* 2001b). Intravenous hydration is recommended using dextrose solution. Peritoneal dialysis and hemodialysis are not effective methods of treatment. For patients with severe toxicity who are suffering from liver failure, a liver transplant may be needed (Behrman, 2000).

Children under six-years-old have a low risk of toxicity from acetaminophen but should be evaluated regardless. Adolescents are at a greater risk of developing toxicity; however, mortality rates are less than 0.5% (Behrman, 2000). Once recovered, patients have shown no sequelae at 3–12 months after ingestion.

Salicylate Poisoning (Aspirin)

Despite safety packaging, which limits the number of tablets per bottle and requires safety caps, aspirin poisoning continues to occur in all age groups. The incidence has decreased some since the increased use of nonaspirin products.

Salicylate toxicity occurs following doses of more than 300 mg/kg (*The Merck Manual*, 2001b). Acute toxicity occurs following one very large dose and is easier to treat than a chronic toxicity that occurs following several days of moderately large doses. Salicylates in oil based agents such as liniments and hot vapor solutions are the most lethal form. Death can result from pediatric ingestion of less than one teaspoonful of an oil-based salicylate.

Symptoms of aspirin toxicity include nausea and vomiting, tinnitus, tachypnea, fever, hyperactivity and seizures (*The Merck Manual*, 2001b). Central nervous system stimulation is replaced quickly by depression and lethargy. Respiratory failure and collapse may occur. Respiratory alkalosis and metabolic acidosis occur simultaneously in older patients. In children less than four years of age, metabolic acidosis occurs rapidly without the occurrence of respiratory alkalosis. There may be serious dehydration and severe loss of sodium and potassium.

Salicylate serum concentrations should be obtained. Serial serum levels will indicate if there is continued absorption occurring. Serial levels can also measure the efficacy of treatment. Arterial blood gases, sodium, potassium, bicarbonate, blood urea nitrogen, glucose, urine pH and specific gravity will also be followed to evaluate the severity of toxicity and the effectiveness of treatment.

Aspirin poisoning requires early gastric emptying. Syrup of ipecac should be given within 30 minutes of aspirin ingestion, if there have been no changes in mental status (*The Merck Manual*, 2001b). If treatment begins after 30 minutes, then activated charcoal is given. The charcoal dose is 15 GM in 4 ounces of water, and it can be given orally or via nasogastric tube. The activated charcoal will

absorb salicylate, and it can prevent intestinal absorption for several hours after administration. Hydration and maintenance of urine output are important treatment measures. Dextrose 5% in normal saline is started, then replaced with 5% dextrose in water with bicarbonate (*The Merck Manual*, 2001b). The bicarbonate will reverse the metabolic acidosis and increase the urine output. The increased urine output will improve the elimination of salicylate through the urine. Serum potassium may be affected by the bicarbonate; therefore, it should be monitored. If ventilation is required, hyperventilation will increase removal of CO2 from the body.

Hyperthermia should be treated with acetaminophen, and seizures should be treated with lorazepam or diazepam. Treatment of fever and seizures will reduce the risk of muscle disintegration. Hemodialysis may be needed to increase urinary elimination of salicylate in patients resistant to bicarbonate, patients with severe neurological impairment or patients with impaired renal function.

CAUSTIC INGESTIONS

The skin, eyes, respiratory tract and gastrointestinal tract can all be affected by caustic injury. Ingestion injuries can be life threatening or can cause long-term morbidity. Most of the caustic burns to the esophagus are caused by lye and occur most often to children under the age of five (Curley & Moloney-Harmon, 2001). Children tend to consume a lesser amount of solid caustics because they stick to tissues and cause a burning sensation that keeps the child from ingesting more (*The Merck Manual*, 2001b). Liquids on the other hand are easily consumed and can cause more damage to the esophagus and stomach; however, liquid ingestions may not cause any damage to the lips, tongue or throat.

Acids and Alkaline Substances

First-degree ingestion burns can cause increased blood flow to the burned area and superficial shedding of epithelium. Second-degree burns produce blisters and shallow ulcers. Third degree burns are deep ulcerations in the mucosa. Ingestion of liquid agents can produce injuries that extend to the stomach.

In severe cases, children feel pain immediately. Children will usually cry and drool. They are unable to swallow fluids or solids. The burned areas become edematous and may cause obstruction. There is swelling, increased secretions and dysphagia. The pulse will be rapid and weak, respirations will be shallow and shock may occur.

Acids produce coagulation necrosis in the stomach and esophagus, which causes eschar formation. Acids can also cause metabolic acidosis. Toilet bowl cleaners can burn the mouth and throat; however, they are usually spit right back out, so ingestion is rare (Curley & Moloney-Harmon, 2001). Detergents and bleach cause irritation but do not cause necrosis.

Ammonia is a common alkali that causes ulcers or full thickness burns to the esophagus, if ingested and also causes irritation and pulmonary edema following inhalation (Curley & Moloney-Harmon, 2001). Alkaline agents affect the mouth, esophagus and stomach. They cause necrosis, inflammation and penetration into the muscle layer of the esophagus and stomach. Several days later there may be destruction of mucosal fats and proteins, thrombosis of blood vessels, cell necrosis and tissue degeneration. Tissue sloughing occurs four to seven days after ingestion when bacteria invade the wounded area. Strictures can develop up to 42 days after the exposure. Nursing assessment should include inquires about the type of agent, the concentration, the pH of the agent and the amount of exposure.

Treatment

Many patients with ingestion injuries will require hospitalization. Patients may present with impending airway obstruction. Gentle or fiber optic intubation is needed to avoid soft tissue perforation. Emesis should not be induced because re-exposure can cause more burns. Gastric lavage is also contraindicated. Liquid ingestions can be treated with nasogastric suctioning (Curley & Moloney-Harmon, 2001). Activated charcoal is not used because there is usually poor absorption, and the charcoal can interfere with endoscopic examination (Curley & Moloney-Harmon, 2001). Second-degree burns, third-degree burns and perforations are treated with antibiotics, antacids and parental nutrition. A follow-up endoscopy is done two to three weeks after the ingestion. Long-term sequelae may require esophageal surgery.

Patients with first-degree burns are assessed for their ability to tolerate liquids and are then slowly advanced to a regular diet. If the gag reflex is intact, the chemical can be diluted with water or milk immediately after the ingestion. Milk is preferred because it contains tissue-repairing protein. The ingestion of solid or granular alkaline material can be diluted with 5 ml/kg of tap water, if done within 30 minutes of the ingestion. Once again, care must be taken to avoid the induction of emesis. Acids are not diluted with water because of the excessive heat production. All skin exposure should be washed well.

Small children, symptomatic patients and patients with mental changes are admitted for observation. An endoscopy will be done to determine the extent of injury and to predict complications of stricture formation or the need for esophageal replacement. If strictures are present, they may require dilation therapy for several months to several years. Treatment includes making the patient NPO and infusing IV hydration for up to 24 hours. Antibiotics are given for fever or other symptoms of infection.

Nurses will observe for increasing distress, which may include drooling, mouth lesions, stridor, hoarseness, subcutaneous air, respiratory distress, acute peritonitis and hematemesis. Airway edema and obstruction can occur up to four days after an alkaline ingestion. Delayed perforation can occur up to four days after an acid exposure. Other potential complications such as infection and strictures can occur more than one week after ingestion injuries. Death can result from circulatory shock, asphyxia, perforation of the esophagus or pulmonary irritation.

HYDROCARBONS

Annual ingestions of hydrocarbons such as gasoline, kerosene and paint thinners number more than 25,000 in children under five-years-old (*The Merck Manual,* 2001b). Hydrocarbons are organic compounds that can cause systemic toxicity (see *Table 6-1*). About 60% of hydrocarbon exposures involve children, and 90% of hydrocarbon related deaths involve children under the age of five. Hydrocarbons primarily effect the respiratory system; although, they can also effect the central nervous system, the gastrointestinal system, the heart and the skin. Hydrocarbons rarely have adverse effects on the liver or kidneys (Curley & Moloney-Harmon, 2001). Death most often occurs from aspiration pneumonitis.

Inhalation abuse of hydrocarbons in adolescents can result in sudden cardiac death. Viscosity and surface tension are important factors that determine the severity of toxicity. The lower the viscosity, the greater the risk of aspiration. Small amounts of inhaled hydrocarbons can spread rapidly throughout the lungs. Chemical pneumonitis can develop from as little as a few milliliters of a hydrocarbon (Curley & Moloney-Harmon, 2001).

TABLE 6-1
Common Hydrocarbon Substances
• Furniture polish
• Lamp oil
• Lighter fluid
• Propane
• Paints
• Paint removers
• Cyclohexane
• Carbon tetrachloride
• Cholorform
• Methylene chloride
• Freon
• Trichloromethane
• Cyclopropane
• Isobutane
• Glue
• Nail polish
• Turpentine

Animal experiments show that death can occur from only 2.5 mL of inhaled hydrocarbons compared to 350 mL of ingested hydrocarbons (*The Merck Manual,* 2001b).

Aspiration can occur during ingestion or with emesis. A possible systemic effect from some hydrocarbons is neurotoxicity (Curley & Moloney-Harmon, 2001). Some hydrocarbons are also associated with anemia caused from bone marrow damage. Death from pneumonitis usually occurs within 24 hours of inhalation injury, whereas nonfatal pneumonitis heals in about one week.

Adverse effects of hydrocarbon ingestion include:

• Pulmonary dysfunction;

- Tachypnea, dyspnea, oxygen desaturations and cyanosis;

- CNS dysfunction with euphoria, agitation, restlessness, confusion, seizures and coma;

- Cardiovascular dysfunction, ventricular dysrhythmias, tachycardia and fibrillation;

- Gastrointestinal effects of oropharyngeal irritation, gastric irritation, vomiting and hematemesis;

- Hepatic dysfunction, elevated liver enzymes and hepatomegaly; and

- Renal dysfunction and albuminuria (Curley & Moloney-Harmon, 2001).

Symptoms

Symptoms of hydrocarbon ingestion or inhalation may include coughing, choking, vomiting, cyanosis and breath holding (*The Merck Manual,* 2001b). The cough usually continues and becomes persistent. An older child may complain of burning in the stomach prior to vomiting. All hydrocarbons cause GI distress, nausea, vomiting, hematemesis and diarrhea. These effects of hydrocarbon toxicity are dose related. Gastric emptying may be done if there are no contraindications. Emesis and gastric lavage are not recommended because of the risk for aspiration.

Aspiration after vomiting leads to hydrocarbon pneumonitis and rapid development of a low-grade fever. Hydrocarbons disrupt surfactant and cause injury to the epithelium and pulmonary capillaries. Bronchospasms and alveolar collapse result in atelectasis. Pulmonary edema may also occur (Curley & Moloney-Harmon, 2001). Symptoms include coughing, retractions, grunting, tachypnea, dyspnea, cyanosis and severe hypoxia. Rales, rhonchi, wheezing or decreased breath sounds may also be observed. Positive x-ray findings for densities, pneumonitis, atelectasis and consolidation can occur as early as two hours after aspiration (Curley & Moloney-Harmon, 2001). Complications of pul-

monary injury include cysts, emphysema, pleural effusion, pneumothorax, pneumomediastinum and pneumopericardium.

Some hydrocarbons are absorbed by the GI tract and the lungs, which causes CNS depression, headaches, dizziness, ataxia, lethargy, changes in mental status and seizures (Curley & Moloney-Harmon, 2001). There may also be signs of narcosis and inebriation. Neurological effects may result in convulsions and coma.

Inhalation of some hydrocarbons can cause fatal ventricular fibrillation (Curley & Moloney-Harmon, 2001). Some hydrocarbons can also cause fatty degeneration of the liver resulting in necrosis and damage to the kidneys causing acute renal failure. Renal failure can occur between one and seven days after exposure. There is also a potential for bone marrow disorders.

Treatment

Copious bathing and eye irrigation may be needed for eye and skin exposures. Children must be monitored for signs of pulmonary aspiration such as coughing choking, gagging and oxygen desaturation. If there is no respiratory distress, atrial fibrillation or ventricular fibrillation, the patient may be managed at home (*The Merck Manual,* 2001b).

Severe cases may require hospitalization in the ICU. Aspiration requires immediate intubation and ventilation (Curley & Moloney-Harmon, 2001). In severe cases a chest x-ray done 1.5 to 2 hours after inhalation will show aspiration pneumonia (*The Merck Manual,* 2001b). It is rare for pneumonia to develop after 24 hours of inhalation exposure. Most incidence of pneumonia will be evident within 6–18 hours. Nurses will maintain mechanical ventilation, monitor for a patent airway, provide pulmonary toilet and monitor ABGs until symptoms subside. ABGs, white blood cell counts and urinalysis should be followed to assess for respiratory changes, infection and kidney involvement. Milk may be given to reduce stomach irritation. Intravenous fluids and oxygen may be needed. Early pneumonitis after exposure is chemically induced; therefore, antibiotics are not effective.

If a patient has intentionally ingested toxins, a psychiatric consult is required. Nurses should promote safety by following up accidental ingestions with safety education such as proper storage of toxic substances and adequate supervision of young children. (Curley & Moloney-Harmon, 2001). Nurses' preventative teaching for caregivers and children will decrease the risk of recurrence.

EXAM QUESTIONS

CHAPTER 6
Questions 34–39

34. Symptoms of toxicity caused by salicylate poisoning are

    a. tachypnea, tinnitus and respiratory failure.

    b. stridor, constipation and liver failure.

    c. hypothermia, right upper quadrant pain and paralysis.

    d. wheezing, dermatitis and pneumonitis.

35. The symptoms of a hydrocarbon ingestion injury include

    a. stomach pain and respiratory distress.

    b. dermatitis and disseminated intravascular coagulation.

    c. dry mouth and diverticulosis.

    d. excessive swallowing and perforation of the duodenum.

36. Which of the following is used to treat caustic ingestion injuries?

    a. antihistamine

    b. antacids

    c. antidiuretic

    a. antihypertensives

37. Complications that may occur as a result of a caustic ingestion include

    a. strictures of the colon.

    b. perforation of the larynx.

    c. thickening of the esophageal epithelium.

    d. esophageal perforation.

38. Which of the following preventive measures should be included in parent teaching after an ingestion accident?

    a. Teach parents to store caustic agents in milk cartons.

    b. Remind parents to ensure adequate supervision of young children.

    c. Instruct parents to induce vomiting after any caustic ingestion.

    d. Explain to parents treatment is only needed if there are visible burns.

39. Which of the following is accurate regarding a hydrocarbon ingestion or inhalation?

    a. Vomiting should be induced after ingestion of a hydrocarbon.

    b. Inhalation or aspiration of hydrocarbons have no adverse effects on surfactant.

    c. Symptoms of hydrocarbon exposure may include nausea, vomiting, hematemesis, respiratory distress and cyanosis.

    d. The earliest that positive x-ray findings can be seen is eight hours after hydrocarbon exposure.

CHAPTER 7

BURNS AND THE PEDIATRIC PATIENT

CHAPTER OBJECTIVE

After completing this chapter, the reader will be able to recognize the most common causes of pediatric burn injuries, the significant physiological effects and the potential psychological effects of severe burn injuries, and the important nursing implications of burn wound care and fluid resuscitation.

LEARNING OBJECTIVES

After studying this chapter, the learner will be able to

1. identify the most common etiologies of pediatric burn injuries.

2. recognize the importance and methods of accurate estimation of burn size in the pediatric patient.

3. recognize the significance of airway edema in a pediatric burn patient.

4. recognize the components of a pediatric inhalation injury.

5. identify the most reliable indicators of adequate fluid resuscitation.

6. indicate the primary objectives of wound care.

7. choose some of the long-term psychological effects of a burn injury in the pediatric population.

INTRODUCTION

More than 1,000 children under 15 years of age die in house fires every year (Deitch & Rutan, 2000). Fire and burn injuries are the second leading cause of death for children ages one through four in the U.S., with the most common cause of death being smoke inhalation (Curley & Moloney-Harmon, 2001). From 8–24% of burn unit admissions are related to child abuse (Curley & Moloney-Harmon, 2001). Common causes of house fire accidents are related to cigarette smoking, careless cooking, unsafe heating, faulty wiring or accidents with candles or matches. Two-thirds of nonfatal childhood burns are scalds caused from household accidents (Deitch & Rutan, 2000).

Burn care has improved since the development of specialized burn centers, and improvements in burn treatment have significantly improved mortality. Improved fluid resuscitation, early wound excision and early wound closure have contributed to improved burn outcomes. Early transfer to a specialized burn center may shorten the length of hospitalization and reduce complications for the burn patient (Curley & Moloney-Harmon, 2001). Approximately 80% of all burn victims survive, however, burn injuries can be especially devastating because they often result in disfigurement, emotional distress, pain and major financial expenses (Deitch & Rutan, 2000).

CLASSIFICATION OF BURN INJURIES

Superficial (first-degree) burns involve the epidermis only, with minor tissue damage and intact skin (Curley & Moloney-Harmon, 2001). Pain and redness are the symptoms. A sunburn is a superficial burn.

Partial thickness (second-degree) burns involve the epidermis and varying levels of the dermis (Curley & Moloney-Harmon, 2001). These are very painful with touch, temperature changes and exposure to air. The area appears red, blistered and moist. The appearance of a deep dermal burn is mottled with red, pink or waxy areas, blisters and swelling.

Full thickness (third-degree) burns involve the epidermis and dermis and can extend into subcutaneous tissue with destruction of blood vessels, nerve endings, sweat glands and hair follicles (Curley & Moloney-Harmon, 2001). These appear red to tan, waxy white, brown or black and are dry, hard and leathery (eschar). Pain is caused from surrounding areas of superficial and partial thickness burns, debridement that exposes nerve endings and eventually from healing nerves (Curley & Moloney-Harmon, 2001). Some full thickness burns involve muscle, fascia and bone. Full thickness burns require skin grafting with autografts or skin substitutes (see *Table 7-1*).

ETIOLOGY

Infants and children with mental or physical disabilities are at a greater risk of severe injury because they cannot protect themselves (Curley & Moloney-Harmon, 2001). Children from age two through school age have been burned after playing with matches and lighters. In early adolescents, flame burns involving flammable liquids such as gasoline from lawn mowers and other equipment are not uncommon. Adolescents are also at risk for burns related to smoking cigarettes. Older adolescents have discovered internet recipes for explosives and other flammable mixtures and are at risk for burn injuries from experimentation (Curley & Moloney-Harmon, 2001). Chemical and contact burns can occur at all ages. Hot irons, ovens, wood stoves and radiators are common causes of contact burns (Curley & Moloney-Harmon, 2001). Fabrics that melt complicate burns that are sustained through clothing (Curley & Moloney-Harmon, 2001). Some burns are seasonal such as burns from fireworks, barbecues and sunburn in the summer months. Wood stoves, space heaters or kerosene heaters are common causes of burn injuries in the winter months (Curley & Moloney-Harmon, 2001). Although most burns in the pediatric population are from contact with flames or hot liquids, household electrical injuries are seen in young children. High-voltage electrical injuries are seen in adolescents following risk-taking behaviors (see *Table 7-2*).

Scald Burns

Scalds account for over 50% of pediatric burn injuries (Curley & Moloney-Harmon, 2001). These are characterized by a splash on the upper body and lap accompanied by splatter burns. Hot foods and liquids from microwave use, hot coffee and soup are common causes of scald burns. These burns are very painful and can be very deep depending on the length of exposure (Curley & Moloney-Harmon, 2001). Kitchen grease burns are severe because the grease cools slowly and is difficult to wash off. Hot tap water is another common household cause of scald burns. Because a child's skin is thinner than an adult's skin, a child exposed to bath water of 140°F can suffer severe tissue damage (Curley & Moloney-Harmon, 2001). A two minute exposure in water at 126°F will create a full thickness burn; however, only five seconds of immersion in water at 140°F will create a full thickness burn (Hopkins, 2000). Bath burns usually

TABLE 7-1
Burn Depth Categories

	Superficial Partial Thickness (First Degree)	Partial Thickness (Second Degree)	Full Thickness (Third Degree)
Cause	Scald, flash, flame, contact, chemical, ultraviolet light	Scald, flash, flame, contact, chemical, ultraviolet light	Scald, flash, flame, contact, chemical, electrical
Surface appearance	Dry, no blisters Minimal or no edema Erythematous	Moist blebs, blisters Underlying tissue mottled pink and white Good capillary refill	Dry, leathery eschar Mixed white, waxy, pearly Khaki, mahogany, soot-stained
Pain and temperature	Very painful Rapid heat loss	Very painful	Rapid heat loss Insensate Less rapid heat loss
Histologic depth	Epidermal layers only	Epidermis, papillary and reticular layers of dermis May include fat domes of subcutaneous layer	Down to and may include subcutaneous tissue May include fascia, muscle and bone
Healing time	2 to 5 days with no scarring May have some discoloration	Superficial, 5–21 days with no grafting Deep partial, 21–35 days with no infection If infected, converts to full thickness	Small areas may heal from the edges after weeks Large areas require grafting

Source: Curley M. & Moloney-Harmon, P. (2001). *Critical care nursing of infants and children* (2nd ed.). Philadelphia: W. B. Saunders.

involve the lower body. Parent safety teaching about scald burns should stress constant adult supervision because children can turn faucets on but cannot always turn them off. Water heater temperatures should be set between 120°F and 130°F. An adult should always check the bath water temperature before putting a child in the tub (Curley & Moloney-Harmon, 2001).

Electrical Burns

Low voltage injuries are sustained from household accidents, and high voltage injuries are sustained from power lines (Curley & Moloney-Harmon, 2001). The more mobile a child becomes, the greater the child's risk of a burn injury. Toddlers can suffer electrical burns by inserting objects into outlets or by chewing on appliance cords (Curley & Moloney-Harmon, 2001). Saliva is an excellent conductor, and it creates a current pathway from the cord through the child's tissues.

Adolescents occasionally sustain electrical burns from climbing power poles or trees, from lightening or from household appliances. Adolescent electrical burns are typically from high voltage sources and often result in amputation,

TABLE 7-2
Burn Causes

Type of Burn	Description/Comment
Flame	Most common type of burn; when clothing burns, the exposure to heat is prolonged, and the severity of the burn is worse.
Scald/contact	Mortality is similar to that in flame burns when total body surface area (BSA) involved is equal.
Chemical	Tissue damaged by protein coagulation or liquefaction rather than hyperthermic activity.
Electrical	Injury is often extensive involved skeletal muscle and other tissues in excess of the skin damage. Extent of damage may not be initially apparent. The tissues that have the least resistance are the most heat sensitive. Bone has the greatest resistance, nerve tissue the least. A cardiac arrest may occur from passage of the current through the heart.
Inhalation	Present in 30% of victims of major burns and should be considered when there is evidence of fire in enclosed space, singed nares, facial burns, charred lips, carbonaceous secretions, posterior pharynx edema, hoarseness, cough, or wheezing. Inhalation injury increases mortality.
Cold injury/frostbite	Freezing results in direct tissue injury. Toes, fingers, ears, and nose are commonly involved. Initial treatment includes rewarming in tepid (105–110°F) water for 20–40 minutes. Excision of tissue should not be done until complete demarcation of nonviable tissue has occurred.

Source: Hopkins, J. (2000). *Harriet Lane handbook* (15th ed.). [Available online: http://home.medconsult.com/dad/book/body/0/871/29.html]. Accessed July 24, 2001.

deep muscle damage and serious morbidity. The majority of adolescent electrical injuries are sustained by males ages 11–18. If the electricity comes into contact with clothing, it can ignite the clothing resulting in a combination of electrical injuries, flame injuries and possibly inhalation injuries (Curley & Moloney-Harmon, 2001).

The physiologic damage of electrical injury is difficult to predict. Direct electrical contact on the body causes several types of injuries (see *Table 7-3)* (Curley & Moloney-Harmon, 2001). Extensive destruction of cells during electrical contact can cause potassium to move from cells into the circulatory system causing severe hyperkalemia. Hyperkalemia can reach toxic levels and may cause life-threatening dysrhythmias (Curley & Moloney-Harmon, 2001). The break down of muscle tissue causes excretion of myoglobin. Myoglobin occludes the kidney tubules and places the child with electrical injuries at risk for renal failure (Whaley & Wong, 1999).

Electricity typically creates a small entrance wound, travels through the body, then creates a more severe exit wound. The electrical current follows the path of least resistance and serious electrical injury results from the current passing through organs, muscles, nerves or vessels. Edema, compartment syndrome and tissue destruction are often not visible (Curley & Moloney-Harmon, 2001). The internal damage can be so severe that amputation is required. Direct electrical contact can cause significant internal injuries (see *Table 7-3*).

Details of the injury such as the type and strength of voltage, duration of contact, presence of water and the occurrence of falls or other trauma are important factors in determining the extent of injury. Electrolytes, skeletal enzymes and cardiac enzymes will be followed closely. Nursing assessment will include cardiac monitoring and inspection distal to the injury for signs of compartment syndrome (circulation, sensation and movement) (Curley & Moloney-Harmon, 2001).

Chemical Burns

Chemical ingestion burns can cause severe gastrointestinal and respiratory damage. Chemical skin contact can cause full thickness burns (Curley & Moloney-Harmon, 2001). Toddlers may suffer chemical injuries from household cleaning products such as lye, ammonia, sulfuric acid or laundry detergents. Older children are at risk for chemical accidents in school laboratories. Chemicals cause coagulation necrosis which can progress over time (Curley & Moloney-Harmon, 2001). The severity of the injury depends on the chemical content, the concentration and the duration of contact with the skin. The skin should be rinsed immediately and continuously with water for 20 minutes or until the child can receive treatment in a burn center (Curley & Moloney-Harmon, 2001).

Burns from Child Abuse

The Child Abuse Prevention and Treatment Act, passed in 1974, requires professionals to

---

TABLE 7-3
Electrical Contact Injuries

- Blood vessel aneurysms
- Destruction of red blood cells
- Damaged muscles
- Vascular thrombosis
- Cardiac arrhythmias
- Myocardial damage
- Neurologic impairment
- Ophthalmologic injury
- Tympanic membrane rupture
- Fractures
- Ruptured tendons

Source: Curley, M. & Moloney-Harmon, P. (2001). *Critical care nursing of infants and children*. Philadelphia: W.B. Saunders.

---

report suspected abuse or neglect of a child. Approximately 20% of pediatric hospital admissions for burns are related to reports of child abuse (Deitch & Rutan, 2000). Therefore, signs of child abuse should be included in every nursing assessment of a pediatric burn patient. Most abusive burn injuries occur in children less than 3 years of age (Deitch & Rutan, 2000). Nurses should be suspicious of parents who do not volunteer information about the injury. Abusive parents may be vague, evasive or contradictory about how the injury occurred. There may also be a time lag in seeking treatment. (See Chapter 9 for symptoms of child abuse burns.)

Inhalation Injuries

Inhalation injury and the potential complications of infection and pulmonary failure are primary causes of death after a burn injury (Deitch & Rutan, 2000). Children may be found dead in closets within the burned shell of their home, untouched by the flames. A child that is exposed to a fire in an enclosed space is at risk for smoke inhalation. It is not always easy to identify someone with an inhalation injury. Some characteristics of a child with an inhalation injury include burns of the face or neck; singed eyebrows, nasal hairs, hairline or facial hairs; soot in the mouth, nose or sputum; brassy cough, hoarseness or stridor; and a serum carboxyhemoglobin level greater than 15% (Curley & Moloney-Harmon, 2001). The effects of smoke inhalation are caused by heat, toxic fumes and reduced oxygen supply.

Heat

Victims of smoke inhalation require close observation and immediate intervention for respiratory distress. Heat damage usually occurs only in the upper airway because the mucous membranes lower the temperature of inhaled gases before they reach the vocal cords (Curley & Moloney-Harmon, 2001). Only heat from steam is able to pass through the larynx causing burns below the vocal cords. Inhaled hot gases produce edema throughout the upper airway, which results in airway obstruction. The edema increases rapidly and peaks between 6 and 12 hours after the exposure (Curley & Moloney-Harmon, 2001). The airway should be protected with an endotracheal tube (ET tube) until the edema resolves (Curley & Moloney-Harmon, 2001).

Toxic Fumes

The second danger of inhalation injuries is caused by toxic fumes created by partially burnt materials. Carbon monoxide (CO) is a colorless, odorless gas that is released during a fire where there is a limited supply of oxygen. Carbon monoxide is toxic because it binds with hemoglobin, which prevents hemoglobin from binding with oxygen (Curley & Moloney-Harmon, 2001). Carbon monoxide has an affinity for hemoglobin that is 200 times greater than oxygen, which greatly reduces the amount of oxygen in the blood (Weibelhaus, Hansen & Hill, 2001). Reduced oxygen in the red blood cells can cause a variety of symptoms depending on the serum carboxyhemo-

globin level. Symptoms range from mild headaches at levels less than 20, to severe effects such as cardiac arrest, at levels greater than 60 (see *Table 7-4*) (Curley & Moloney-Harmon, 2001). The presence of CO in the blood may create bright cherry red lips and skin; although, pallor and cyanosis are more likely to be seen. The toxicity of carbon monoxide can be reduced with the administration of 100% oxygen. The amount of CO in the blood is reduced by 50% for every 30 minutes of 100% oxygen administration (Weibelhaus et al., 2001). For a severely toxic child, hyperbaric oxygen may be given. The child is placed into a hyperbaric chamber where 100% oxygen is administered at higher than atmospheric pressures (Curley & Moloney-Harmon, 2001). The hyperbaric oxygen removes carbon monoxide faster than normal atmospheric pressures.

Other toxic gases such as sulfide, cyanide or chloride can also reach the lungs and cause corrosion of the lung tissues. The corrosion causes an excessive discharge of mucous in the lungs. This is followed by necrosis and sloughing of tissues. Atelectasis results hours or days after the initial injury. These toxic gases may also be absorbed into the blood stream and cause systemic effects (Curley & Moloney-Harmon, 2001).

Nurses cannot rely on pulse oximeter readings when carbon monoxide levels are elevated because carbon monoxide in the blood creates inaccurate pulse oximeter readings (Hopkins, 2000). Arterial blood gases must be obtained for an accurate measurement of arterial oxygen.

Reduced Oxygen Supply

A reduction in available oxygen is the third risk factor of inhalation injuries. As the environmental oxygen is reduced, the child's PaO2 will drop. Oxygen concentrations may be reduced as low as 16% or less (Curley & Moloney-Harmon, 2001). A PaO2 of 50 to 60 is common with inhalation injuries.

TABLE 7-4
Physiologic Effects of Carbon Monoxide Exposure

Carboxyhemoglobin Level (%)	Physiologic Effects
<20	Headache, dyspnea, confusion, lapse of attention, loss of peripheral vision
20–40	Irritability, faulty judgment, dim vision, nausea, vomiting, easily fatigued
40–60	Tachycardia, tachypnea, confusion, hallucinations, ataxia, syncope, convulsions, coma
>60	Often fatal

Source: Curley M. & Moloney-Harmon, P. (2001). *Critical care nursing of infants and children* (2nd ed.). Philadelphia: W. B. Saunders.

Pneumonia, bacteremia and septic shock can complicate the recovery from an inhalation injury. Long-term complications may include chronic effects of the bronchi or trachea. Prolonged intubation or tracheotomy may cause stenosis of the trachea, chronic dilation of the bronchi or degeneration of bronchial tissue (Curley & Moloney-Harmon, 2001).

MANAGEMENT OF BURN INJURIES

The ABCs of resuscitation always come first. However, for health care providers at the scene of a burn accident, stopping the burning process comes before assessment of the airway, circulation and breathing.

There are three phases of burn management. The initial phase is the shock phase, which begins at the time of injury and lasts for about 48 hours or until fluid stabilization. There will be a decrease in cardiac output, less oxygen consumption and a drop in temperature.

Next is the acute phase, which ends with wound closure. The acute phase involves an increased metabolic rate with persistent tachycardia, tachypnea, hyperthermia and body wasting.

The metabolic rate continues to increase for over a week and it remains elevated until the wounds are closed (Curley & Moloney-Harmon, 2001). The increased metabolism is accompanied by increased cardiac output, increased oxygen consumption and increased blood flow to the burn wound, which is necessary in order for the wound to heal.

The last phase is the rehabilitation and reconstructive phase, which can last for the rest of the patient's life (Curley & Moloney-Harmon, 2001). There are several physical and psychological sequelae that require major adaptation by the pediatric burn patient.

Airway Edema

Immediate and ongoing assessment of the airway is very important in the pediatric burn patient. A child with burns of the face or with inhalation injuries may need immediate intubation. A delay in intubation could make intubation impossible once airway swelling has occurred (Curley & Moloney-Harmon, 2001). The smaller diameter of the pediatric airway places children at a higher risk for airway obstruction (Deitch & Rutan, 2000). One millimeter of swelling in a child's 4 mm trachea results in a 75% decrease in patency, while a similar amount of swelling in an adult airway would reduce the airway by only 44% (Deitch & Rutan,

2000). Hyperextension of the neck is contraindicated in the pediatric patient (Deitch & Rutan, 2000). A straight laryngoscope blade should be used in children less than 6-years-old. A quick measurement of endotracheal tube size for children is equal to the diameter of the child's little finger (Deitch & Rutan, 2000). Securing an endotracheal tube in a burn patient can be very difficult and may require creative techniques to avoid additional tissue injury (Curley & Moloney-Harmon, 2001). Ventilation with 100% oxygen is provided for all patients with inhalation injuries or a carbon monoxide level >15%.

Temperature Instability

Due to their greater body surface area, pediatric patients are particularly vulnerable to alterations in temperature. Because core body temperature is often elevated after a major trauma, a depressed or normal temperature may indicate sepsis or exhausted physiologic capabilities and should be viewed as an ominous sign (Deitch & Rutan, 2000). A large burn with loss of skin and lipid layers places a child at risk for hypothermia. To prevent hypothermia, exposure during examinations, procedures or dressing changes needs to be minimized. The room should be kept free from drafts, and a warmer than normal temperature (98.6°F to 99.6°F) should be maintained. Wet dressings should be covered and linen needs to be kept dry. Additional methods of preventing hypothermia include warm blankets, head covering, reflective blankets and warming shields.

Fluid Maintenance

Fluid Loss

Hypovolemic shock can occur quickly, especially in infants and small children. There is a significant amount of fluid evaporation from the burned areas (Deitch & Rutan, 2000). A 10 kg child with a 20% total body surface area (TBSA) burn may have an evaporative loss of about 475 mL or 60% of the circulating volume. The same burn in a 70 kg adult causes the loss of about 1.1 L or only 20% of the circulating volume (Deitch & Rutan, 2000). Following a severe burn, there is also a significant fluid shift from the vascular spaces to interstitial spaces. Fluid and protein shifts occur during the first several hours after the burn. If the fluid and protein shifts are not treated, the patient will go into shock from hypovolemia. Inhalation injuries cause additional fluid loss and can increase fluid resuscitation needs by 30% or more (Curley & Moloney-Harmon, 2001).

Early venous access is crucial. Even a 30-minute delay in fluid resuscitation can result in profound shock. However, if resuscitation is done correctly, cardiac output will return to normal within 36 hours (Curley & Moloney-Harmon, 2001). A large-bore intravenous (IV) catheter is essential because fluid resuscitation is crucial to initial burn treatment (Curley & Moloney-Harmon, 2001). Two peripheral venous sites, femoral venous access or saphenous venous access is recommended. Fluid resuscitation should be calculated by body surface area and should be titrated to achieve a urine output of .75–1.5 ml/kg/hour (Deitch & Rutan, 2000). For the first 24 hours, fluid replacement ranges between 2 to 4 ml/kg of body weight multiplied by the TBSA of the burn. These calculations are a guideline and may be adjusted based on the patient's response to fluid replacement. Intravenous fluids should be isotonic and should replace lost electrolytes. Lactated Ringer's is the most suitable fluid for the first 24 hours; although, infants may require glucose (Deitch & Rutan, 2000). A child younger than 2-years-old may require IV bicarbonate to resolve metabolic acidosis. After the first 24 hours, the fluids should be changed to 5% dextrose with sodium to maintain normal levels.

Hematuria may be present from the hemolysis of red blood cells (Whaley & Wong, 1999). Red blood cells are destroyed in burned tissues. Blood loss during the injury should be replaced on the second to fifth postburn day. The usual amount of blood replacement in a 24-hour period is 10ml/kg over 3–4 hours, unless there is active blood loss (Deitch & Rutan, 2000).

An indwelling urinary catheter is essential for accurate output measurements. Hourly urine output is an important indicator of adequate fluid resuscitation. A urine output of 1–2 ml/kg/hr indicates adequate fluids for a child. In the first few days, oliguria is more likely the result of inadequate fluids rather than renal failure (Whaley & Wong, 1999). Another indicator of sufficient fluids is the child's mental status. A change in mental status may be related to hypovolemia. Urinary output, hemodynamics and respiratory status require diligent nursing attention during fluid resuscitation (Curley & Moloney-Harmon, 2001).

Fluid Overload

Fluid overload in the pediatric patient can cause pulmonary edema, cerebral edema and tissue edema (Curley & Moloney-Harmon, 2001). Tissue edema reduces oxygenation of the burned area. Cerebral edema is of particular concern in children. Nurses should maintain elevation of the head, especially during the first 48 hours postburn (Deitch & Rutan, 2000). Frequent neurological exams should also be done during the first 48 hours.

Approximately 48 hours after an inhalation injury occurs, pulmonary edema can develop from the toxic gases, and symptoms similar to adult respiratory distress syndrome (ARDS) will be seen (Curley & Moloney-Harmon, 2001). The increased fluid loss caused by inhalation injuries increases fluid needs; however, fluid replacement is complicated by the presence of pulmonary edema (Curley & Moloney-Harmon, 2001). Pulmonary edema can also be caused by hydrostatic pressure. In the absence of inhalation injury, this indicates fluid overload (Deitch & Rutan, 2000). The balance between fluid replacement and pulmonary edema can be very complicated.

Auscultation of breath sounds should be done routinely with vital signs to assess for the presence of rales. Pulmonary edema requires treatment with diuresis and fluid restrictions.

WOUND CARE

The primary goal of wound care is to promote wound healing, preserve muscular function and produce the best cosmetic results (Deitch & Rutan, 2000). In order to promote wound healing, nurses can help preserve as much viable tissue as possible. Necrotic tissue is removed, and every effort is made to prevent infection. Viable tissue may be lost after exposure to bacteria, fungus and certain topical agents and cleaning solutions. Inappropriate topical agents can be detrimental. Early excision of eschar and grafting as soon as possible is important for optimal healing. Full thickness burns need skin grafting with an autograft or skin substitute. The ultimate goal is wound closure with intact durable skin.

Cooling the burn can decrease burn severity but is only effective the first 30 minutes following the injury. Cooling will also lessen the pain. Clean towels are soaked in cold water and applied to burns if they are <10% of TBSA. For burns >10%, use only a clean dry towel to prevent hypothermia (Hopkins, 2000). Chemical burns should be treated immediately with water lavage for 20 minutes.

Burn Assessment

As soon as possible after the injury, clothing and jewelry are removed and a total survey is performed. Large burns are assessed by checking one area at a time because complete exposure contributes to rapid heat loss for a small child. The wound is assessed for depth, and the total body surface area (TBSA) is estimated. Nursing assessment of burn depth includes the appearance of the burn, the amount of pain the patient is having and tissue pliability. The cause of the burn and the length of exposure also help to determine the depth of a burn (Curley & Moloney-Harmon, 2001). Wound severity changes over the first 72 hours, so these initial estimates may change (Curley & Moloney-Harmon, 2001). Burn depth can increase after the initial burn is sustained. Infection or mechanical injury can complicate the injury by increasing the depth of the burn (Curley & Moloney-Harmon, 2001). Debridement dressings and shearing forces can cause a loss of viable tissue. Hypotension, hypoxia and poor perfusion to the wound can also reduce viable tissue creating a deeper wound. Nurses should be judicious about giving prognostic information to parents during the first couple of days because of the many factors that may alter the severity of the burn wound (Curley & Moloney-Harmon, 2001; Hopkins, 2000). It is important for nurses to always assess for secondary injuries or traumas that may have been sustained while trying to escape a fire burn (Hopkins, 2000).

An accurate estimation of the burned area and burn depth is essential in treating the pediatric patient (Deitch & Rutan, 2000). The calculation of TBSA is an important factor in calculating fluid replacement and nutritional needs (Curley & Moloney-Harmon, 2001). The well-known "Rule of Nines" is not accurate for children less than 15-years-old. *Figure 7-1* provides a more accurate measurement (Deitch & Rutan, 2000). The most accurate mapping of a burn wound occurs after the initial bathing and removal of sloughing tissue. Children with burn injuries of greater than 10% of the TBSA should be referred to a burn unit (Deitch & Rutan, 2000). Children with burns of more than 10–15% of the TBSA require immediate fluid resuscitation (Deitch & Rutan, 2000). A burn of more than 25% of the TBSA affects all of the organ systems in the body (Curley & Moloney-Harmon, 2001). Burns of more than 50% of the TBSA involve critical care treatment that lasts for weeks or months (Curley & Moloney-Harmon, 2001). Superficial partial-thickness injuries are not part of TBSA calculations because the skin integrity of these areas is not broken.

Cleaning and Debridement

Wounds should be bathed daily and observed for signs of infection. Wounds are cleansed with an antibacterial soap and sterile water or sterile normal saline. All loose tissue is debrided. Most burn specialists recommend removal of all nonviable tissue as soon as possible. Debridement can be done with special dressings, blunt or sharp debridement methods, by hydrotherapy or excision under anesthesia (Curley & Moloney-Harmon, 2001). A wide mesh gauze (WMG) is often used for debridement. Pain relief prior to any debridement method is an essential aspect of burn care. Pain should be reassessed and treated throughout the debridement procedure. Viable tissue is pink, moist and warm. Sensation of viable tissue should be present depending on the depth of the burn (Curley & Moloney-Harmon, 2001). Early surgical excision and grafting during the first 48 hours can decrease blood loss and reduce hospital stay (Deitch & Rutan, 2000). However, early excisions should only be done by professionals familiar with the procedure, and only for full thickness burns (Deitch & Rutan, 2000).

Dressings and Grafts

The prescribed topical agent is applied unless there are plans for immediate transfer. If the patient is being transferred to a burn center, the first dressing is usually a clean dry dressing. Application of a topical agent is done with a gloved hand or liberally spread onto the fine mesh gauze. The initial dressings are wrapped loosely to accommodate additional swelling. Also, while applying these dressings access to check for peripheral pulses distal to the burned areas should be left available. Elevation of the head and extremities may minimize swelling. All wounds should be checked daily for signs of infection.

When dressings are changed, the outer dressings are removed and then dressings that have

FIGURE 7-1
Calculating TBSA

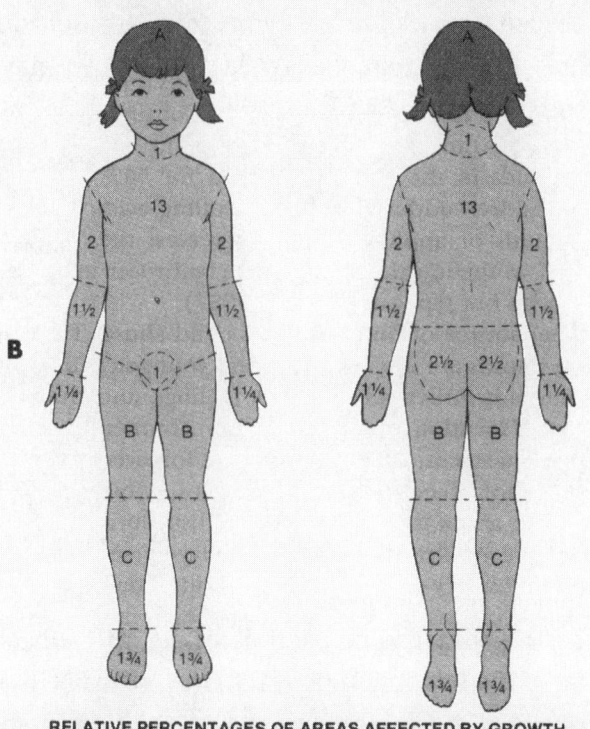

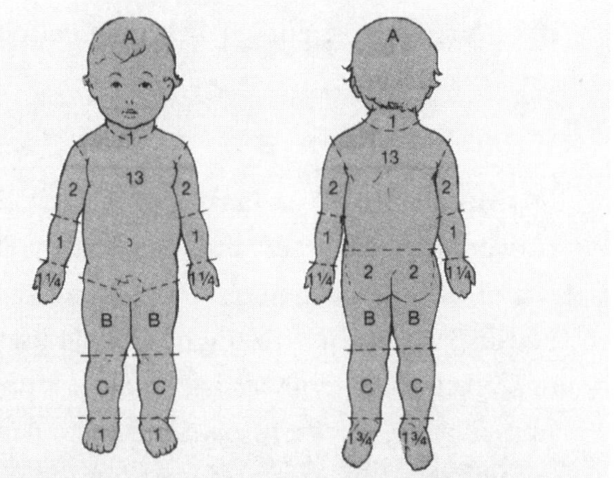

RELATIVE PERCENTAGES OF AREAS AFFECTED BY GROWTH

AREA	BIRTH	AGE 1 YR	AGE 5 YR
A = ½ of head	9½	8½	6½
B = ½ of one thigh	2¾	3¼	4
C = ½ of one leg	2½	2½	2¾

RELATIVE PERCENTAGES OF AREAS AFFECTED BY GROWTH

AREA	AGE 10 YR	AGE 15 YR	ADULT
A = ½ of head	5½	4½	3½
B = ½ of one thigh	4½	4½	4¾
C = ½ of one leg	3	3¼	3½

Estimation of distribution of burns in children. **A.** Children from birth to age 5 years. **B.** Older children.

adhered to the wound can be loosened with tepid sterile water. Dressings serve to absorb exudate, protect and debride the wound and provide patient comfort. Dressings are placed so that no two burned areas are touching each other, such as between fingers and toes or behind the ears. Dressings are applied from distal to proximal parts to promote venous return. Care is taken to avoid impairment of circulation or limit motion. Elastic bandages are placed in a figure eight to increase circulation and decrease edema.

Many biologic dressings are available including biosynthetic-collagen dressings, human cadaver allografts and porcine xenografts. A biologic dressing is applied to a clean wound to promote healing and reduce evaporative water loss. A biologic dressing creates a warm, moist environment, which is conducive to tissue growth; however, this environment is also likely to promote bacterial growth as well. Meticulous nursing care is required to reduce the patient's exposure to microorganisms. Burn wound infections will cause an increase in wound depth.

The best wound covering is a skin graft from the patient's own skin. The donor site of a split thickness graft of the epidermis and dermis heals within 10 to 14 days and can be reharvested to create another graft. A full thickness graft includes the epidermis, dermis and sometimes the fat and muscle. The donor site of a full thickness graft will require a split thickness graft for closure. Full thickness grafts are reserved for the face, hands or joints (Curley & Moloney-Harmon, 2001).

Artificial grafts are being developed, and several new artificial skin products are available. One example is Integra®. Integra is sutured into place and reduces evaporative water loss. It is removed after three weeks, and a thin graft can be applied. A second example of an artificial graft is epithelial cell cultures. For this graft, a stamp size skin biopsy is taken from the patient and sent to a special laboratory. After ten days, the cells have grown in a special culture and are treated with an enzyme and prepared for further growth. After another ten days, there is enough cultured epithelial sheets for patient use. These sheets are sutured into place, but these cells are very fragile and require special care for several weeks to prevent damage to the cells. Epithelial cells are used for a child with extensive full thickness burns (Curley & Moloney-Harmon, 2001).

Eschar

Circumferential burns of the extremities act as a tourniquet, decreasing blood flow to the area. As edema increases, the tissues are compressed and the patient will experience numbness and tingling, decreased motor function, reduced sensation and increased pain (Curley & Moloney-Harmon, 2001). The pressure is released by surgical escharotomy or fasciotomy. Fingers and toes are also at risk for compartment syndrome and may require escharotomies. An escharotomy is an incision through the tissue into the subcutaneous fat. A fasciotomy is done for injuries that extend to the muscle. This is a deeper incision through the fascia, the fibrous tissue that covers the muscle compartments. The fasciotomy allows room for the edematous muscle (Curley & Moloney-Harmon, 2001).

Full thickness circumferential burns of the chest replace the normally elastic skin with nonelastic eschar (Curley & Moloney-Harmon, 2001). Eschar on the chest creates a tight corset-like effect. As edema continues to accumulate, tissues are compressed against the chest wall reducing circulation and compromising ventilation. An escharotomy can be done to relieve the tightness. This is usually done during the first 24 hours after the injury (Curley & Moloney-Harmon, 2001).

If an escharotomy is not done, the pressure on tissues can cause compartment syndrome, necrosis and gangrene. Benefits of escharotomy must be weighed against the potential blood loss that may occur if the procedure is done (Curley & Moloney-Harmon, 2001). Edema peaks at 24 hours post burn; therefore, frequent neurological checks are important for the first 24 hours.

Pain Management

Morphine and fentanyl are the first choice for pain control in the pediatric burn patient (Deitch & Rutan, 2000). IV narcotics are preferred for pain because absorption through edematous tissues is unpredictable (Curley & Moloney-Harmon, 2001). Immediately postburn, pain medication should be administered by a continuous low dose infusion with bolus doses as needed (Deitch & Rutan, 2000). Older children may be capable of using a patient controlled analgesia (PCA) method of pain control. Doses typically start small and titrate up as needed. For less severe burns, regularly scheduled oral doses of narcotics or acetaminophen may be sufficient.

Midazolam or lorazepam are given in addition to pain medication to relieve anxiety, especially for intubated patients. Nurses should use an appropriate pain scale for children such as a series of line drawn faces, from smiling to crying, or an objective pain scale *(Figure 7-2)* (Deitch & Rutan, 2000). When pain assessment tools cannot be used, physiologic indicators, such as respiratory rate or heart rate, can help determine pain levels. (See Chapter 5 for more information on pediatric pain control.)

Mobility can be painful because of the healing burns and contractures. Activities of daily living, range of motion exercises and position changes also increase pain and anxiety and may require additional pain medication (Curley & Moloney-Harmon, 2001). Burn patients need to be premedicated prior to bathing, dressing changes, physical therapy or chest PT. Bolus pain medication doses are required for any activity that may cause increased pain. Distraction, guided imagery, hyp-

FIGURE 7-2
Wong-Baker FACES Pain Rating Scale

0	1	2	3	4	5
No Hurt	Hurts Little Bit	Hurts Little More	Hurts Even More	Hurts Whole Lot	Hurts Worst

Explain to the person that each face is for a person who feels happy because he has no pain (hurt) or sad because he has some or a lot of pain. Face 0 is very happy because he doesn't hurt at all. Face 1 hurts just a little bit. Face 2 hurts a little more. Face 3 hurts even more. Face 4 hurts a whole lot. Face 5 hurts as much as you can imagine, although you don't have to cry to feel this bad. Ask the person to choose the face that best describes how he is feeling. Rating scale is recommended for persons age 3 years and older.

From Wong, D., Hockenberry-Eaton, M., Wilson, D., Winkelstein, M. & Schwartz, P. *Wong's Essentials of Pediatric Nursing,* 6/e, St. Louis, 2001, P. 1301. Copyrighted by Mosby, Inc. Reprinted with permission.

nosis, and music can also be used in addition to, or in place of narcotic medication. Explanations and allowing the child appropriate choices may also reduce anxiety. Relaxation and distraction are useful methods that can involve the family members in patient care.

COMPLICATIONS

Contractions

Like adults, children are prone to contractions. The hands and neck are especially at risk for contractions (Deitch & Rutan, 2000). Immobility from bed rest, pain, dressings, splints, muscle wasting and loss of stamina all contribute to the development of contractions (Curley & Moloney-Harmon, 2001). Contractions can severely limit mobility; therefore, rehabilitation must start as soon as possible (Curley & Moloney-Harmon, 2001).

Rehabilitation begins on the day of admission with active or passive range of motion exercises (Deitch, 2000). Active and passive range of motion should be done with every dressing change and throughout rehabilitation. Routine position changes are done, and efforts are made to maintain joints in their extended positions. When joints are not being exercised, they should be maintained in maximal extension with the use of splints (Deitch & Rutan, 2000). Physical and occupational therapy play a very important role in the care of a burn patient. For optimal progress, nurses can schedule analgesics to be given prior to all exercise activities.

Infection

Infection control is a primary concern for the burn nurse. Local and systemic infections are common complications for burn patients. Burn patients are susceptible to infections because of their open wounds and poor nutritional intake. Wound healing and the increased metabolic rate of a burn patient create an increase in nutritional needs (Curley & Moloney-Harmon, 2001).

A nasogastric tube is placed initially for gastric decompression; however, enteral feedings should be started as soon as possible to ensure normal function of the digestive system. Enteral feedings may begin as early as three to six hours post-burn (Deitch & Rutan, 2000). A nutritionist consult is often made the day of admission. Adequate caloric intake is measured by calorie counts, albumin levels, biweekly weights and the status of wound healing. Oral feedings are preferred but may not be sufficient. Feeding tubes are often surgically placed. Some centers use a combination of tube feedings and hyperalimentation to provide adequate nutrition (Curley & Moloney-Harmon, 2001).

Maintaining an aseptic environment is very important. The single most important factor in preventing wound infection is good hand washing. Patients are typically in a private room. A laminar flow room is preferred. Isolation gowns, gloves, hats and masks are necessary to protect burn patients from microorganisms. Burn wounds need to be kept warm, moist and as clean as possible. At the first sign of inflammation or sepsis, a wound culture is obtained. Infection destroys viable tissue and deepens the wound. Topical agents are used to prevent the growth of microorganisms. The choice of topical agent depends on the wound and the type of agent (Curley & Moloney-Harmon, 2001).

Some common topical agents for burn wounds are Silvadene, silver nitrate, mafenide acetate, Povidone iodine and Dakin's solution® (see *Table 7-4)*. Silvadene® is cooling to the skin and is the least painful agent. Silvadene must be washed off completely with each dressing change. Silvadene should not be used with sulfa allergies or with toxic epidermal necrolysis. Silver nitrate solution 0.5% stings briefly with application. Petroleum gauze is used to protect the surrounding normal skin from staining. Mafenide acetate leaves a burning feeling for 15 to 20 minutes and must be washed off with each dressing change. Povidone iodine causes a stinging pain with application. Dakin's solution stings and can macerate normal tissue. It should be stored in a dark place.

REHABILITATION

Physical Rehabilitation

Burn care treatments have improved significantly in recent years. Severely burned patients are more likely to survive today than they were in the past. Approximately 80% of severely burned patients survive and many are able to perform basic activities of daily living (Curley & Moloney-Harmon, 2001). This increase in survival presents a new challenge for nursing care. Efforts to help maintain a meaningful and functional life for the severely injured burn patient are more important than ever.

The management of scar formation is an important aspect of rehabilitation for the burn patient. Scar tissue collagen when "active" is vascular and appears red, raised and firm. Scar tissue will contract and result in contractures, deformities and disfigurement if left untreated (Whaley & Wong, 1999). Scarring usually peaks at four to six months after wound healing but becomes mature or inactive in one to two years. Treatment with continuous pressure by elastic bandages or pressure garments decreases the blood supply and pushes the collagen into a smoother and more normal appearance. These pressure garments or wraps are removed for only short periods of time and are often custom-made for the child. Because they may be worn for months or a year, the fit may need to be altered with growth (Whaley & Wong, 1999).

Other treatments for active scar tissue include use of moisturizers and/or the administration of diphenhydramine or other medications to minimize itching (Whaley & Wong, 1999). Massage while applying the moisturizer may also help to stretch the scar tissue and prevent contractures. Because scar tissue does not grow with the child, surgery may be needed to release a scar contracture. Other surgery may be indicated for reconstruction to restore function or appearance (Whaley & Wong, 1999).

TABLE 7-4
Topical Antibacterial Agents

Agent	Action	Side Effects	Use
Silver sulfadiazine (Silvadene)	Broad antibacterial, painless, fair eschar penetration	Sulfonamide sensitivity, occasional leukopenia, contraindicated in pregnancy	Q12hr; cover with light dressings; leave face and chest open
Bacitracin ointment	Limited antibacterial action, poor eschar penetration, transplant, easy to apply	Rapid development of resistance; conjunctivitis if contact with eye	Q12 hr, apply to small areas; acceptable with facial burns
Mafenide (Sulfamylon®)	Excellent antibacterial for Gram-positive and Gram-negative and *Clostridium*, rapid eschar penetration	Painful, sulfonamide sensitivity, carbonic anhydrase inhibition may lead to acidosis	Q12hr; cover with light dressings; leave face, chest, abdomen open
Aqueous silver nitrate solution	Universal antibacterial action, poor eschar penetration	Strong tissue staining, hypochloremic alkalosis	Q12hr, light gauze dressing
Iodophores (Efodine®)	Universal antibacterial action, poor eschar penetration	Strong tissue staining, iodine absorption	Q12hr, light gauze dressing

Source: Hopkins, J. (2000). *Harriet Lane handbook* (15th ed.). [Available online: http://home.medconsult.com/dad/book/body/0/871/29.html]. Accessed July 24, 2001.

A study at the Shriner's Hospital in Galveston, Texas examined pediatric patients with massive burn injuries to determine their quality of life. In this study, 103 pediatric patients were studied to evaluate their ability to achieve independence with activities of daily living. These patients all suffered 80% or more TBSA burns. Of the 103 patients studied, 67% of them survived, and 80% of the survivors did achieve independence with activities of daily living (Meyers-Paal et al., 2000). Physical dependence was related to the loss of one or more fingers, one or more limb amputations, joint fusion or brain anoxia (Meyers-Paal et al., 2000).

Psychological Rehabilitation

Along with physical rehabilitation efforts, nurses need to be aware of the burn patient's psychological needs. The adaption to a change in body image is influenced by gender, social support, burn severity and developmental stage (McQuaid, Barton & Campbell, 2000). Body image is dynamic especially as children progress through developmental stages. Normally, changes in body image are very gradual. However, a new body image is abruptly forced upon a burn patient. The sudden dramatic change in body image that follows a burn injury can be psychologically disruptive (McQuaid et al., 2000). In addition to the initial change in body image, a new body image must be found with each new reconstructive surgery. Patients with face and hand scars have the most trouble dealing with the change in their appearance (Curley & Moloney-Harmon, 2001). Burn patients will experience mourning for the loss of their previous body image (McQuaid et al., 2000). Maintaining contact with friends and teachers during hospitalization will ease the return to a normal life.

In a study of adult burn victims, post traumatic stress disorder (PTSD) was seen one year post burn in about 50% of the patients (Ehde, Patterson, Wiechman & Wilson, 2000). These burn survivors suffered from problems sleeping; they avoided thoughts about the burn injury; and they felt distress when reminded of the burn injury (Ehde et al., 2000). Only one out of every five survivors in this study were completely free from PTSD symptoms one year after their burn injury.

The psychosocial adjustment for the pediatric patients studied at the Shriner's Hospital appeared to be normal. However, borderline test scores indicated social competence concerns. Based on these test scores it was determined that teaching interpersonal and social skills would be beneficial. The Shriner's Hospital plans to begin a social skills training program for burn patients (Meyers-Paal et al., 2000).

One study showed that severely burned children between ages one and twelve-years-old had moderate to severe psychological problems such as fears, anxiety, poor self-esteem, poor body image and problems with interpersonal relationships (McQuaid et al., 2000). The presence of these psychological problems did not translate directly as poor post-burn adjustment.

Body image is present as early as two years old. By age six, children can differentiate between stereotypical attractiveness and unattractiveness. Studies show that children between the ages of 9 and 14 choose their friends based on appearance

(McQuaid et al., 2000). Therefore, children with physical deformities may have difficulty making friends. This will make adjustment after a burn injury even more difficult. The reaction of peers to a school-age child with burn injuries influences the child's body image (McQuaid et al., 2000). Staring and teasing can make adaption more difficult. Negative peer reactions can cause depression, low self-esteem and psychological dysfunction (McQuaid et al., 2000).

Surprisingly, studies show that children with more severe burns may be more socially competent. This may be because they are more likely to receive sufficient support. Also, children with hidden scars live with the fear of discovery, such as exposure in gym class or in the summer. If scars are hidden, body image revision may be delayed or incomplete.

Adolescence is considered a major life stage. Studies show that adolescents with and without severe burn injuries had a lower body image than younger children. Body awareness is heightened during adolescence because of the physical changes that occur during this developmental stage (McQuaid et al., 2000). A study of burned children under 11-years-old showed that children with no previous self-esteem problems developed a problem with self-esteem up to six years after their burn injury (McQuaid et al., 2000). This suggests that when children are nearing adolescence body image issues become more important.

Research suggests that adolescent girls are more appearance oriented than are adolescent boys. Therefore, cosmetic issues are more important to girls. This puts girls at a greater risk for depression, low self-esteem and negative body image than boys with an equivalent burn severity (McQuaid et al., 2000). Adolescent boys on the other hand were more inhibited after burn injuries. They felt less masculine and felt more loss over a lack of physical function (McQuaid et al., 2000). The overall adjustments for male and female adolescents are similar (McQuaid et al., 2000).

Little is known about vocational issues of competence and employability for burn patients. These are issues that require further study (Meyers-Paal et al., 2000). Social support, especially parental support, is vital in burn rehabilitation (McQuaid et al., 2000). Adaption to body image after a burn injury is influenced by overall psychological adjustment, social support, temperament, preburn psychology and socioeconomic status of the patient's family (McQuaid et al., 2000). Research suggests that if a child's life has meaning and purpose, then body image disorders will become insignificant. Studies show this is the case for the majority of children with burn injuries (McQuaid et al., 2000).

CONCLUSION

Smoke detectors in the home and lowering the temperature of tap water will help prevent the two most prevalent causes of pediatric burn injuries. All nurses can help to promote these safety factors. One of the nursing challenges of burn care is communicating with patients who are unable to communicate as they normally would. Communication may be impaired because of sedation, ventilation, pain or the patient's age. Nurses can provide emotional support to the family as well as to the patient. The patient and family should always be informed of all procedures prior to the procedure, and an explanation regarding the long-term plan of care for the patient should be provided. Other members of the health care team should be consulted as needed. The multidisciplinary team for a burn patient may include a respiratory therapist, physical therapist, occupational therapist, dietitian, psychiatrist, social worker and chaplain. Referrals for family members to social services and mental health professionals should be made as needed.

EXAM QUESTIONS

CHAPTER 7
Questions 40–44

40. The type of burn that occurs most frequently in the pediatric population is a(n)

    a. frostbite of the toes, fingers and ears.
    b. scald burn from hot liquids, grease or tap water.
    c. chemical burns from ingestion of household products.
    d. electrical burns from low-voltage appliances or high-voltage line.

41. Burn size must be estimated accurately in order to

    a. calculate the amount of fluid volume needed.
    b. predict patient outcome.
    c. meet the criteria for transfer to a burn center.
    d. determine the type of dressing to use.

42. The most emergent complication of inhalation injuries is

    a. burn injuries to the face.
    b. systemic gas effects, such as dizziness.
    c. airway obstruction from edema.
    d. the development of pneumonia.

43. The most reliable indicator of adequate fluid resuscitation is a

    a. normal blood pressure for age.
    b. urine output of >2 ml/kg/hr.
    c. decreasing peripheral edema.
    d. return to normal body temperature.

44. The single most important factor in preventing wound infections is

    a. good nutrition.
    b. daily wound care.
    c. good handwashing.
    d. a private room.

CHAPTER 8

NEAR-DROWNING

CHAPTER OBJECTIVE

After completing this chapter, the reader will be able to indicate the prevalence and potentially devastating outcome for drowning and near-drowning victims. The reader will also be able to identify near-drowning specific pulmonary therapy and potential multisystem complications, and engage in public education of drowning prevention by describing the prevalence, devastation, high risk factors and preventive measures of submersion accidents.

LEARNING OBJECTIVES

After studying this chapter, the learner will be able to

1. specify potential multi-system complications.

2. select public education for drowning prevention.

3. specify the prevalence of drowning and the high risk factors of associated with drowning.

4. choose the appropriate preventive measures for submersion accidents.

5. recognize the usual sequence of events in a submersion accident and the resulting physiologic effects.

6. identify specific pulmonary therapy for near drowning.

7. recognize the most frequent cause of mortality and morbidity following submersion accidents.

EPIDEMIOLOGY

The facts about drowning are startling. Many Americans are unaware of the prevalence and risks involved with drowning and near-drowning (Behrman 2000; Quan, 1999).

- Approximately 500,000 people drown worldwide each year.

- In the U.S., approximately 50,000 near-drownings require medical intervention annually.

- Fifty percent of all pediatric submersion victims are declared dead at the scene.

- In the U.S., drowning is the fourth leading cause of death for children under age 19.

- Children under five years of age are at the highest risk of drowning.

- Teenagers ages 15 to 19 are at the second highest risk of drowning.

- Drowning is more common in males than in females.

- African American children suffer drowning accidents twice as often as Caucasians.

- There are far more near-drowning victims than there are drowning victims.

- Many near-drowning victims that survive have neurologic sequelae.

- Forty percent of submersion victims are less than 4-years-old.

- Pools account for half of all submersion accidents in the United States.

- Child abuse and homicide account for about 8% of submersion injuries.

Children under five-years-old are at the greatest risk for drowning (Quan, 1999). Infants younger than one-year-old are often left unattended in bathtubs. Children from one to four-years-old frequently fall into residential swimming pools, especially during meal times (Quan, 1999). Children can also drown in buckets, toilets, washing machines and sinks. When small children fall headfirst into a bucket, they cannot get back up because their cephalic center of gravity limits their ability to tip the bucket over. Also, toddlers do not have the reasoning skills to sit or stand up to avoid drowning. There is a high mortality rate for drowning in buckets because the contents of the bucket are often caustic. Children with epilepsy have an even greater risk of drowning (Behrman, 2000).

The next highest risk age group is teenagers. Teenagers between the ages of 15 and 19 often drown in lakes and ponds where there is no adult supervision. Teenage drownings are often associated with high-risk behaviors, including alcohol or drug use (Rivara, 1999). Alcohol clouds judgment and decreases motor coordination. Alcohol is also associated with arrhythmias that can cause sudden cardiac arrest in submersion victims. Positive blood alcohol is found in 10–50% of adolescent drownings (Quan, 1999). Suicide should also be considered with adolescent drownings.

DEFINITIONS

Death by asphyxiation within 24 hours of a submersion accident is termed drowning (Behrman, 2000). Near-drowning refers to a submersion victim that survives more than 24 hours. The outcome for near-drowning victims ranges from complete recovery to death.

Secondary drowning also occurs 24 hours after submersion and refers to a death caused by submersion complications, such as adult respiratory distress syndrome (ARDS) or pneumonia.

Despite efforts toward prevention and improved cardio-respiratory resuscitation, near-drowning is often associated with high mortality and morbidity. Thanks to technology, victims of drowning accidents are more likely to survive. However, there are no current therapies that will treat a prolonged hypoxic insult to the brain. Unfortunately, health care professionals have no control over the most important factors of a successful central nervous system (CNS) outcome. The length of submersion, the time lapsed between rescue and resuscitation and the level of consciousness after initial resuscitation are all important factors that determine the outcome.

Diving Reflex

The diving reflex is seen in some aquatic mammals and involves bradycardia and slowing of other systems. The diving reflex may provide cerebral protection during prolonged submersion; although, this protection for humans is probably minimal (Behrman, 2000). It has not been proven that the diving reflex explains the remarkable rare survival of children after submersion in icy water (Quan, 1999). Some authors report that since children are more likely to develop hypothermia, the diving reflex may be more prominent in children.

Immersion Syndrome

Immersion syndrome is the sudden death of a victim after contact with water. Bradycardia or tachycardia causes syncope or arrhythmia. This occurs with a sudden contact with water that is at least 40°F less than body temperature. The greater the temperature difference, the higher the risk of syncope or loss of consciousness.

Dry Drowning

According to Sachdeva (1999) aspiration does not occur in about 10–15% of humans who drown. Sachdeva (1999) believes that these victims of submersion accidents have acute laryngospasms that result in a dry drowning. There is no aspiration of water, and death is caused by profound obstructive asphyxia. Quan (1999) reports that an estimated 10–20% of drownings are "dry drownings." He states that laryngospasms are a precursor to aspiration, causing obstruction and hypoxia. Behrman (2000) agrees that pulmonary aspiration does not occur in all cases of near-drowning.

THE RESCUE

Contrary to media portrayals, a drowning is usually silent. Victims do not call for help. Breathing takes precedence, and a drowning victim is not able to call or wave for help. Victims are usually upright with arms extended. They usually thrash and slap the water. Bystanders may not recognize that the splashing is struggling. It may appear that the victim is playing. Victims may submerge and surface several times. Children can only struggle for 10–20 seconds before final submersion. Adults may struggle for up to 60 seconds before submersion.

Panic and struggle are followed by breath holding then large amounts of water are swallowed. Further attempts to breathe cause aspiration of water into the lungs. As little as 1–3 mL/kg of aspirated water leads to a profound reduction in gas exchange. Aspiration decreases surfactant and decreases pulmonary compliance by 10–40%. Atelectasis occurs, and within one to three minutes, hypoxia quickly affects the brain, heart and other organs and tissues.

The duration of hypoxia determines the severity of injury. Resuscitation becomes more difficult as hypoxemia and ischemia cause irreversible damage. Hypoxemia causes CNS depression and terminal apnea. Initial tachycardia is followed by severe hypertension and reflex bradycardia. Within three to four minutes, the myocardium becomes ischemic and ventricular fibrillation (V.Fib) and asystole occur. This leads to cerebral anoxia and ischemia. Without prompt intervention, multisystem failure will follow. The affects of hypoxia on other organ systems are delayed and become evident over time. Cerebral edema can occur from 6–12 hours after submersion. Most deaths following submersion accidents are due to cerebral causes. Complications of hypoxia are often responsive to treatment, but complications can result in long-term sequelae.

Airway and Breathing

For complete cardiopulmonary resuscitation instruction refer to basic cardiac life support (BCLS) guidelines. Resuscitation techniques specific to submersion victims are discussed here. Rapid effective resuscitation provides the greatest chance for a complete recovery. Waiting for paramedics can take up to ten minutes. Immediate resuscitation by those at the scene is essential. Panicky struggling victims are dangerous to the rescuer. The rescuer could drown saving the victim and therefore, should always approach the victim with a buoy. If the victim is unconscious, the buoy can be used under the victims head to keep it above the water.

Immediate response from bystanders is critical. Mouth-to-mouth breathing should be started in the water before return to shore. After initiating mouth-to-mouth, the rescuer should bring the victim to shore as quickly as possible. Rescuers should not try to remove water from the victim's lungs because usually only small amounts of water are aspirated. If aspiration does occur, fresh water is rapidly absorbed into the vascular system, and salt water causes continuous production of pulmonary fluid. Remove only visible emesis. The Heimlich maneuver should not be done, unless there are symptoms of an airway obstruction. The Heimlich maneuver leads to an increased risk of vomiting and therefore increased risk of aspiration. BCLS should continue until paramedics arrive.

Paramedics

It is important to provide ventilation in spite of copious amounts of frothy pulmonary edema. If the pulmonary status is stable, then stopping ventilation to suction is acceptable. However, if oxygen saturations fall below 90%, ventilation should resume and is effective regardless of the pulmonary fluid. Oxygen should be administered at the highest concentration available. Intubation and positive pressure ventilation with bag and mask may be required. The use of cricoid pressure during intubation will prevent aspiration. Rescuers should continue CPR until arrival at the nearest emergency room (ER). Intravenous (IV) or intraosseous access should be established as soon as possible. Although fluid resuscitation is a priority, care should be taken to avoid excessive fluid that may exacerbate cerebral edema.

Hospital Care

A complete history of the submersion accident is important in determining injuries and predicting outcomes. Assessment information includes the location of the submersion, type of water, precipitating events, duration of submersion and water temperature. It should be determined whether there was a pulse present after the rescue, how long apnea persisted, if breathing resumed spontaneously or if there were resuscitation efforts. All victims who required oxygen at the scene, were submerged for more than 1 minute or were cyanotic or apneic should be hospitalized. These victims should be observed for 24 hours for delayed pulmonary edema, which occasionally occurs up to 12 hours after submersion. Cerebral edema can also cause late onset neurological deterioration. Victims that required CPR, had an abnormal CXR

or abnormal ABGs should be admitted to an intensive care unit. The goal of medical and nursing care is to restore oxygenation, ventilation and perfusion in order to minimize and prevent secondary injury. Therapeutic interventions focus on pulmonary, cardiovascular and cerebral functions. Physicians may stop resuscitation after 30–45 minutes if there has been no response.

Causey, Tilelli & Swanson (2000) believe that submersion victims with mild symptoms do not require 48–72-hour hospital observation. In a retrospective single-center study of submersion victims over a three-year period, 48 patients were evaluated. These patients had a Glasgow Coma Scale (GCS) greater than or equal to 13, no need for advanced life support and normal room air oxygen saturation at four to six hour post submersion. All of these patients were discharged with a normal neurological baseline, and none of them experienced secondary drowning or symptoms of adult respiratory distress syndrome (ARDS). There were three patients with a GCS of 14 or 15 who were not included in the study because they developed increased respiratory symptoms less than four hours after arrival to the emergency room (ER), and they required additional respiratory support. All three of these patients made a full recovery. Causey et al., (2000) believe these three cases further support the theory that the risk of secondary drowning or respiratory deterioration is highest within the first 4–6 hours after arrival to the ER. Causey et al., (2000) conclude that prolonged hospital admissions or observations are not necessary for mildly symptomatic, alert submersion victims with a GCS greater than or equal to 13.

PULMONARY CONSIDERATIONS

Salt Water Versus Fresh Water

Although there are some physiological differences between fresh and salt water drowning, the treatments are essentially the same. Both types of aspiration can cause surfactant destruction and reduction of gas exchange. There are typically no significant changes in electrolytes because the amount of water aspirated is usually very small. As little as 1–3 mL/kg can lead to severe reduction in gas exchange and hypoxemia. There must be more than 11 mL/kg of fluid aspirated in order to cause significant changes in blood volume. Significant electrolyte changes will not occur unless there is an aspiration of 22 mL/kg. Aspiration of polluted water or cleaning liquids are exceptions.

Salt Water

Salt water is hypertonic, similar to 3% normal saline. It would take large amounts of aspirated salt water to create an osmotic gradient drawing interstitial and intravascular fluid into the alveoli. This reduction of vascular fluid could result in hemoconcentration. However, the aspiration of large amounts of water is extremely rare; therefore, the only effects typically seen are the inactivation of surfactant and resulting atelectasis.

Fresh Water

Fresh water washes out surfactant causing alveolar collapse, hypoxemia and pulmonary insufficiency. Fresh water is hypotonic and is absorbed from the alveoli into capillaries. Severe cases, when large amounts of water are aspirated, can lead to hemodilution, hyponatremia and hypokalemia. However, the aspiration of large amounts of water is very rare.

Pulmonary Complications

Aside from aspiration of pool or lake water, aspiration of gastric contents or toxic chemicals, organisms and foreign bodies can all cause pulmonary injury. Aspirated water inactivates surfactant causing atelectasis. Pulmonary edema may develop from aspiration, hypoxemia, myocardial dysfunction or hypothermia. Pulmonary infections or pneumonia may occur from aspiration of contaminated water or emesis. Infection can also occur following intubation or from hypothermia. Antibiotics are not recommended for prophylactic use after near-drowning. Antibiotics are reserved for use only following positive culture growth.

Observation for ARDS is recommended for 8–12 hours after submersion. Fifty percent of asymptomatic children develop symptoms four to eight hours after submersion, even if they presented with a normal chest x-ray (Behrman, 2000). For those with severe symptoms, volutrauma, barotrauma and spontaneous pneumothorax may also occur. Those with minor respiratory symptoms maybe asymptomatic by 18 hours after the submersion.

Pulmonary Treatment

Respiratory distress varies depending on the extent of hypoxic-ischemic injury and the amount and type of fluid aspirated. Near-drowning patients may present with a cough, shallow rapid breathing, chest pain and burning, pink frothy sputum, shortness of breath, retractions, rales or rhonchi. Apnea in severe submersion accidents is usually caused by central nervous system dysfunction.

Airway, breathing and circulation assessments are followed quickly by assessment of core temperature. Hypoxia may require increased FiO2. Oxygen should be administered to keep saturations >90%. Mild to moderate hypoxia can be treated with continuous positive airway pressure (CPAP) via mask and endotrachial tube. Respiratory distress should be treated with positive end-expiratory pressure (PEEP) or CPAP. Pressures should be started at 5–10 cm H2O and increased to 10–15 cm H2O if needed. To maintain proper pulmonary function, hypercapnia should be avoided, using normal ventilation or mild hyperventilation to maintain a PaCo2 @ 35–40 mm Hg. Excessive hyperventilation is not indicated and may lead to cerebral hypoperfusion. This may lead to ischemic injury. Chest x-ray, pulse oximetry and serial arterial blood gases are the most important diagnostic tools. Nurses will assess for level of consciousness, adequate perfusion and respiratory distress.

Corticosteroids are not recommended for lung injury caused by submersion. Diuretics for pulmonary edema may be considered but are not usually necessary. Pulmonary toilet including chest physiotherapy is recommended. A bronchoscopy is done if a foreign body is suspected. It is important to manage ARDS and watch for volutrauma and barotrauma. If apnea, cyanosis, hypoventilation or labored respiration persists, endotracheal intubation should be preformed. Hypoxemia can increase the risk of arrhythmias such as ventricular tachycardia, ventricular fibrillation and asystole. Even after severe pulmonary injury, lung function usually returns to normal in most near-drowning victims.

CENTRAL NERVOUS SYSTEM (CNS)

Improved technology usually results in recovery of lung function; however, recovery of cerebral function is not always possible. The brain is very sensitive, and CNS injury is the most frequent cause of mortality and long-term morbidity following submersion accidents. It is believed that hypoxemia beyond three to five minutes causes irreversible CNS injury. Cerebral cell death from hypoxemia and ischemia is irreversible. Neurological care is controversial but is primarily supportive in nature. Further research is needed for advances in cerebral resuscitation.

Supportive Therapies

Frequent neurological checks and GCS evaluations are important in order to determine early prognosis and the effectiveness of treatment. Adequate oxygenation, ventilation and perfusion are imperative in preventing exacerbation of neurological damage. Cell death from hypoxemia and ischemia is not treatable. Severe anoxic encephalopathy is seen in 10–30% of intensive care patients who survive a submersion accident. Chronic neurologic sequelae after near drowning includes lowered mentation, cerebral dysfunction, quadriplegia, extrapyramidal syndromes, optic and cerebral atrophy, cortical blindness, peripheral neuromuscular damage or a persistent vegetative state. Further CNS hypoperfusion can occur from increased intracranial pressure, cerebral edema, cerebral arteriolar spasms and by oxygen-derived free radicals.

Increased blood pressure and bradycardia are early signs of increased intracranial pressure (ICP). Anything that increases cerebral edema will also increase ICP. Excess free water can swell cerebral cells, increasing cerebral edema and ICP. Vasodilator drugs can exacerbate increased ICP. Historically, ICP has been treated with hyperventilation, mild hypothermia, diuretics and barbiturates. However, studies have shown that these traditional therapies are not effective; therefore, ICP is no longer measured. If ICP is measured, an ICP measurement equal to or greater than 20mm Hg indicates a poor outcome. Head computed tomography (CT) scans are not indicated following a near-drowning.

Other causes of CNS damage may be investigated such as drugs or alcohol, head injury or spinal cord injury. Supportive measures include avoiding hypercapnia, fever and seizures. Seizures should be identified and treated promptly. Hyperglycemia can exacerbate CNS injury. Patients with a blood sugar greater than 300 are at a greater risk of severe morbidity or death. However, control of hyperglycemia with insulin after near-drowning is not recommended. Careful monitoring to avoid hypoglycemia is also important. Hypoglycemia should be treated with .5–1.0 mL/kg of 50% dextrose or 2–4 mL/kg of 10% dextrose.

Severe neurological deficits may require rehabilitation or long term care. Nurses should be realistic and supportive when talking and listening to families. Physicians should consider withdrawing all treatments when caring for deeply comatose near-drowning victims who do not show neurological improvement after 24 to 72 hours of aggressive therapy.

HYPOTHERMIA

Core temperatures of <35° Celsius is common after submersion accidents. Very young children and the elderly are at greatest risk for hypothermia. Children have an increased risk for hypothermia because they have less subcutaneous fat and a large body surface area compared to their weight (Curley & Moloney-Harmon, 2001). Mild hypothermia should be treated to prevent severe hypothermia. Hypothermia can cause progressive bradycardia, impaired myocardial contractility and decreased vasomotor tone. This leads to inadequate perfusion, hypotension and shock. Severe and lengthy drops in temperature may lead to ARDS, decreased hepatorenal metabolism, hypoglycemia, hyperglycemia, thrombocytopenia, platelet dysfunction or disseminated intravascular coagulation. Impaired reticuloendothelial function causes increased susceptibility to infection and sepsis. Resuscitation continues until the core temperature is above 32°C.

Temperature >32 Degrees Celsius

At temperatures above 32°C, the body will attempt to restore a normal temperature. With moderate hypothermia at 32–35°C, there is increased oxygen consumption from shivering and increased muscle tone. Rescuers should remove wet clothes, dry the skin and cover the victim with warm blankets. The victim should be moved to a heated environment as soon as possible. Adequate circulation greatly improves rewarming. Passive rewarming with a warm room and dry blankets may be sufficient for mild hypothermia (Curley & Moloney-Harmon, 2001).

Temperatures <32 Degrees Celsius

Below 32°C, thermoregulation fails and spontaneous rewarming will not occur. Shivering ceases and cellular metabolism decreases. Hypothermia below 32°C can be caused by contact with cold water, by swallowing or aspirating fluid or from heat loss after removal from cold water. For victims not in cardiac arrest with core temperatures less than 34°C, external rewarming measures should be applied only to the trunk to avoid "after drop." Rewarming may cause an initial drop in temperature. This "after drop" is caused by the return of colder blood from the extremities to the warmer central core. After drop may compromise cardiac, respiratory or neurologic function. To minimize after drop, the extremities should not be rewarmed during the initial rewarming period.

Passive rewarming may not be sufficient for severe hypothermia. These victims require active internal warming measures as soon as possible (Curley & Moloney-Harmon, 2001). Warmed intravenous (IV) fluid and humidified oxygen should be used when available. Fluids should be warmed to 40–43°C if possible. Active external warming with warmed blankets and radiant warmers will quickly restore the temperature.

Extreme Hypothermia

When temperatures fall below 28°C, hypoventilation, apnea and bradycardia occur, and there is a greater risk for ventricular fibrillation (V.Fib) or asystole. There is an increased risk of V.Fib with resuscitation at 28°C. However, current recommendations are to proceed with CPR as indicated by pulselessness or respiratory insufficiency. For extreme hypothermia, active core warming may be needed. This involves warmed IV fluid at 36–40°C and heated, humidified oxygen. Warmed gastric, bladder or peritoneal lavage may also be used. Even more aggressive rewarming can be accomplished with hemodialysis, extracorporeal and cardiopulmonary bypass. These methods are significantly faster than external methods and may especially be used in cases that present with circulatory collapse.

Rewarming shock may occur. Signs of shock such as slow capillary refill, cool extremities and altered mental status should be assessed. Increased metabolic requirements and increased body temperature cause vasodilatation. A borderline cardiovascular function may not be able to respond to the increased tissue demands. Hypotension, arrhythmias, decreased myocardial function, metabolic acidosis, tissue ischemia and other signs of shock may be exacerbated with rewarming.

Victims in a deep coma with fixed and dilated pupils and absent reflexes at very low body temperatures may appear to be dead. Resuscitation should be continued until core temp is normal, unless the victim is obviously dead (dependent lividity or rigor mortis). The core body temperature should be at least 32–34°C before stopping resuscitation. Core temperature is most accurate if measured at the tympanic membrane.

MULTISYSTEM COMPLICATIONS

Cardiovascular

Near-drowning patients are placed on a cardiac monitor in order to identify and treat arrhythmias. Myocardium anoxia may cause ventricular fibrillation, bradycardia or asystole. Cardiac arrest after submersion may require defibrillation or cardioversion. Normal sinus rhythm may not return until hypothermia is corrected. After three attempts at defibrillation, CPR should be resumed until the body temperature is returning to normal. Cardiac medications can be given at the usual dosage; however, they may need to be given less frequently due to delayed metabolism and drug clearance.

Although anoxia occurs during submersion, cardiac output may continue for a short period of time. Anoxia lasting one to three minutes can shut down the brain and heart. Hypoxia leads to decreased cardiac output and severe hypotension. Fluid resuscitation may be needed, and establishing effective perfusion takes precedence over measures to minimize cerebral and pulmonary edema. Low cardiac output is common and results in increased pulmonary pressure, increased central venous pressure (CVP), pulmonary vascular resistance and increased pulmonary edema causing more severe ARDS.

Cardiovascular function assessment includes heart rhythm, heart rate, blood pressure and strength of peripheral pulses. Level of consciousness, capillary refill and urine output are some of the indicators of adequate tissue perfusion. Two large bore intravenous catheters or a central venous line should be established as soon as possible. An intraosseous catheter placement can be lifesaving and may avoid the delay associated with multiple attempts to gain venous access. Isotonic fluid, Lactated Ringer's solution or normal saline is usually bolused to increase circulatory volume. Diuretics are not recommended. Dobutamine is the treatment of choice for reduced cardiac output. Severe cases may require an arterial catheter for frequent arterial blood gas (ABG) checks and blood pressure monitoring. Severe myocardial dysfunction may also require a CVP line for right and left pressure monitoring. A series of echocardiograms may be done to check for adequate cardiac output. Fortunately, cardiac arrhythmias usually resolve when hypothermia, perfusion, ventilation and metabolic problems are corrected.

Renal

Significant fluid shifts are uncommon, and altered renal function usually normalizes with treatment. However, acute renal failure may occur with hypoxic ischemic injury. Acute tubular necrosis or cortical necrosis are potential complications. Hourly intake and output measurements are used to assess renal function and the effectiveness of fluid resuscitation. Assessment includes lab values for serum electrolytes, blood urea nitrogen (BUN), creatinine, glucose and complete blood count.

Massive salt-water ingestion or aspiration can lead to electrolyte changes and fluid shifts because of high sodium concentration. Hypernatremia may occur as fluid is drawn from the vascular spaces into the lungs and gastrointestinal tract. Hemoconcentration may be seen from reduced intravascular volume.

Victims may swallow large amounts of water and ensuring adequate perfusion with IV fluids may lead to fluid and electrolyte changes. Water intoxication can cause hyponatremia and hemodilution. Free water overload may occur from excess antidiuretic hormone, which accompanies pulmonary or brain injury. A foley catheter is necessary for accurate measurements of urine output.

Trauma

Traumatic injury may have precipitated the submersion accident. Head injury and cervical spine injuries should be assessed by the nurse, especially with water sports. If a cervical injury is suspected, a cervical collar should be used and cervical alignment maintained.

Infection

Near-drowning victims are at risk for acquiring nosocomial infections. Patients should be monitored for bacteremia and sepsis. Blood and respira-

tory cultures should be done early, and tracheal aspirate cultures should be repeated daily. Fever during the first 48 hours is normal and resolves spontaneously in approximately 80% of cases without the use of antibiotics (Behrman, 2000). If the fever is high, cooling techniques may be required to prevent CNS injury. Antibiotics may be recommended following obvious aspiration of contaminated fluid. Otherwise, antibiotics should only be given following positive culture results.

Gastrointestinal

Gastrointestinal effects may reverse after conservative treatment. Vomiting is seen in more than 75% of victims during resuscitation and nearly 25% of victims aspirate their gastric contents. A nasogastric tube is indicated to prevent aspiration (Behrman, 2000). Cricoid pressure during ventilation, and nasogastric or orogastric decompression may prevent further distention. Abdominal distention, gastric pH and occult blood are assessed to determine gastrointestinal dysfunction. Patients should remain NPO until stable, and gastric pH should be controlled.

Psychological Effects

Psychiatric and psychosocial sequelae are common, and counseling for the child and family should be considered. Grief, guilt, and anger are common reactions. Approximately 80% of parents of a submersion victim are divorced within a few years of the accident (Behrman, 2000). Problems with jobs and substance abuse are frequently seen. Professional counseling and the support of a social worker should be considered for all families of a near-drowning victim.

For patients who are not recovering from multisystem failure, a hospice consult will assist the family in preparing for the inevitable. If brain death has been determined and the decision has been made to stop treatment, nurses should examine their own feelings and beliefs then ask for assistance if needed. Parents are invited to hold their child when treatments are discontinued. Nurses should turn off all alarms and audible monitor signals before discontinuing ventilation or medications. Monitors should be turned away from the family, and the physician needs to be notified when time of death should be pronounced.

Experimental Therapies

Several new therapies have been tried. None have been proven to be effective in adults, and they are not recommended in children. These include high frequency ventilation, nitric oxide, artificial surfactant, partial liquid ventilation, extracorporeal life support and defoaming of pulmonary edema with butyl alcohol vapor following salt-water aspiration.

PROGNOSIS

Initially, all near-drowning victims should receive aggressive support. Early and precise prognosis is important in order to guide triage decisions, counsel families and reduce unnecessary interventions. Health care professionals should help guide family decisions regarding withdrawal of support.

Approximately 90% of pediatric submersion victims who survive have good outcomes (Behrman, 2000). Studies have shown that children with a normal sinus rhythm, reactive pupils or neurologic responsiveness at the scene almost always have a good outcome. Victims with a submersion duration of less than five minutes are usually neurologically intact or have mild impairment. Eighty-seven percent of victims with restored cardiovascular function within 10 minutes of submersion have a good outcome (Behrman, 2000). Stuporous or obtunded victims that respond to painful stimuli at two to six hours after submersion often have a normal outcome. With appropriate treatment, many comatose children show neuro-

logic improvement within the first 24–72 hours after submersion (Behrman, 2000).

Longer submersion time is associated with a poorer outcome. Prolonged submersion victims rarely benefit from resuscitation. Studies have shown that 93% of victims that required CPR and were submerged for more than 10 minutes died or had severe neurologic impairment (Behrman, 2000). Studies have also shown that 100% of victims that received resuscitation for more than 25 minutes died (Behrman, 2000). In comatose victims, CNS injury is a major concern. A GCS score of <5 indicates increased mortality or severe CNS damage. Those with a poor outcome such as quadriplegia may have medical cost of up to $100,000.00 annually. Decorticate or decerebrate posturing at two to six hours after drowning indicates either brain death or severe neurological impairment. Fifty percent of victims in a coma will die or have severe neurological damage or brain death (Behrman, 2000). Health care professionals should consider withdrawl of life support from a comatose victim after 24 to 72 hours of aggressive therapy, if there has been no improvement in mental status.

The Glasgow Coma Scale is not conclusive but may be helpful in predicting recovery. Children with a GCS of >6 on admission to the hospital typically have good outcomes; whereas those with a GCS of <5 have a high risk of poor neurologic outcome. Improved GCS within the first several hours of hospitalization may indicate a better prognosis. Neurologic examination and progression during the first 24–72 hours are currently the best indicators of neurologic outcome. Serial neurological exams should be done with consideration of withdrawing support from patients who fail to show improvement over 72 hours. Families should be counseled during early stages and discuss whether to increase efforts from standard therapies to experimental or new therapies. Victims with good short-term outcome are still at risk for secondary drowning or ARDS, which can result in a vegetative state.

If two or less of the following indicators are present, there is a 90% chance of a good outcome. If there are three or more of the following indicators present, there is only a 5% chance of normal recovery (Orlowski & Szpilman, 2001).

- <3 years old
- Submersion for more than 5 minutes
- No resuscitation for 10 minutes
- Coma on admission to ER
- ABG pH of 7.10 or below

PREVENTION

Barkin and Gelberg (1999) examined primary care physicians' counseling protocols on drowning prevention. About 465 pediatricians and family practitioners were sent a questionnaire and 325 responded. About two thirds of them did not know how common drowning deaths are, and only 1/3 stated that they counsel families on drowning prevention. Barkin and Gelberg (1999) suggest that drowning prevention receives little attention because it has low visibility. Visibility is low because many victims are declared dead at the scene and never receive medical care.

A recent study examined the effectiveness of fenced-in pools as a safety measure for young children. Results showed that a four-foot high, large mesh chain link fence can be scaled by 75% of 2-year-olds in an average time of 25.6 seconds and by 100% of 4-year-olds in an average time of 11.5 seconds (Behrman, 2000). Increasing the fence height to 5 ft and narrowing the mesh to 1.25 inches minimally decreased the scaling success rate (Behrman, 2000).

In the U.S., there are 50,000 new pools built every year. There are already 2.2 million residential pools and another 2.3 million nonresidential pools in the U.S. (Orlowski & Szpilman, 2001). This may explain why nearly half of all U.S. drownings occur in pools. Approximately 46% of drownings occur in people who know how to swim (Orlowski & Szpilman, 2001). Most occur in young, healthy productive people with a long life expectancy. Trauma, boating accidents, skin diving, scuba diving and cramps can all increase the risk of submersion accidents. Cardiopulmonary disease or syncope can precipitate submersion. Homicide, suicide and immersion syndrome are possible causes of submersion deaths. Cervical spine injury from diving in shallow water is a frequent cause of drowning or long term neurological sequelae.

In 1998, thirty states required children from 6 to 12 years of age to wear life vests while boating. Given the high-risk for teenagers, this age restriction should be increased. A law against driving under the influence (DUI) for boaters exists in all 50 states but is frequently not enforced. Advertisers should be prohibited from promoting the use of alcohol while boating.

Preventive Measures

- Pools should be appropriately fenced in.
- Fences around pools should have self-closing gates with self-latching closures mounted near the top of the fence.
- Fences around pools should have a safe height and mesh size.
- Pool covers or solar blankets should not be depended on as safety measures.
- Parents should supervise all school age children every moment during swimming.
- Parents should be taught that any body of water, no matter how innocuous, poses a drowning risk—especially in children <4 years old.
- Bathtubs, buckets, toilets and washing machines can all be hazardous for small children.

- Swimming lessons do not drown-proof children and may provide false security.

- Water safety for children, teenagers and parents should include wearing flotation devices while boating and never swimming alone.

- Teens should be taught how alcohol and drug use contributes to submersion and drowning incidence.

- Swimmers should swim near lifeguards.

- No one should dive into water less than nine feet deep.

Risk Factors

- Children less than 5-years-old are at the highest risk of drowning.

- Toddlers are most at risk during meal times.

- Individuals who overestimate their swimming ability are at risk.

- Teenagers between 15 and 19-years-old are at an increased risk of drowning.

- Alcohol and drugs increase drowning risk.

- Males are more at risk than females.

- African Americans are more at risk than Caucasians.

- Individuals with seizure disorders are always at risk.

- Residential swimming pools increase drowning risk.

- Any body of water presents a drowning risk.

- Broken fences and locks indicate increased risk.

NURSING INTERVENTION

There are two important aspects of nursing care of a submersion victim. The first is to complete frequent neurological checks during the first 24 to 48 hours. This is important prognostic information that may determine whether to continue aggressive therapy or to discontinue treatments. The second important aspect of nursing care is to do frequent assessments of pulmonary status. Any deterioration in pulmonary status should be treated promptly to prevent further hypoxic insult. This is essential in providing a positive neurological outcome.

Nurses should always consider intentional causes of submersion injury, especially when the history is incompatible with the developmental ability of the child. A careful history should be taken if abuse is suspected.

Nurses can play an important role in drowning prevention. Nurses can create flyers or posters for hospital, office or public health settings to educate families about the risks of drowning and the devastation of many near-drowning outcomes. Nurses can also discuss the risks of drowning during routine office exams or prepare a presentation at local schools. Health care professionals have little control over the most important outcome factors, which include submersion duration and rapid resuscitation. Therefore, the best defense for health care professionals is offense. Drowning prevention should be taught at every opportunity.

Case Report

A veteran staff nurse was working the night shift when a five-year-old patient came out of her room to tell the nurse that her roommate woke up and would like a glass of water. The nurse smiled at the patient, peaked in the room briefly to see the other patient resting with her eyes closed. The nurse said she would return shortly and continued passing her twelve o'clock meds wondering what could have prompted that child to come up with such a tale. The five-year-old's roommate was a 6-year-old girl who had been basically unresponsive since admission. The six-year-old had fallen through an ice-covered lake and was submerged for 20 minutes. She spent the last week in the ICU and was moved to the floor until transport to a long-term rehab facility could be arranged. The child's mental status involved nonpurposeful movements and occasional moaning with no signs of improvement since admission.

Moments later, the nurse was interrupted again by the five-year-old for the roommate's water. The five-year old said her roommate was sitting up now and was very thirsty. Upon entering the room, the nurse stood momentarily in shock to see this near-drowning victim sitting up, alert and indeed asking for water. The nurse brought the water then promptly dialed the young girl's mother at home (Stafford, 2001).

SUMMARY

The most important thing that nurses can do is to promote prevention in the office, public health or hospital setting. The importance of rapid response at the scene should be emphasized. Despite improved pulmonary therapy, prolonged hypoxia and ischemic injury remains a major problem after submersion accidents. This makes submersion accidents particularly devastating to victims and their families. It is important for nurses to remember that 46% of drownings occur in people who know how to swim (Orlowski & Szpilman, 2001). The majority of submersions occur in young, healthy productive people with a long life expectancy. Public education about the hazards and prevalence of near-drowning injuries is the best method of reducing its devastating effects.

EXAM QUESTIONS

CHAPTER 8
Questions 45–56

45. Which of the following statements best describes the pathophysiology of salt water and fresh water aspiration?

   a. Salt water aspiration has no adverse effects on surfactant or gas exchange.

   b. Both types of aspiration diminish surfactant and reduce gas exchange.

   c. Only fresh water aspiration causes a reduction of surfactant and atelectasis.

   d. Neither salt water nor fresh water negatively affect gas exchange or the presence of surfactant.

46. The location of most drowning accidents in the U.S. is

   a. lakes and rivers.

   b. pools.

   c. buckets.

   d. sinks and tubs.

47. The age group most at risk for drowning is

   a. 1- to 4-years-old.

   b. 5- to 10-years-old.

   c. 10- to 15-years-old.

   d. 15- to 19-years-old.

48. Which of the following statements is true regarding drowning prevalence in the U.S.?

   a. Annually, approximately 5,000 people drown.

   b. 25% of all pediatric submersion victims are declared dead at the scene.

   c. Many near-drowning victims that survive have neurologic sequelae.

   d. Drowning is the third leading cause of death by injury in children under 19.

49. Which of the following actions should be taken at the scene of a submersion accident?

   a. Rescue breathing is started once the victim is out of the water.

   b. The Heimlich maneuver is performed to remove any obstruction before rescue breathing begins.

   c. Rescue breathing should be started in the water if possible.

   d. The victim's airway is suctioned to prevent pulmonary edema before any rescue breathing is begun.

50. The correct pulmonary management of a submersion victim is to

   a. suction all frothy mucous before starting rescue breathing.

   b. oxygenate to keep saturations >90%.

   c. hyperventilate to keep $PaCo_2$ <35.

   d. begin IV corticosteroid and prophylactic antibiotic therapy.

51. Which of the following factors cause cerebral cell death following a submersion accident?

    a. increased ICP, decreased perfusion and ischemia

    b. a PaCo2 between 35–40 from hyperventilation with oxygen

    c. IV administration of fluid boluses and vasopressors

    d. administration of corticosteroids for lung injury

52. The primary goal of fluid resuscitation is

    a. establishing effective perfusion.

    b. minimizing cerebral edema.

    c. minimizing pulmonary edema.

    d. resolution of hypothermia.

53. In a recent study, 100% of submersion victims died after receiving CPR for

    a. 15 minutes.

    b. 20 minutes.

    c. 25 minutes.

    d. 30 minutes.

54. What is the correct statement regarding hypothermia following a submersion accident?

    a. Hypothermia can cause tachycardia and hypertension.

    b. Young children and geriatric patients are at the lowest risk for hypothermia.

    c. Hypothermia can cause bradycardia and hypotension.

    d. Hypothermia causes increased perfusion.

55. Which of the following is correct regarding cardiovascular complications following a submersion accident?

    a. Cardiac medication should be given more often.

    b. After three minutes of hypoxia, tachycardia will result.

    c. Fluid resuscitation takes precedence over minimizing cerebral edema.

    d. Epinephrine is the treatment of choice for cardiac complications.

56. To prevent drowning

    a. diving should be safe in water over 6 feet deep.

    b. CPR should be done only by parents or lifeguards.

    c. the use of life vests while boating is only necessary for young children.

    d. parents should be taught that buckets and sinks are a potential drowning risk.

CHAPTER 9

CHILD MALTREATMENT

CHAPTER OBJECTIVE

After completing this chapter, the reader will be able to recognize the significance of child abuse including the prevalence of abuse, consequences for victims, and their relevance to the nursing profession.

LEARNING OBJECTIVES

After studying this chapter, the learner will be able to

1. identify the prevalence of child abuse and the common causative factors.

2. recognize the devastating long-term effects of child abuse.

3. select some preventive measures that will contribute to the reduction of child abuse.

4. choose physical symptoms that are indicative of abusive injuries.

5. specify patient symptoms and characteristics of sexual abuse.

6. indicate the behaviors and characteristics of a child suffering from child neglect.

7. recognize appropriate factors related to parent teaching following a child abuse injury.

INTRODUCTION

History

The Society for the Prevention of Cruelty to Children was created in 1874. This occurred when the Society for the Prevention of Cruelty to Animals (SPCA) was the only resource available to help an abused child who was abandoned in a church (Jain, 1999). The SPCA demanded legal protection of this beaten child on the grounds that the child belonged to the Animal Kingdom (Curley & Moloney-Harmon, 2001). The Child Abuse Prevention and Treatment Act (CAPTA) that was passed in 1974 required mandatory reporting of child abuse in every state by physicians, nurses, educators, social workers and police officers (Jain, 1999).

Prevalence

- There are three million cases of child abuse reported in the United States each year (Bethea, 1999; Jain, 1999).

- Each year, 160,000 children suffer severe or life-threatening injury and up to 2,000 children die as a result of abuse (Bethea, 1999; *The Merck Manual,* 2001c).

- Approximately 75% of the violence in this country is domestic violence (Bethea, 1999).

- More children are victims of maltreatment than all other serious illnesses combined (Curley & Moloney-Harmon, 2001).

- Reports of child abuse have increased significantly in the last 15 years; however, it is unknown if this represents an increase in abuse or just an increase in abuse reporting (Curley & Moloney-Harmon, 2001).

DEFINITIONS

Child abuse and neglect are the physical or mental maltreatment of any child under the age of 18 (*The Merck Manual,* 2001c; Jain, 1999). The Department of Health and Human Services (DHHS) defines four types of maltreatment to include neglect, physical abuse, sexual abuse and emotional abuse. Many children fall into more than one category (Jain, 1999). Negligence includes the failure to provide medical, educational or physical care.

- Physical abuse involves inflicting a physical harm to a child through beating, burning, choking, biting, shaking, pushing, restraining, kicking or any other mechanism meant to hurt a child.

- Sexual abuse involves oral, anal or genital penetration. Molestation involves genital contact without intrusion, sexual exposure or touching areas other than the genitals with sexual intentions (Jain, 1999).

- Emotional abuse can be a lack of protection from harmful influences. This may include spousal abuse in the child's presence. Emotional abuse may involve close confinement as a method of punishment, verbal abuse or demeaning words.

- Neglect means not meeting a child's basic needs of life. Neglect includes emotional, physical and educational neglect. Neglect symptoms are not as objective as physical abuse, and it is often not reported. However, all forms of abuse can lead to devastating long-term consequences (Jain, 1999). Neglect is

often seen when there is a substance abuse problem in the home. Chronic depression of a mother may contribute to neglect (*The Merck Manual,* 2001c). Physical neglect may include delaying or not seeking medical attention for routine care or not providing a safe living environment. Educational neglect means not enrolling a child in school as mandated by state laws, not addressing special educational needs or condoning truancy. Emotional neglect is much more difficult to identify and may manifest as learning or social problems.

CAUSES OF ABUSE

Some parents may have unrealistic expectations of their child. They may become frustrated and lose control when their child does not meet their expectations. Abuse is often caused by a parent's lack of impulse control. Parents may feel isolated, unprotected and vulnerable when they do not have support from family, friends, neighbors or peers.

Abuse is more prevalent during times of stress. There are many factors that add stress to a family's life, and there are also factors that prevent parents from handling stress. If a family's basic needs for food, shelter, clothing, safety and medical care are not met there is added stress and an increased risk for abuse. Any family crisis can precipitate abuse, and drugs or alcohol may provoke abusive behaviors (*The Merck Manual,* 2001c).

Characteristics of an Abuser

- All social classes and races can inflict abuse or neglect, but children living in poverty suffer 12 times more often than those who do not (*The Merck Manual,* 2001c).

- Most child abuse occurs at home by someone the child knows (Bethea, 1999). Except for sexual abuse, about 77% of abusers are parents and 11% are other relatives (Jain, 1999).

- Childcare providers are only responsible for about 2% of intentional abuse injuries (Bethea, 1999).

- Most abusers are between the ages of 20 and 40 years old (Jain, 1999).

- Approximately 40% of confirmed child abuse cases are related to substance abuse (Bethea, 1999).

- Child abuse is much more likely to occur in homes where there is spousal abuse, and fathers are more likely to inflict the abuse than mothers (Bethea, 1999).

- Uneducated parents or parents with few coping skills are more likely to abuse their children.

- If a parent has a psychiatric disorder, there is a greater risk of abuse.

- Families who are socially isolated or have poor social support have an increased risk of abuse.

Children at Risk for Abuse

Some children are more susceptible to abuse than others. Although abuse crosses all socioeconomic levels, poverty is the most frequent and persistent risk factor for child abuse (Bethea, 1999). It is uncertain if cases of abuse in low-income homes are more evident as a result of greater scrutiny by public agencies or if they are directly related to the stress of poverty (Bethea, 1999). Children with disabilities are also at an increased risk for mistreatment (Committee on Child Abuse and Neglect & Committee on Children with Disabilities, 2001).

Neonaticide (the murder of a baby during the first 24 hours of life) accounts for 45% of child deaths that occur during the first year of life (Bethea, 1999). Girls are abused a little more often than boys. Fewer reports of abused children under two-years-old may be related to the limited contact that infants and toddlers have with the community compared to older children (Jain, 1999). Abuse is more likely to occur in children under 12-years-old. Perhaps because after the age of 12, children

are more likely to find a way of escaping an abusive home.

Children at Risk of Abuse

- Children under five-years-old;
- Premature infants;
- A difficult child;
- An irritable child;
- A demanding child;
- Children with a physical or mental handicap;
- A sick or chronically ill child;
- A stepchild or an adopted child;
- A child raised only by a father; or
- A child with three or more siblings (Jain, 1999).

CLINICAL SIGNS OF ABUSE

Physical Abuse

Physical signs of abuse can be lesions, bruises, hematomas, burns, welts, fractures or abrasions. Multiple injuries in different phases of healing are indicative of abuse. Repeat injuries may indicate inadequate supervision or neglect (*The Merck Manual,* 2001c). A careful exam can provide important clues. Single soft tissue injury in infants and multiple soft tissue injuries in toddlers may indicate abuse (Jain, 1999).

Certain child behaviors can be indicative of a history of physical abuse. Nurses caring for an abused child may notice wariness of any physical contact, fear of parents or of going home or failure to cry from painful injuries. Children who have suffered maltreatment may also act out with aggressive behaviors, or they may exhibit withdrawal behaviors such as depression (Whaley & Wong, 1999).

Bruises

Normally bruises occur on the shins and fore-head of a toddler, so bruises on other body parts such as the back, genitals, chest or abdomen may be suspicious of abuse. A small bruise may be the only sign of a healing, underlying fracture that was not treated at the time of injury (Jain 1999). The size, location, and color of all bruises should be documented in the nurse's notes. When abuse is suspected, the amount of swelling needs to be recorded, and photos of bruises should be taken.

- Loop marks or parallel marks may indicate the use of a cord, belt or rope (Hopkins, 2000; Jain, 1999).

- The color can help determine the age of a bruise *(see Table 9-1)*.

- A bruise in the shape of a hand or finger prints indicates abuse.

- Abrasions at the corners of the mouth and cir-cumferential bruises around the wrists and ankles may be from a binding injury (Jain, 1999).

Bites

All human bites on young children raise the suspicion of abuse.

- Human bites tend to crush instead of lacerate. A human bite is usually superficial with soft tissue bruising, whereas an animal bite is usu-ally a deep puncture wound with soft tissue tearing.

- Teeth measurements greater than 3 cm is sug-gestive of an adult human bite. Marks that show individual teeth and the pattern of the dental arch can help identify the abuser.

- Saliva samples can be taken from fresh bites. Samples must be taken before the wound is cleansed and must be given to legal authorities for forensic evaluation (Jain, 1999; Hopkins, 2000). The sooner local law enforcement is called regarding suspected abuse, the more

TABLE 9-1
Bruise Descriptions

Red/Blue/Purple	1 to 4 days old
Green	5 to 7 days old
Yellow	7 to 10 days old
Brown	10 to 14 days old
Resolution	2 to 4 weeks

likely there will be usable evidence for the courtroom.

Burns

As many as 25% of childhood burns are inflicted intentionally. Nurses can differentiate accidental spill burns from intentional burns by looking at the pattern of the burn. All clear, even burns are suspicious of abuse.

Characteristics of Accidental Burns

- An accidental burn is most severe at the point of first contact, then the burn narrows where the liquid traveled down the body. There are usually splatter marks near the burn.

- The most common location of accidental burns for children is the chest.

- Accidental burns of the hands are usually patchy and irregular from the child's quick release of a hot object.

Characteristics of Intentional Burns

- The edges of an intentional burn are clearly marked with little or no splash marks.

- "Glove" or "stocking" burns are caused when a hand or foot is put into hot water and held there for several seconds.

- Intentional burns are usually symmetrical. Symmetrical burns on both buttocks or legs and symmetric burns on both palms or soles all suggest intentional injury (Hopkins, 2000).

- Well marked burns of the buttocks are often punishment for a toilet training accident.

- Diapers are protective; therefore, burns around the edge of a diapered area are also suspicious.

- A cigarette burn is 7–8 mm and is a distinctive circular burn (Jain, 1999).

Abdominal Trauma

Abdominal trauma is not a common symptom of abuse, but when it occurs, there is a high incidence of mortality (Hopkins, 2000; Jain, 1999).

- A duodenal hematoma causing upper gastrointestinal obstruction is suspicious of intentional blunt trauma. The injury may involve a tear, laceration or perforation of internal organs.

- There is often a delay in seeking medical attention, and the parents may seek treatment only after the child develops obvious signs of sepsis or hemorrhaging.

- By the time treatment is sought, there is a high risk of morbidity or mortality.

- Death usually occurs from sepsis or hemorrhage.

Fractures

Certain types of fractures are indicative of abuse. Any fracture in an infant is highly suspicious. Stair related falls are not typically a cause of fractures. An accidental fall injury usually involves one body part; often this will be the face or head. Long bone fractures from an accidental fall down stairs are rare. Skeletal injuries at different stages of healing are often found when a child is seen in the emergency room for an unrelated injury. There may be minimal swelling because of the delay in seeking treatment.

- Epiphyseal or metaphyseal chip fractures are typical abuse injuries. These can occur following jerking or shaking a child's limb.

- Spiral fractures are suspicious, especially if no history of rotational force is given.

- Transverse fractures, along with a suspicious history, may indicate abuse.

- Rib fractures are usually not displaced and occur posteriorly.

- Pleural thickening, pleural fluid and contusions may suggest an undetected rib fracture. These can be caused by direct blows or severe squeezing of the rib cage.

- A fracture of the cervical spine is unlikely from a fall of less than five feet (Jain, 1999).

- Skull fractures sustained from mild to moderate trauma are usually linear, nondisplaced, unilateral and in the parietal bone. They are usually benign unless associated with an underlying epidural hemorrhage.

- Abusive skull fractures suggest a greater force than is typically sustained in minor household trauma. Fractures more than 3 cm wide or complex fractures are suspicious. Skull fractures from abuse are more likely to be bilateral, crush injuries or depressed injuries and involve a bone other than the parietal bone. Abuse fractures may cross a suture line and be associated with other injuries (Jain, 1999; Hopkins, 2000).

Head Injury

Child abuse is the most common cause of serious head injury in infants, and head injury is the most common cause of mortality in victims of child abuse. Most household trauma does not produce enough force to cause significant intracranial pathology. An abusive head injury may or may not present with external evidence of trauma. However, if there are no obvious signs of accidental injury with a diagnosis of head injury, abuse should be suspected. Symptoms of head trauma are as follows.

- Excessive crying, poor feeding or irritability may be present.

- There may be lethargy or seizures.

- Coma or varying states of unresponsiveness may occur.

- Hypertonicity or hypotonicity is a potential symptom.

- Bradycardia, apnea or cardiorespiratory arrest may result.

- Bleeding from the ears or leakage of cerebral spinal fluid from the nose or ears indicates trauma. CSF leakage indicates a basilar skull fracture (Hopkins, 2000).

- Raccoon eyes or periorbital ecchymosis is a sign of an orbital roof fracture (Hopkins, 2000).

- Battle's sign is ecchymosis behind the ear and is a sign of a mastoid fracture (Hopkins, 2000).

- Subdural hematomas are strongly correlated with intentional trauma. They are rare in other situations except for major trauma (Jain, 1999).

- Retinal hemorrhage is very suspicious of child abuse (Jain, 1999).

Shaken Baby Syndrome

- The initial symptoms of shaken baby syndrome may be vague and may include listlessness, poor feeding, and irritability. The initial diagnosis is often a viral syndrome.

- There is often minimal external signs of trauma in the infant (Jain, 1999).

- There is an association of retinal hemorrhages and subdural hematomas.

- There may be long bone or rib fractures.

- Seizures, apnea or lethargy can be signs of intracranial injury in children less than six months old (Hopkins, 2000).

- Shaken baby syndrome has a 30% morbidity and mortality rate (Jain, 1999).

Retinal Hemorrhage

Retinal hemorrhages are suggestive of abuse and always require evaluation for head trauma. Ophthalmic examination is a vital part of screening for abuse. Retinal hemorrhages are not conclusive of abuse but are strongly associated with inten-

tional injury. Retinal hemorrhages occur in 65–95% of infants with shaken baby syndrome (Jain, 1999). There are only occasional reports of retinal hemorrhages after accidental trauma, and differentiating accidental and abusive causes may be difficult.

Although retinal hemorrhages in young children have almost become diagnostic of child abuse, three recent case studies have shown that accidental household trauma can also cause retinal hemorrhage, and a suspicion of child abuse should not be made based on retinal hemorrhage alone (Christian, Taylor, Hertle & Duhaime, 1999). All other evidence presented with these three case studies was consistent with accidental trauma. There was no delay in treatment, no change in stories, a negative skeletal survey and a negative physical exam (Christian et al., 1999). These case studies indicate the importance of a complete history of events and a thorough medical examination when child abuse is suspected.

Symptoms of Emotional Abuse

Emotional abuse is less easily identified. Emotional abuse may result in failure to thrive or developmental delay. An emotionally abused child may be distrustful, distant or superficial in relationships. Infants may exhibit a lack of a social smile or lack of normal "stranger anxiety." Rocking, sucking or biting behaviors may be seen in infancy (Whaley & Wong, 1999). Older children may show passiveness and overt concern with pleasing adults. A school age child may have difficulty interacting with teachers and peers. There may be antisocial behaviors, aggression, cruelty or destructiveness (Whaley & Wong, 1999). A child may struggle with relationships following emotional abuse (*The Merck Manual,* 2001c).

Symptoms of Sexual Abuse

Clinical signs of sexual abuse may be physical or behavioral. Behavioral changes may include public masturbation, inappropriate sexual play or seductive behavior. There may be a sudden onset of fears such as fear of strangers, of the dark or of leaving home. Sexual abuse may result in hostility, aggression or depression (Whaley & Wong, 1999). Some physical signs of sexual abuse are as follows.

- After sexual abuse a child may be irritable or fearful and may have insomnia.

- Difficulty walking or sitting may indicate genital trauma. Vaginal bleeding and external genitalia injury are suspicious of abuse. Anal lacerations, bruising, hemorrhoids, scars and absence of anal wink can be evidence of forced penetration.

- Vaginal discharge, vaginal pruritus, recurrent urinary tract infections, infections such as genital warts or a sexually transmitted disease of any sort in a child under 12-years-old is suggestive of sexual molestation.

- Oral trauma may involve lacerations inside the mouth from forced feeding or forced oral sex. There may be burns in the mouth from hot food. Lacerations or bruises around the corners of the mouth may indicate a gag injury (Jain, 1999; Hopkins, 2000; *The Merck Manual,* 2001c).

Symptoms of Neglect

Signs of neglect may include malnutrition, poor hygiene and ill fitting or dirty clothing. Poor dental hygiene and lack of immunizations may also be signs of neglect. Up to 50% of failure to thrive infants have been neglected (*The Merck Manual,* 2001c). Infants may have delayed emotional growth with no interest in their environment when they have had little interaction or stimulation. This lack of interest may be mistaken for mental retardation. Older children may have poor school attendance or poor school performance.

DIAGNOSIS

The first priority is to identify and treat the child's immediate medical problems. Suspicious symptoms indicate the need for a thorough physical examination. A complete history of events prior to and during the injury will help to determine the cause of injury. Diagnostic testing may include a head CT scan for intracranial pathology. An MRI may be done to assess for lesions and to help date the time of injury. An ophthalmologic exam will reveal retinal hemorrhages, if they are present (Hopkins, 2000).

A skeletal survey is done for bone trauma and should be done for all children who are potential abuse victims. A skeletal survey includes separate views of every bone. A complete survey includes anterior and posterior views of the arms, legs, feet and hands and the skull. An axial skeleton view may also be obtained. Skeletal surveys are done at specially equipped facilities. Special film and methods are used to detect subtle abnormalities (Jain, 1999). A bone scan may also be done for fractures that are difficult to detect.

MEDICAL TREATMENT

Medical treatment is provided per usual trauma protocol. (See Chapter 5 for specific pediatric considerations.) After treatment of physical injuries, long-range plans must be considered for high-risk families. Nurses should approach families in a helpful manner and ask about the family setting to assess the family's needs. A social worker or case manager should be consulted to determine what type of assistance is available. Nurses should report to social services or welfare, if needed. Many facilities have multidisciplinary teams available to address the variety of needs of an abusive family. A sexual abuse victim in particular may require counseling.

Temporary removal from the home may be required if the home setting is too high-risk for the child to return. Recurrences of abuse occur frequently, and permanent removal may be needed. Removal requires a court petition. However, if immediate removal from the home is needed, Child Protective Services should be contacted for immediate foster care placement. If immediate placement cannot be made, a hospital admission may be needed until placement can be found (Jain, 1999). Families of abused children often relocate to avoid follow-up. Broken doctors appointments are also very common.

NURSING RESPONSIBILITY

Documentation

All health care providers are required to report suspected abuse or neglect to the local police (Hopkins, 2000). Documentation must always be legible. Clinical documentation can make the difference between an abused child being placed into a safe home or being returned to an abusive parent. Both the reported mechanism of injury and the suspected mechanism of injury need to be charted. The reported mechanism of injury needs to be documented in the patient or caregiver's own words using quotation marks. Along with the child's responses, nurses should document their questions to indicate the use of nonleading questions. Physicians should include a detailed physical examination. It is helpful to have drawings to indicate the location of injury. Measurements, color, shape and texture of all injuries should be recorded in as descriptive a manner as possible. The more legible and descriptive the nurse's notes are the less likely the nurse will be needed to testify in court. Nurse's notes should stand alone as complete evidence of the incident.

Photographs are an important method of documentation of abuse injuries. Photographs provide documentation of the extent of the injuries and are admissible evidence in court. Photographs need to be labeled with the date, patient's name, chart number and the physician's name. Also, nurses need to document in the nurse's notes that photographs were taken and documentation of the person who the photographs were released to needs to be included. A polaroid camera is sufficient for taking photos of abusive injuries (Jain, 1999).

History of Events

Nurses should obtain a history from all possible sources. The caretaker in the emergency room, the caretaker at the scene, and the child. If possible, the child should be interviewed alone. Open-ended questions should be used with the child to encourage the child to elaborate on the answers. The child's story should be documented in their own words (Jain, 1999). Interviews from adults should be obtained separately. Nurses should then take note if the histories are consistent or contradictory. When did the injury happen? Were there any delays in seeking treatment? Are the events of the incident consistent with the developmental abilities of the child? Is the history consistent with the injury? Nurses need to inquire about the activities immediately prior to the event to help determine the risk of abuse. A period of colic, poor feeding or toilet training accidents may precipitate abuse. Have there been previous injuries, previous hospitalizations or other medical problems? Is there any history of drug use in the family, previous abuse, marital stress or financial hardships (Jain, 1999)? Nurses should be suspicious of abuse if there are inconsistencies in the events prior to the injuries (see *Table 9-2*).

Mistakenly reported abuse can be devastating to families. Nurses can avoid over reporting by learning the physical signs and symptoms of abusive injuries. Learning how to obtain a complete

---

TABLE 9-2
Signs of Abuse

- There is inadequate detail or delay in providing a history of the injury.

- The explanation changes over time or is contradictory.

- The injury is inconsistent with the story of how it occurred.

- The physical examination results do not match the mechanism of injury.

- The parental reaction to the injury is inappropriate.

- The events preceding the injury are incompatible with the developmental ability of the child.

- There is a delay in seeking treatment.

- There is evidence of neglect or failure to thrive.

- The child displays emotional instability.

- There is a prior history of suspected abuse.

Source: Hopkins, J. (2000). *Harriet Lane handbook* (15th ed.).[Available online: www.home.medconsult.com/das/book/body/O/871/30.html.] *The Merck Manual.* (2001c). [Available online: http://www.merck.com/pubs/manual/section19/chapter264/264a.htm.]

---

history of the events leading to the injury and obtaining a family history to assess for risk factors are important nursing skills. All of this information is used to determine the likelihood of an injury being caused by abuse.

Intervention

Nurses are actively involved in treatment plans for these children. Health supervision visits can be used to assess a family's strengths and need for assistance. The American Academy of Pediatrics supports the role of health care professionals in the prevention, identification and treatment of child abuse and neglect (Committee on Child Abuse and Neglect & Committee on Children with Disabilities, 2001).

Case Report

D. Hart (2001), a registered nurse, recalled a five-month-old baby girl that was admitted for shaken baby syndrome. The baby suffered severe head injuries, and although everything was done to save her, she was diagnosed with brain death on the day of admission. The baby was intubated and ventilator dependent. The nurses and physicians tried to explain the prognosis and futility of continued medical treatment to the young parents.

The parents gave conflicting information, and none of the information about the injury appeared to be accurate. The case was reported to the local police for suspected child abuse, and the couple hired a lawyer. The days turned into weeks, and weeks turned into months. After one year of nursing care for this unresponsive child, nurses had to make arrangements for home care and medical equipment so that the family could take the baby home. She was not a candidate for rehabilitation. Although there was not enough evidence to convict the couple with child abuse, a child death may have warranted a trial. Nurses felt strongly that the young couple chose to keep their baby alive with the support of medical technology to avoid prosecution for murder.

CONSEQUENCES OF ABUSE

Victims of child abuse suffer long after the intentional injuries stop. Childhood abuse may lead to criminal, psychiatric and dysfunctional behaviors as an adult. There is also an increased risk of an abused child becoming an alcoholic or drug addict as an adult (Jain, 1999). These children are at risk for developmental delays, separation anxiety, aggressive behaviors, depressive and affective disorders, post-traumatic stress disorders, panic attacks, schizophrenia and abuse of their own children and spouse (Bethea, 1999). All health care professionals are required to report suspected child abuse and neglect to the police. Although they are less likely to be reported, emotional, educational and nutritional neglect can lead to negative long-term effects for a child. (Jain, 1999). Long term consequences of child abuse are as follows.

• Being arrested as a juvenile;

• Committing a violent crime as an adult;

• Prostitution after sexual abuse;

• Suicide;

• Depression;

• Psychiatric disorders;

• Violent behaviors;

• Drug and alcohol use; and

• Developmental disabilities (Jain, 1999).

PREVENTION

Child protection agencies have been overwhelmed, and recent efforts have begun to focus on the prevention of child abuse. It may seem impossible to make a dent in the number of abused children; however, accumulatively every five minutes worth of intervention can add up to effective prevention. Studies have shown that physicians spend as little as one minute discussing anticipatory guidance with parents. Parenting classes could fill this gap. Evening and weekend office hours for working parents can decrease family stress. Respite care for families with chronically ill children can also help to reduce family stress.

Many of the same supportive measures provided following abuse can be offered proactively to prevent an abusive situation. Prevention can address all of the stressful aspects of family life: Financial, educational, substance abuse, childcare and safety.

Identifying High-Risk Families

Child abuse often stems from parental problems. The best way for nurses to help abused children may be to offer assistance and understanding to their parents. All pediatric patients should be assessed for high-risk parents. It should be determined if there is a lack of support from family or friends. First time parents, teen parents, parents with a high-risk pregnancy or premature delivery may also be prone to abuse or neglect their child. Financial concerns, single parenting or having several young children are possible high-risk situations. Nurses can create a supportive, non-threatening relationship with parents in an effort to help them work through their problems and in the long run, make great strides in protecting victims of child abuse.

Nurses need to identify and counsel parents who suffer from spousal abuse. Five or ten minutes should be taken with each parent to ask questions and provide them an opportunity to share their burdens. Parents who were victims of abuse themselves need to be identified; they are likely to treat their children with abuse or neglect. These parents often talk about their abusive past. Nurses can ask parents how they are feeling about parenthood (see *Table 9-3*). Parents should be asked about their support systems. Do they have family or friends that offer assistance?

TABLE 9-3
Sample Questions

- What is it like for you taking care of this baby?

- Do you have family or friends to help you with your children?

- What activities do you do that are just for you?

- What do you do when your child is making you crazy?

- What are the most difficult parts of your day?

- How are things going with you and your partner?

Source: Bethea, L. (1999). Primary prevention of child abuse. *American Family Physician, 59* (6). [Available online: http://home.medconsult.com/das/article/bod...&sp=10686679&sid=50639722/N/214060/1.html.] Accessed July 25, 2001.

Nurses can encourage physicians to accept a few charity cases every year to help high-risk families reduce financial stress (Bethea, 1999). Nurses can suggest that their offices write off care for charity when there is extreme need and allow payment schedules for low-income families.

Community Resources

Nurses can watch for high-risk families and be knowledgeable about available interventions. Nurses need to become familiar with the resources both nationally and in their community (see *Table 9-4).* Nurses should not hesitate to make referrals to social workers for assistance. A list of community resources, homeless shelters, food stamps, home health agencies, financial counselors, psychologists, local mental health facilities, alcohol and drug treatment centers and parenting centers should be maintained (Bethea, 1999).

A referral to a home care agency may provide a professional in the home just to assess the safety in a questionably abusive home. Following a change to early obstetric discharges, many hospitals offer new parents home nurse visits. These visits may be useful in identifying families with specific needs. Parenting classes either before or after delivery are a good opportunity for nurses to

encourage safety measures and appropriate discipline techniques.

Nurses need to identify and help seek treatment for parents with substance abuse, psychological problems or financial concerns. Nurses can provide an empathetic ear and make referrals whenever possible (Bethea, 1999). Daycare or respite programs may provide a few hours relief to parents of a physically handicapped or mentally impaired child. There may be parent-aide programs, or Parents Anonymous groups that can provide valuable social support (*The Merck Manual,* 2001c).

Many hospitals have domestic violence or abuse committees. Nurses can be instrumental in initiating hospital or office protocols for handling child abuse. Hospital or office nurses could consider setting up a 24-hour hotline for parents.

Parent Teaching

Nurses should take every opportunity to stress good parenting skills and appropriate discipline techniques. Nurses need to discourage corporal punishment and encourage the use of time out (Bethea, 1999). Parenting classes should be offered as a proactive means of abuse prevention (Bethea, 1999). Classes can be specific for infants, toddlers or school age children. This type of community support offers an outlet for frustrations and ques-

---

TABLE 9-4
National Resources

National Committee to Prevent Child Abuse

332 S. Michigan Ave., Suite 1600

Chicago, IL 60604-4357

Telephone: 312-663-3520; fax 312-939-8962

www.childabuse.org

National Council on Child Abuse and Family Violence

1155 Connecticut Ave. NW, Suite 400

Washington, DC 20036

Telephone: 202-429-6695 and 800-222-2000

American Humane Association, Children's Division

63 Inverness Dr. East

Englewood, CO 80112

Telephone: 303-792-9900

---

tions. It also lets parents know that they are not alone.

It is always best to give specific advice to parents instead of general undefined directions (Bethea, 1999). For example, nurses can suggest the use of an egg-timer for time out so that a busy parent does not forget when the time is up, causing failure of this appropriate discipline technique. Appropriate safety measures in the home should be encouraged to reduce accidents that may occur from neglect. Nurses should ask parents of toddlers if their home is childproofed with outlet covers and cleaning products out of reach.

Discipline Techniques

Discipline is one of the most controversial issues of well-child care. Parents tend to use the same methods of discipline that were used by their own parents, and parents often have unrealistic expectations about discipline. Parents are often unaware of the most effective discipline techniques. The following effective discipline strategies are recommended by the American Academy of Pediatrics.

- Maintain a positive supportive loving relationship between parents and children.

- Provide positive reinforcement for desirable behaviors.

- Use withdrawal of privileges for undesirable behaviors.

- Use punishments to reduce or eliminate undesirable behaviors.

Nurses can help improve discipline by observing methods currently used and offering practical advice to address the specific needs of each family. If nurses pick up any clues that there may be marital problems, violence or substance abuse in the home, the nurse should suggest a referral for counseling. Nurses should try to remain empathetic and consider the context of the family when discussing discipline techniques.

Nurses can remind parents who use verbal reprimands to keep their comments directed at the child's behavior and avoid direct insults to the child. For example, it would be better to say to a child "When you wipe your hand on your shirt it gets dirty, please stop that." than to say "Look at you. You're so sloppy!"

Explain to parents that the use of time out and removing privileges requires consistency and patience. These methods take longer to see results in behavior, but when the changes occur, they last longer and are worth the time invested. Clear expectations of the child's behavior is important. The time out or removal of privilege should occur immediately so that there is a clear connection between the undesired behavior and time out. It is helpful for parents to set a timer so that they do not forget about the child. If a tantrum occurs, parents need to remain calm to avoid escalating the tantrum. Parents should be taught to ignore the tantrum unless it becomes destructive or harmful.

Punishment is controversial. In the U.S., about 90% of parents use spanking as a regular method of discipline (Behrman, 2000). Long-term effects of corporal punishment are unknown. Some forms of physical punishment are definitely abusive. Physical punishments should never leave lasting marks on a child, such as bruises. If spanking is used, it should not be done with anything other than the parents hand and should be avoided if the parent is angry.

CONCLUSION

There are four levels to consider when determining the causes of child abuse. Individual, family, community and society (Bethea, 1999). Within their practice, nurses can encourage improvements on an individual or family level. On a community or societal level, nurses can contribute by getting involved and becoming proactive. Nurses can get involved with local government and advocate for respite care, substance abuse and mental health funding, and domestic assault shelters. There are more shelters and community resources available today than there were 20 years ago, and with increased awareness, there will be continued improvement of resources in the future.

Above all, nurses must report all suspected abuse. Nurses can stop the cycle of child abuse. Nurses must not look for excuses not to call. Nurses cannot rely on the physician or social worker to make the call. A list of local police numbers should be readily available for all the districts in the area. If a nurse does not make the call, the nurse should always follow-up and ask if it has been done. Nurses and physicians are required by law to report abuse, and all health care professionals should be able to recognize the signs of physi-

cal and emotional abuse (*The Merck Manual,* 2001c).

Although child abuse involves a large number of children, nurses should not take a defeatist attitude toward prevention (Bethea, 1999). Nurses that take the initiative to talk with families are able to develop a trusting relationship, assess for high-risk children and make a difference in a child's life (Bethea, 1999).

EXAM QUESTIONS

CHAPTER 9
Questions 57–65

57. A potential long-term effect of child abuse is

    a. child abuse can lead to adult criminal activity and depressive disorders.

    b. abused children are less likely to commit violent crimes as an adult.

    c. drug and alcohol use are not characteristic of an adult who suffered child abuse.

    d. children who were abused have a decreased risk for developmental disability.

58. Which of the following statements provides accurate information regarding child maltreatment prevalence?

    a. Over 1,000 children die from abusive injuries each year, and 1 million cases of abuse are reported each year.

    b. Over 2,000 children die from abusive injuries each year, and 3 million cases of abuse are reported each year.

    c. Over 5,000 children die from abusive injuries each year, and 5 million cases of abuse are reported each year.

    d. Over 7,000 children die from abusive injuries each year, and 7 million cases of abuse are reported each year.

59. Child maltreatment involves children under the age of

    a. 2.

    b. 10.

    c. 16.

    d. 18.

60. Which of the following are two behaviors that can be indicative of an abused child?

    a. going to strangers easily and starting to cry after an injection

    b. not crying after an injection and displaying aggressive behaviors

    c. crying for attention when left unattended for long periods

    d. smiling and playing with toys when left in crib for short periods

61. In which situation would physical abuse be suspected?

    a. According to a mother, a two-year-old fell down the stairs. In the ER he was diagnosed with a concussion.

    b. A three-month-old had a one-day history of irritability, poor feeding and lethargy and was seen in the ER for a seizure.

    c. A ten-year-old girl was treated for a hairline fracture of the tibia after playing soccer without shin guards.

    d. A five-year-old was brought into the ER for a second-degree scald burn of the chest and first-degree burns of the abdomen.

62. Which of the following health care goals address child abuse prevention?

    a. routine annual physical exam

    b. well-child visits with safety education

    c. parenting classes and respite care promotion

    d. school based programs about bike helmets

63. Which of the following questions should nurses ask to assess for families at risk for abuse?

    a. How much does your baby eat?

    b. What is it like for you taking care of this baby?

    c. Does your baby sleep through the night?

    d. Are you getting enough sleep at night?

64. Teaching appropriate discipline techniques can reduce the risk of abuse. What is the discipline method recommended by the American Academy of Pediatrics?

    a. Provide positive reinforcement for desirable behavior.

    b. Spank with a wooden spoon immediately after any undesirable behavior.

    c. Place the child in a closet following undesirable behavior.

    d. Withhold food to encourage desirable behavior.

65. The percentage of American families using spanking as a regular method of discipline is

    a. 10%.

    b. 50%.

    c. 75%.

    d. 90%.

CHAPTER 10

ADOLESCENTS PART I: ADOLESCENT SEXUALITY AND COMMUNICATION

CHAPTER OBJECTIVE

After completing this chapter, the reader will be able to recognize effective communication techniques, identify the importance of preventive sexual education, and indicate the risks associated with a sexually active adolescent.

LEARNING OBJECTIVES

After studying this chapter, the learner will be able to

1. specify the prevalence of pregnancy and sexually transmitted diseases (STDs) in the adolescent population.

2. recognize effective communication techniques useful in dealing with adolescents.

3. identify examples of adolescent problem solving skills.

4. specify three risk factors that may contribute to early teen sexual activity.

5. select three patient education facts that are important for contraceptive education about implants.

INTRODUCTION

Adolescence is a cultural phenomenon. Many non-Western societies have no period of adolescence. Several cultures simply have a rite of passage, which clearly marks the change from childhood to adulthood. The transition is quick, and adult responsibilities are gradually added (Strasburger, 2000). In America, adulthood is not clearly defined. American adolescents can drive at 16, vote at 18 and legally drink alcohol at 21. These stages of maturity or rites of passage are confusing. Perhaps the cloudy transition into adulthood in combination with the natural curiosity of childhood are responsible for the high-risk behaviors of many adolescents. Nurses and other health care professionals are in a good position to assist teenagers through these difficult years by providing information and by teaching problem solving skills.

ADOLESCENT COMMUNICATION

Adults who communicate frequently with adolescents need to be aware of typical adolescent growth and development issues. While defining their own identity, teenagers no longer want to be seen with their parents. They are critical of their parents' opinions, and they have an average of two conflicts with their parents every three days. Teenagers seek validation of their identity from their peers. Peer relationships are the most important relationships during adolescence. Adolescents are self-centered and often have an "It can't happen to me." mentality (Strasburger, 2000). According to Piaget, consistent problem solving skills and abstract thinking is not seen until 18 years of age. Adolescents from 12 to 14-years-old cannot comprehend the negative consequences that can result from sex, and 15 to 17-year-olds think that negative consequences are not likely to happen (Davis, 2001).

Adolescents are exposed to far more appealing messages of sexual activity on television and in movies than the more realistic negative consequences. (Davis, 2001; Strasburger, 2000). For many adolescents, the media serves as their primary source of sexual education. In addition to poor media examples of sexual behaviors, teenagers are not likely to be logical about sexual decisions (Behrman, 2000). Sexual activity is often sporadic and frequently coercive, which contributes to the lack of contraceptive use. Nurses can provide teenagers with skills needed to make smarter sexual choices.

Adolescent/Nurse Communication

Problem Solving

Knowledge based education alone is not enough for adolescents (Davis, 2001). Adolescents need skill building, problem solving and communication based education (Davis, 2001). Health care professionals need to focus on age-appropriate education. Surveys show that the topics that nurses and doctors discuss are not usually the ones that teenagers want to hear (Davis, 2001). Although 66-70% of teenagers wanted to discuss sexually transmitted diseases (STDs) and contraception, one study showed that these topics were discussed less than 22% of the time (Davis, 2001).

A practical example of problem-solving-skill-education involves the use of condoms. For teenagers who are sexually active, contraceptive counseling should focus on practical advice instead of repeated education on why contraception is important. Condom counseling, for example, should focus on the problems that adolescents have, not the benefits of use. Nurses need to ask teenagers specific problem solving questions. Why wasn't a condom used? Was it not available? Did it break? Did it take too long to put on? Did the boyfriend not like it? *(See Figure 10-1* and Appendix C for sample forms for early and mid-adolescence).

Condom use is an important method of reducing the risk of pregnancy and sexually transmitted diseases (Lindberg, Sonenstein, Ku & Levine, 1997). Results of a national study of condom breakage showed that inexperienced condom users had an increased rate of breakage. However, sex education was associated with an 80% decrease in the risk of breakage among young men who used condoms infrequently (Lindberg et al., 1997). Both experience with condom use and knowledge about condoms reduces the risk of condom breakage (Lindberg et al., 1997). Nurses can incorporate condom instructions into adolescent contraception discussions.

Nurses can also support adolescent use of condoms by providing parents with information and skills to discuss sexuality early, before sexual activity begins (Miller & Whitaker, 2001). Together, nurses and parents can teach teenagers to practice ways to say no to sex, or when appropriate, to plan ahead with barrier methods (Strasburger, 2000).

Communication Techniques

Traditional parent-child communication about sexual activity has been based on "the talk" (Pranzarine, 2001). Research has shown that the most effective methods of communication with adolescents are frequent, brief, informational chats during teachable moments using interactive communication techniques (Pranzarine, 2001). All

FIGURE 10-1 *1 of 2*
Sample Adolescent Assessment Form

Early Adolescence Visits (11, 12, 13, 14 Years)	ID#:		Date:
Name:		DOB:	Sex:
Parent Name:		Phone:	

Wt. (___%)	Ht. (___%)	BMI	T	P	R	BP

Questions for Parent

● How is _____ doing in school? What does he do after school?

● What has _____ been taught in school or at home? about drugs, sex, and other health objects?

● Have you clearly stated rules about how you want _____ to act?

Questions for Adolescent

✳ Who is your best friend? What do you and your friends do for fun?

✳ Tell me some of the things you're really good at.

✳ Do your friends try to pressure you to do things that you don't want to do? How do you handle that?

✳ How much time each week do you spend watching television or playing video games?

✳ Has anyone talked with you about what to expect as your body develops?

✳ Have you started dating? Do you have any worries or questions about sex?

✳ Who do you live with? How do you get along with your family?

School Performance

✳ How are you doing in school? How often do you miss school?

✳ What activities or sports are you involved in?

Family's Questions

● What questions or concerns would you like to discuss today?

Interval History

Medications:

Allergies:

Recent injury/illness:

Special health care needs:

Visits to other health care providers, facilities:

Changes/stressors in family or home:

Physical Exam

	Normal		Normal
General	[ ]	Neurologic	[ ]
Skin (acne)	[ ]	Reflexes	[ ]
Head	[ ]	Signs of abuse	[ ]
Eyes	[ ]	Tanner stage	[ ]
Ears	[ ]	***Females***	
Nose/throat	[ ]	Condyloma/lesions	[ ]
Mouth	[ ]	Instruction in breast	[ ]
Teeth	[ ]	self-exam	
Neck	[ ]	***Males***	
Lungs	[ ]	Gynecomastia	[ ]
Heart	[ ]	Hernias, condyloma/	[ ]
Abdomen	[ ]	lesions	
Back (scoliosis)	[ ]	Testicular cancer	[ ]
Extremities	[ ]	Instruction in testicular	[ ]
Feet	[ ]	self-exam	

If abnormal, please explain:

FIGURE 10-1 *2 of 2*
Sample Adolescent Assessment Form

Early Adolescence Visits (11, 12, 13, 14, Years)	**Date:**
Name:	

Anticipatory Guidance

Healthy habits

* [ ] Adequate sleep, exercise
* [ ] Athletic conditioning, fluids
* [ ] Weight training, changes
[ ] Limit TV
[ ] Seat belts, helmets, sunscreen
[ ] Protective sports gear
[ ] Smoke-free environment
* [ ] Weapons
[ ] Learn to swim
[ ] Challenges, self-confidence
[ ] Listen to friends/adults
* [ ] Stress, nervousness, sadness
[ ] Three meals a day, nutritious snacks
[ ] Family meals
[ ] Food choices (fruits, vegetables, grains)
[ ] Iron, calcium
[ ] Sugar, high-fat foods
* [ ] Weight management
[ ] Brush teeth
[ ] Fluoride, dental sealants
[ ] Dental emergency care
* [ ] See dentist
[ ] Body changes
[ ] Sexual feelings normal
[ ] How to say no, abstinence
[ ] Birth control, safer sex
[ ] Cigarettes, spit tobacco
[ ] Diet pills, steroids
[ ] Alcohol , drugs
[ ] Peer counseling

Social competence

* [ ] Family time
[ ] Respect parents' limits/consequences
[ ] Social activities, groups, sports
[ ] Peers, sibling relationships
* [ ] Peer pressure, peer refusal

Responsibility

[ ] Respect others
[ ] Ethical role model
[ ] Rules, chores, responsibilities
[ ] New skills, talents, interests

School achievement

[ ] School transitions
[ ] Attendance, homework
[ ] Frustrations, dropping out
* [ ] School activities ·
[ ] Future plans, college, career

Community interaction

* [ ] Religious, cultural, volunteer activities
[ ] Social responsibility
[ ] Referrals

Screening

PPD (once at 14-16)

If risk: Vision   R _____ L _____

Hearing   R _____ L _____

PPD   Hyperlipidemia

Hematocrit or hemoglobin (females)

If sexually active:

Annual pelvic exam (females)   Gonorrhea, chlamydia

Syphilis, HIV   Urine dipstick for leukocytes ___

Immunizations

Immunizations up to

Side effects discussed? [ ]

Hepatitis B #   [ ]
Tetanus and diptheria toxoids   [ ]
Measles, mumps, rubella #   [ ]
Varicella #   [ ]

Summary

● Summarize visit.
● Arrange continuing care

_____

Referral	**Phone Numbers**	
Health Insurance	_____	[ ]
SSI	_____	[ ]
WIC	_____	[ ]
Food Stamps	_____	[ ]
Social Services	_____	[ ]
Housing	_____	[ ]

Other:

Notes:

Signature: _____

Provider Form – BACK

Bright Futures is sponsored by **MCHB, HRSA**, and, in part, supported by unrestricted educational grants from **Pfizer Pediatric Health**. Bright Futures material is produced by **NCEMCH** and is not copyrighted.

nurses in contact with adolescents can take advantage of teachable moments. Whenever adolescent topics presents themselves, nurses should make age-appropriate comments or ask questions to illicit conversation (Panzarine, 200). Music, magazines and videos create teachable moments because their content is frequently related to sex, violence or drugs. The more nurses talk about sexual issues, the more comfortable they will become with the topic.

Nurses can incorporate sex education into the routine care of children and adolescents (Committee on Psychosocial Aspects of Child and Family Health & Committee on Adolescence, 2001). Adolescents as young as 11 are not too young for age appropriate sexual information. Nurses need to find out what adolescents already know by asking open-ended questions. Questions such as: What are your concerns? What is the worst thing you have heard about...? Nurses need to clear up misinformation and be careful not to laugh if an adolescent's misinformation surprises them (Panzarine, 2000). Adolescents should be asked about what their friends or kids at school are doing. Direct personal questions are uncomfortable and are less likely to be answered until trust is developed. Teenagers should be encouraged to call back with questions. One study showed that 70% of the teenagers who called with questions continued to use their contraception.

Nurses do not have to have all the answers. It is okay for nurses to look up information and come back later with the answers. Many adults are hesitant to discuss contraception with teenagers that are not sexually active. However, studies have shown that early adolescence (11-years-old) is the best time to teach safe sex practices, well before the onset of sexual activity. Talking about contraception does not cause teenagers to engage in sexual activity (Panzarine, 2000). Studies have shown that early education about contraception actually delays the first sexual encounter.

Communication studies show that verbal explanations prior to nonverbal actions will reduce patient uncertainty. Reduced patient uncertainty is associated with positive health outcomes. If nurses request permission to perform an examination after they have already started the examination, the verbal request appears to be perfunctory, inauthentic or ungenuine. When a nurse asks "Are there any more questions?," she should not be walking out the door as she says it (Robinson & Stivers, 2001).

Nurses and physicians are in a position to identify youth that are at a higher risk for early sexual activity. For instance, studies show that boys and girls from abusive families are more likely to engage in early sexual activity (Anda et al., 2001). Family practitioners especially may be aware of contributing family factors that increase the risk factors for some adolescents. Another example of high-risk teenagers are those who have been adopted. Children adopted by a relative or nonrelative are both at risk for early sexual activity (Carpenter, Clyman, Davidson & Steiner, 2001).

When a high-risk adolescent is identified or when a teachable moment occurs, nurses can approach the adolescent with effective age-appropriate communication techniques *(see Table 10-1)* (Davis, 2001).

Nursing Role

Nurses can teach adolescents problem solving skills and communication-based education. Activities should include lessons on social pressures, negotiation and refusal skills (Kirby, 1999). The most effective teaching methods are appropriate for the adolescent's age, sexual maturity and culture (Kirby, 1999). Communicating the consequences of teenage pregnancy, helping teenagers deal with peer pressure and promoting parent-child communication are among some of the most effective methods in reducing adolescent sexual activity (Doniger, Adams, Utter & Riley, 2001). Educating teenagers during regular office visits would be

---

TABLE 10-1
Effective Adolescent Communication Techniques

- Keep encounters interactive.

- Avoid yes and no questions.

- Reduce speaking time for the nurse (less than one minute at a time).

- Increase speaking time for the adolescent.

- Avoid using the word should.

- Ask open-ended questions.

- Assess cognitive development of the adolescent.

- Appreciate and validate adolescent concerns.

- Keep the conversation focused and pertinent.

- Use role-play to teach early teenagers how to say no to sex.

- Focus on why a condom was not used, not why it should be used.

- Offer practical suggestions like put birth control pills by your toothbrush to help you remember.

- Provide counseling on missed pills, breakthrough bleeding and financial issues.

- Many teenagers fear the pelvic exam. Postpone the pelvic for a second visit.

- Describe the sensations felt during the pelvic before you begin.

- Provide information about long acting and emergency contraception.

Source: Davis, A. (2001). Adolescent contraception and the clinician: An emphasis on counseling and communication. *Clinical Obstetrics and Gynecology, 44*(1), 114–121.

---

ideal; however, some adolescents are rarely seen by their health care providers. Parents adhere poorly to annual physicals especially before teenagers become sexually active.

Some researchers suggest preventive office visits for parents and adolescents throughout the teenage years. These visits would reinforce the reproductive education provided in schools as well as provide practical answers to individual questions about STDs, contraception, violence and drugs. Nurses can help teenagers learn problem solving skills and improved communication skills. Parents could be supplied with information to help reinforce teenage education at home. Parents could also be taught communication skills that will enhance parental teaching of morals, values and religious beliefs.

The American Medical Association (AMA) along with several other professional organizations published guidelines for adolescent preventive visits. These visits would provide preventive counseling for adolescents and their parents. Information would be provided regarding sexuality, substance abuse, mental health and violence. The inconsistent messages of the media could also be addressed.

The nursing role as a patient advocate is important for adolescents. If there are no preventive office visits or sessions in place at local facilities, nurses can take an active role in initiating improved contact with adolescents. Nurses can work with physicians to begin a task-force that will brain storm and find ways to incorporate more adolescent education. Visits with adolescents who come for sports physicals could be scheduled additional time. Nurses should take five minutes to assess teenagers for high-risk behaviors and when identified, encourage parents to schedule a preventive visit. Nurses can voice their opinions on local, state and federal issues regarding media ratings and prime-time TV scheduling.

The nurse-patient relationship is a very important aspect of care. Patients often determine their satisfaction based on their communication with nurses and physicians, and they are more satisfied when health care providers engage in active listening (Cardello, Ray & Pettey, 1995). Health care providers that are perceived as attentive, and animated and not too dominant or contentious were perceived most favorably by patients (Cardello, Ray & Pettey, 1995).

Parent/Nurse Communication

A survey of 1,000 students showed that students believed that information was an important deterrent for teen pregnancy (Hacker, Yared, Strunk & Horst, 2000). Teenagers prefer to talk to someone they know, and parents are teenagers' first choice for an information source (Aquilino & Bragadottir, 2000; Hacker et al., 2000). However, teenagers are often embarrassed, and parents are often ill-equipped to discuss sexual intercourse and contraception (Hacker et al., 2000). Parents need information and guidance with adolescent communication, and nurses can provide this guidance (Panzarine, 2000).

Parents who are confident are more likely to talk to their teenagers about sex, and adolescents who talk about sex with parents are less likely to initiate sex (DiIorio et al., 2000). Parental communication about sexuality is important not only because it can reduce teenage pregnancy but also because it provides an aspect that school based education cannot: Important morals and values

about relationships and sexual activity (DiIorio et al., 2000).

A study by Miller and Whitaker (2001) showed that information regarding sexuality and STDs from a health care source contributes to mother-adolescent communication about condoms. This study showed that parent-child communication can influence adolescent use of condoms and leads to decreased sexual risk (Miller & Whitaker, 2001).

Studies show that parents who participate in adolescent activities have teenagers with delayed sexual activity (Davis, 2001). There are about 12 hours a week less parent-child interactive time today than there was in the 1960s. Teenagers need to be encouraged to involve parents in their sexual decisions. Davis (2001) recommends that physicians schedule two parental counseling sessions every year. Nurses can distribute handouts from the American Medical Association (AMA) to provide information and encourage parental communication about sex (Davis, 2001). Nurses need to teach parents about the risk factors, such as latch key hours from 3:30 to 5:30 in the afternoon when there is no adolescent supervision. Alcohol and drugs also lead to increased sexual activity. Parents need to be warned to keep alcohol in a locked location. Even the most well behaved teenagers have a natural curiosity about alcohol.

Parent-teenager discussions about sexuality are associated with increased teenager-partner communication about sexual risk and condoms but only if the parents are skilled and comfortable with communicating about sexual issues (Whitaker, Miller, May & Levin, 1999). The influence of parent-teenager communication about sex depends on both what the parents say and how they say it. Programs that foster parent-teenager communication about sexuality should focus on both of these aspects (Whitaker et al., 1999).

Despite the importance of communication, parents are either not talking to teenagers early enough or not at all (Miller & Whitaker, 2001). Adolescents' poor communication skills may further complicate parent-adolescent communication (Grobler, Myburgh & Poggenpoel, 1999). Adolescents are known for poor listening skills, struggling for power, poor focusing and externalizing topics (Grobler et al., 1999). Sometimes parent communication skills are not productive. Expressions of hostility, criticism, poor information exchange and lack of conflict resolution prevent healthy family communication (Tasman, 1997). Nurses can teach valuable communication skills to both parents and adolescents.

Adolescent risk factors can be greatly reduced with changes in the media, increased parental involvement, increased access to assistance and improved delivery of medical care. Nurses can help by teaching teenagers to problem solve, recognize risks and communicate effectively with their parents (Davis, 2001).

ADOLESCENT SEXUALITY

Introduction

The U.S. leads all industrialized countries in the number of births to 15 to 19-year-olds (Behrman, 2000). U.S. teenage pregnancies are 10 times greater than in Japan or the Netherlands and are double those in Canada or Britain (Davis, 2001). There were 800,000 adolescent pregnancies in the U.S. in 1994 (Behrman, 2000). Almost one out of every 10 American adolescent females becomes pregnant every year. The majority of teen pregnancies are unintended. One-half of pregnant adolescents give birth, and the other half will have an abortion (Davis, 2001; Behrman, 2000).

Adolescent sexual activity is a serious problem in the U.S., and there are many negative social and economic consequences (Davis, 2001). Sexually transmitted diseases (STDs), pregnancy and inter-

rupted education are just of few consequences of early sexual activity. School based programs do not provide confidential, individual risk assessment or targeted sexual preventive counseling. Less than one-half of primary care physicians routinely ask adolescents about their sexual activity and even fewer ask about STDs or the use of condoms or sexual abuse. More than one-half of adolescents who saw their physician with a parent present stated that fear of discussing sexual issues prevented them from getting the care that they needed (Committee on Psychosocial Aspects of Child and Family Health & Committee on Adolescence, 2001).

Studies show that the media has a strong effect on teenage sexual activity and that media is a major source of sex education for teenagers (Strasburger, 2000). Teenagers receive inconsistent messages from television and movies. Teenagers view 14,000 instances of sex every year on television, and only about 165 instances of STD or pregnancy are shown as a consequence (Davis, 2001; Strasburger, 2000). Very few programs or movies deal with contraception, self-control or abstinence. Magazines, MTV and rock music all promote sex without communicating the risks associated with sexual activity (Davis, 2001).

According to Strasburger (2000), the U.S. does not have more sexually active teenagers than other countries, but the U.S. does have more teenagers not using contraception. The increased rate of pregnancy in the U.S. may be related to restricted access to contraception. Some progress has been made; the slight drop in teen pregnancies in recent years is attributed 80% to contraception and 20% to abstinence (Davis, 2001). Abstinence-only education funded by the U.S. government is a concern because studies have shown that abstinence-only education does not delay the onset of sexual activity (Strasburger, 2000). Giving information on contraception does not promote or increase the onset of sexual activity either, but providing this information does improve safe sexual practices among adolescents. The worldwide decrease in first birth to youths under 20 is attributed to an increased education level of women (Behrman, 2000).

Teenage Pregnancy

Young teenagers are less likely to be logical about sexual decisions. Sexual activity is sporadic, and there is inconsistent use of contraception (Behrman, 2000). Adoption and marriage are less likely to occur in teenagers. Pregnancy dramatically changes the life of a teenager. Studies show that an adolescent mother is much less likely to finish high school, less likely to find a steady job and is therefore more likely to live in poverty dependent on welfare. For those who do get married, adolescent couples are more likely to have an unstable marriage. Teenagers frequently engage in serial monogamy, which translates to more than one partner in a three-month period. This frequent change in partners increases the risk for pregnancy and STDs.

Along with the negative consequences that pregnancy has on the adolescent, negative effects also extend to the infant of an adolescent parent. Pregnant teenagers are less compliant with prenatal care and are at a higher risk for low birth weight infants or premature delivery (Polaneczky & O'Conner, 1999). Children of an adolescent parent are more likely to have problems in school, reduced cognitive function and accidents in the home (Behrman, 2000). There is an increased risk of criminal behaviors and poor health. Children of adolescent parents are also more likely to become adolescent parents themselves (Polaneczky & O'Conner, 1999).

Teenagers at Risk

Educated nurses will recognize teenagers who are at risk for early or unprotected sexual activity (Panzarine, 2000; Committee on Psychosocial Aspects of Child and Family Health & Committee on Adolescence, 2001; Behrman, 2000) (see *Table*

TABLE 10-2
Characteristics of Teenagers Who are High-Risk for Early Sexual Activity

- Early puberty
- Having sexually experienced friends
- Early dating
- Steady relationships
- Low school expectations or no future goals
- Large amount of exposure to media
- Social or emotional problems
- Behavioral problems
- Alcohol or drug abuse
- Low income families
- Victim of sexual or physical abuse
- Minimal parental supervision
- Marital problems between parents

Sources: Panzarine, S. (2000). Sex, drugs, and rock 'n' roll: Experimenting and taking risks. In S. Panzarine (Ed.), *A parent's guide to the teen years: Raising your 11 to 14-year-old in the age of chat rooms and navel rings* (87–120). New York: Facts on File, Inc. Committee on Psychosocial Aspects of Child and Family Health and Committee on Adolescence. (2001). Sexuality education for children and adolescents. *Pediatrics, 108,* 498–502. Behrman, R. (2000). *Nelson's textbook of pediatric* (16th ed.). [Available online: http://home.medconsult.com/das/book/body/0/873/555/.html]. Accessed July 19, 2001.

10-2). Once high-risk teenagers are identified, nurses can provide age-appropriate preventive sexual education.

Symptoms of Pregnancy

The most common symptom that brings a pregnant adolescent to the doctor is missed periods (see *Table 10-3*). For all the adolescents that present with amenorrhea, the most common diagnosis is pregnancy (Behrman, 2000). However, not all teenagers are aware of amenorrhea with pregnancy because bleeding or spotting can occur during implantation. An adolescent may think that the implantation bleed is a period and may not be aware that she is actually pregnant. In addition to

TABLE 10-3
Symptoms of Pregnancy

- Morning sickness
- Nausea
- Swollen breasts
- Breast tenderness
- Weight gain
- Amenorrhea
- Headache
- Fatigue
- Abdominal pain
- Frequent urination
- Scant or irregular menses

bleeding with implantation, approximately 30% of pregnant adolescents do not completely miss a period (Polaneczky & O'Conner, 1999). Adolescent females with light, short or mistimed menses should be tested for pregnancy (Polaneczky & O'Connor, 1999).

Diagnosis

The diagnosis of pregnancy can be made based on several physical and laboratory findings. An enlarged uterus, cervical cyanosis (Chadwick's sign) and a soft cervix (Goodell's sign) are all indications of pregnancy. Serum and urine pregnancy tests are so accurate that they have replaced other diagnostic methods. A positive serum pregnancy test can be seen in 98% of women seven days after implantation (Behrman, 2000). Serum hCG levels less than 5 mIU/mL are normal (Polaneczky & O'Connor, 1999). The hCG level doubles every two days during the first six to seven weeks of pregnancy. The level of serum hCG is approximately 100 mIU/mL by the time a period is missed. If pregnancy test results are negative, the test can be repeated in two weeks. A negative preg-

nancy test is a nursing opportunity for birth control counseling.

Urine pregnancy tests identify the presence of hCG, but they do not indicate the level of hCG. Pregnancy tests should be confirmed in the doctor's office following a positive home pregnancy test. The first morning void is recommended because it contains the highest levels of hCG. A refrigerated specimen can be saved for 48 hours but should be brought to room temperature prior to testing (Polaneczky & O'Connor, 1999).

The placenta is the only normal tissue that secretes hCG in premenopausal women. Both ectopic gestations and spontaneous abortions cause the hCG level to be lower than a normal pregnancy hCG level would be. A Molar pregnancy or twin pregnancy both have a higher than normal hCG level. If a serum pregnancy test is positive and there are no other signs of pregnancy abnormal pathology may be suspected. An increased serum hCG can be caused from choriocarcinoma, embryonal cell carcinoma of the ovary or neuroendocrine tumors (Polaneczky & O'Connor, 1999). Additional physical pregnancy landmarks can be assessed as early as 10 to 12 weeks gestation (see *Table 10-4*).

Assessment

Assessment should include a medical, sexual and menstrual history, as well as contraceptive use. The diagnosis of pregnancy should be confirmed, the gestational age determined and potential complications identified. Abnormal bleeding or abdominal pain may require a referral to a specialist. Suspicion of ruptured membranes also requires immediate attention. Bleeding or spotting occurs in about 25% of pregnancies. About half of those with bleeding will have spontaneous abortions.

A spontaneous abortion is a miscarriage that occurs before 20 weeks of gestation. Approximately 60% of spontaneous abortions are associated with abnormal chromosomes, such as

TABLE 10-4
Physical Landmarks in Pregnancy

Landmark	Gestational Age (wk from LMP)
Fetal heart audible by Doppler	10–12
Fundus palpable at pubic symphysis	11–12
Fetal movement detectable ("quickening")	16–20
Fetal heart audible by fetoscope or stethoscope	17–19
Fundus palpable at umbilicus	20
Gestational age in weeks approximates number of centimeters from pubic symphysis	20–36

LMP = last menstrual period

Source: Polaneczky, M. & O'Conner, K. (1999). Pregnancy in the adolescent patient. *Pediatric Clinics of North America*, 46. [Available online: http://home.mdconsult.com/das/article/bod...&sp=10872211&sid=67971830/N/148583/1.html]. Accessed November 3, 2001.

trisomies or Turner syndrome. Uterine or cervical abnormalities can also cause spontaneous abortions. An abortion is considered inevitable when bleeding, cramps and cervical dilation are present. Bleeding and cramping with a closed cervix is a threatened abortion. A threatened abortion is still viable, and bedrest is recommended.

Confidentiality and privacy are very important. When nurses obtain a sexual history, they can ask about partners, sexual practices, feelings about sex and contraceptive plans. The younger the teenager the greater the risk that sex was coercive. Screening for abuse is recommended. Pregnant adolescents without complications can be educated and counseled regarding their options. When appropriate, referrals can be made for prenatal care, adoption or abortion. Nurses need to encourage participation of a parent or other trusted adult when discussing pregnancy options. Follow-up with the adolescent must be made to ensure that an adult is involved (Behrman, 2000).

Pregnancy Prevention

Increased use of contraception and delayed sexual activity are the primary goals of pregnancy prevention. When adolescents have increased economic opportunities and increased life options, they typically delay sexual intercourse and display positive sexual behaviors, which decreases the risk of pregnancy. Parents often underestimate the prevalence of adolescent risk-taking behaviors. Nurses can educate parents about typical adolescent behaviors. Studies show that parents who keep a close eye on their teenager's whereabouts are less likely to have a teenager involved in risky behaviors (Strasburger, 2000). According to Strasburger (2000), there is no substitute for humane consistent parenting. Panzarine (2000) recommends suitable topics for early adolescent discussions (see *Table 10-5*). Teaching problem solving skills to adolescents involves not only the need to say no to sex, but also some examples of how to say no (see *Table 10-6*).

TABLE 10-5
Topics to Discuss with Adolescents

Topics to Discuss with Early Adolescents

• Intimate emotions

• Sexual intercourse

• How pregnancy occurs

• Ways to prevent pregnancy

• Abstinence

• Contraception

• STDs

• AIDS

• How to prevent STDs

• How to say no to sex

Topics to Discuss with Older Adolescents

• Anatomy

• Masturbation

• Menstruation

• Erections

• Nocturnal emissions

• Sexual fantasies

• Sexual orientation

• Orgasms

Source: Panzarine, S. (2000). Sex, drugs, and rock 'n' roll: Experimenting and taking risks. In S. Panzarine (Ed.), *A parent's guide to the teen years: Raising your 11 to 14-year-old in the age of chat rooms and navel rings* (pp. 87–120). New York: Facts on File, Inc.

Contraception

Implants. Once an adolescent is sexually active, it is appropriate to encourage the use of barrier protection and contraception. There have been significant advancements in long-term contraceptive methods. Implantable contraception has improved since Norplant® was first introduced (Meckstroth & Darney, 2000). New delivery systems use only one or two implants rather than the six that were used for Norplant. Biodegradable capsules are being investigated to avoid the need for removal of implants. Implants are a good option for adolescents who have trouble remembering to take the pill on a daily basis (Meckstroth & Darney, 2000).

Implants are inserted in a fan shape on the medial aspect of the upper arm and can be left in place for up to seven years. Implants prevent pregnancy by suppressing ovulation, reducing endometrium size and thickening the cervical mucus, which reduces sperm motility. Implants are very effective with pregnancy rates of only 0.2 per 100 (Meckstroth & Darney, 2000). A backup method is recommended for three days to one week after insertion. Implant contraception is easily reversible upon removal. One disadvantage of implants is the surgical procedure needed to begin and end the contraception. Removal can be complicated if the implants were inserted too deep. Adverse events with implants may include irregular or prolonged bleeding, headaches, mood swings, weight gain, depression, acne, nervousness, abdominal pain or arm pain (Meckstroth & Darney, 2000).

Implants are a good choice for adolescents because they are effective, long-lasting and do not require any attention from the user. Nurses can teach adolescents about the use of implants to increase awareness of this effective alternative contraceptive method (Meckstroth & Darney, 2000) (see *Table 10-7*).

Birth Control Patch. The Ortho Evra® patch is the first transdermal birth control patch for women approved by the U.S. Food and Drug Administration (FDA). This patch is changed weekly for three weeks, then left off for one week to allow menstruation to occur. The patch should be replaced with a new patch on the same day of the week. Ortho Evra can be worn

---

TABLE 10-6
Ways to Say "No" to Sex

What if He/She Says...	*You Can Say...*
If you loved me, you'd have sex with me.	If you loved me, you wouldn't pressure me to doing something I'm not comfortable with.
You must not be a real man/woman.	Having sex doesn't make you a man/woman.
Everybody's doing it.	I'm not everybody.
You're the only virgin in the school.	And I'm proud of it.
What are you waiting for?	I'm waiting until it's the right choice for me.
There must be something wrong with you.	If that's what you think, there must be something wrong with you.
If you don't sleep with me I'll find someone who will.	See you later.
I'm tired of waiting for you to be ready.	I'm tired of being pressured to do something I don't want to do.
What are you afraid will happen?	I'm not afraid of anything: I'm just not ready.
Are you going to sleep with me or am I wasting my time?	If that's all you care about, you're wasting my time.

Source: Davis, A. (2001). Adolescent contraception and the clinician: An emphasis on counseling and communication. *Clinical Obstetrics and Gynecology, 44*(1), 114–121.

---

on the lower abdomen, buttocks, upper body or upper outer arm. Once applied, the patch provides regular transdermal delivery of hormones for one week. Studies show that the patch remains attached while bathing, swimming or exercising. Less than 3% of patches fell off during clinical studies. When used as directed, the patch prevents pregnancy.

The adverse effects associated with the patch are similar to those associated with oral contraceptives. Potential adverse effects include an increased risk of thrombosis, myocardial infarction and stroke. Smokers are advised not to use Ortho Evra because they are at a greater risk of serious cardiovascular side effects.

In clinical trials about 5% of women said they had at least one patch fall off, and 2% stopped using the patch because of skin irritation (Ortho-McNeil, 2000). The FDA notes that the patch is not as effective in women weighing over 198 pounds. Ortho Evra will be available for prescription in 2002.

Emergency Contraception. Emergency contraception provides pregnancy prevention after unprotected intercourse. Although the FDA has approved the use of oral contraceptives for emergency contraception, this is an under-used method (Slugg-Moore, 1999). There is a lack

---

TABLE 10-7
Implant Patient Education

- Implants will not move after insertion.

- It will not damage the implants if they are touched.

- There are no restrictions of arm movement.

- Implants will not affect fertility.

- Implants will not cause birth defects.

- Implants may be visible under the skin.

- Backup contraception should be used for three to seven days.

- Local anesthesia is used for insertion.

Source: Meckstroth, K. & Darney, P. (2000). Implantable contraception. *Obstetrics and Gynecology Clinics, 27*(4). [Available online: http://home.mdconsult.com/das/article/bod...&sp=11532116&sid=67971830/N/196568/1.html]. Accessed November 3, 2001.

---

of information about this contraceptive option. There are two products that are marketed as emergency contraception, Preven™ and Plan B™. Plan B is the only emergency contraception containing only progestin, and has fewer side effects. Emergency contraception is taken in two doses. The first dose must be taken within 72 hours of unprotected intercourse. The second dose is taken 12 hours after the first dose. Depending on the menstrual cycle phase, emergency contraception works by either preventing ovulation, preventing fertilization or by preventing implantation (Slugg-Moore, 1999).

Plan B with progesterone is 89% effective (Slugg-Moore, 1999). Preven and oral contraceptives are about 75% effective (Slugg-Moore, 1999). The most common side effect of emergency contraception is nausea. Nausea can be reduced by eating crackers 30 minutes before dosing or by taking Dramamine® 60 minutes before each dose. Less common adverse effects are breast tenderness, headache, abdominal pain, cramps and dizziness.

The best time to talk about emergency contraception is before a crisis occurs. Adolescents should be taught that emergency contraception is an option if a condom breaks or falls off or if a diaphragm dislodges. Emergency contraception should never be used routinely as the only method of birth control. Preven and Plan B kits come with a pregnancy test. Nurses should teach adolescents to take the pregnancy test to make sure they are not pregnant before they take any contraceptive pills (Slugg-Moore, 1999). Nurses need to remind patients that emergency contraception is not just the "morning after pill," it can be taken up to 72 hours after unprotected sex.

When instructing patients to use oral contraceptives for emergency birth control, nurses need to explain that the pills must all come from the same pack. Birth control pills (BCPs) from different brands contain different doses, and for this reason, they cannot be combined (Slugg-Moore, 1999). Adolescents who take BCPs for emergency contraception will start their next menstrual cycle within three to four weeks. This method does not provide contraceptive protection for the remaining menstrual cycle, and an alternative method must be used. For the correct dosing of oral contraceptives as emergency contraception see *Table 10-8.*

Nurses must instruct patients to notify their doctor if they experience severe leg, abdominal

TABLE 10-8
Brands of Oral Contraceptives That can be Used for Emergency Contraception in the United States[a]

Brand	Manufacturer	Pills per Dose[b]	Ethinyl Estradiol per Dose (µg)	Levonorgestrel per Dose (mg)[c]
Plan B	WCC	1 white pill	0	0.75
Preven	Gynétics	2 blue pills	100	0.50
Ovral®	Wyeth-Ayerst	2 white pills	100	0.50
Ogestrel®	Watson	2 white pills	100	0.50
Alesse®	Wyeth-Ayerst	5 pink pills	100	0.50
Aviane®	Duramed	5 orange pills	100	0.50
Levlite®	Berlex	5 pink pills	100	0.50
Nordette®	Wyeth-Ayerst	4 light-orange pills	120	0.60
Levlen®	Berlex	4 light-orange pills	120	0.60
Levora®	Watson	4 white pills	120	0.60
Lo/Ovral®	Wyeth-Ayerst	4 white pills	120	0.60
Low-Ogestrel®	Watson	4 white pills	120	0.60
Triphasil®	Wyeth-Ayerst	4 yellow pills	120	0.50
Tri-Levlen®	Berlex	4 yellow pills	120	0.50
Trivora®	Watson	4 pink pills	120	0.50
Ovrette®	Wyeth-Ayerst	20 yellow pills	0	0.75

Notes:

a Plan B and Preven are the only dedicated products specifically marketed for emergency contraception. Ovral, Ogestrel, Alesse, Levlite, Nordette, Levlen, Levora, Lo/Ovral, Low-Ogestrel, Triphasil, Tri-Levlen, and Trivora have been declared safe and effective for use as ECPs by the U.S. Food and Drug Administration. Outside the United States, several emergency contraceptive products are specifically packaged, labeled, and marketed. Schering markets a four-pill strip, with each pill - identical to an Ovral tablet - containing 50 µg ethinyl estradiol and 0.50 mg norgestrel, under the brand name PC4® in the United Kingdom. Schering also markets a four-pill strip with each pill containing 50 µg ethinyl estradiol and 0.25 mg levonorgestrel under three brand names: E-Gen-C® in South Africa, NeoPrimovlar® in Finland, and Tetragynon® in Denmark, France, Germany, Norway, Switzerland and Sweden. The same pills are sold as Imediat® in Argentina by Gador. Gedeon Richter and HRA Pharma are marketing the levonorgestrel-only products Postinor-2® and Norlevo®, respectively, each consisting of a two-pill strip with each pill containing 0.75 mg levonorgestrel. Norlevo became available over-the-counter without a prescription in France in June 1999.

b The treatment schedule is one dose within 72 hours after unprotected intercourse, and another dose 12 hours later.

c The progestin in Ovral, Ogestrel, Lo/Ovral, Low-Ogestrel, and Ovrette is norgestrel, which contains two isomers, only one of which (levonorgestrel) is bioactive; the amount of norgestrel in each dose is twice the amount of levonorgestrel.

Source: Trussell, J., Koenig, J., Ellertson, C. & Stewart, F. (1997). Preventing unintended pregnancy: The cost-effectiveness of three methods of emergency contraception. *American Journal of Public Health 1997, 87*(6):932–937.

or chest pain; cough; shortness of breath; severe headaches; weakness; numbness; dizziness; blurred vision or vision loss (Slugg-Moore, 1999).

Adolescents may receive sex education from nurses along with their parents or in a coordinated effort. Nurses should encourage parents to discuss sex and contraception beginning early in childhood. Parents should also be encouraged to discuss sexual issues at appropriate age levels. Nurses and parents should use proper terminology with children. Parents need to understand the typical masturbation behaviors that are seen at various stages of childhood. Nurses can initiate conversations about sex with children at appropriate opportunities such as following the birth of a sibling or a pet.

Parents should be encouraged to answer questions accurately. Nurses can assist parents to improve communication with their adolescent by providing accurate information. While providing sexual education, nurses need to respect family values and religious beliefs. Nurses need to promote safety and communication with adolescents' partners. Confidential health services and emergency contraception are important topics for adolescents.

Summary

Although there have been some improvements, teenage pregnancy continues to be a social concern in the U.S. In addition to reproductive education in schools and parental support of contraception, there is an identified need for improved health care intervention. Nurses play an important role in adolescent education. Nurses can extend that role by helping to create preventative adolescent visits, scheduled health prevention sessions, newsletters for adolescents or informational handouts for parents.

SEXUALLY TRANSMITTED DISEASES (STDS)

Individuals less than 25-years-old are at the highest risk for gonorrhea and chlamydia (Behrman, 2000). Physiologic vaginal tissue changes in adolescent females predispose them to an increased risk for infections (Berhman, 2000). Following is a review of the most common sexually transmitted disease syndromes and their most prevalent characteristics. Laboratory confirmation is recommended prior to treatment of these infections.

Urethritis is inflammation of the urethra. Symptoms are urethral discharge, dysuria or both. Discharge is typically yellow-green and purulent if inflammation is caused by gonococci. Chlamydia causes a white mucopurulent discharge.

Vaginitis is an infection of vaginal mucosa. There will be vaginal discharge, pruritus and a foul odor. Bacterial vaginosis is caused by colonization without infection. Trichomoniasis and candidiasis with bacterial vaginosis is the most common cause of vaginal discharge.

Cervicitis involves inflammation of the cervix and causes a vaginal discharge, postcoital or irregular bleeding, mucopurulent discharge and a friable cervix. The most common pathogens are *C. trachomatis* and *N. gonorrhoeae*. Herpes Simplex Virus (HSV) is less common and is associated with ulcerative and necrotic cervical lesions.

PID or pelvic inflammatory disease is an inflammation of the upper genital tract in females. This includes endometritis, salpingitis, tubo-ovarian abscess and pelvic peritonitis. *N. gonorrhoeae* and *C. trachomatis* are the most common pathogens in young adolescents. With increased age and recurrent PID, there may be other pathogens present. Symptoms include lower abdominal tenderness, cervical motion tenderness and dysmenorrhea. Symptoms often begin after menstruation with fever, urinary symptoms, abnormal vaginal bleeding and abnormal vaginal discharge.

Epididymitis involves scrotal swelling, tenderness, and a history of urethral discharge.

Genital ulcer syndromes involve ulcerative lesions in the mucosa exposed to sexual contact including the penis, oral cavity, vulva and rectum. The causative organisms for genital lesions are HSV, *treponema pallidum* (Syphilis), and *Haemophilus ducreyi* (Chancroid). Lesions begin as vesicles but are often ruptured when examined by the nurse. HSV is most prevalent in adolescents.

Genital lesions and **ectoparasites** are lesions that present as outgrowths on the epithelium. Human papillomavirus is associated with cervical cancer and causes the greatest risk for long-term outcome for adolescents. Molluscum contagiosum and condyloma lata are associated with secondary syphilis.

Human immunodeficiency virus and **hepatitis B** are usually asymptomatic and unexpected. Risk factors are more likely than symptoms to alert nurses to suspect these diseases. Suspicions are then verified with laboratory screening.

Bacterial STDs

Gonorrhea

Gonorrhea is caused by *Neisseria gonorrhoeae*. It is the second most frequently reported STD in the United States. There were 324,901 cases reported to the CDC in 1997 (Centers for Disease Control [CDC], 2001). The CDC believes that only one-half of gonorrhea cases are reported, so the actual incidence is probably much higher. *N. gonorrhoeae* causes mucosal infections in the cervix, rectum and throat. If gonorrhea is not treated, it can cause pelvic inflammatory disease

(PID), tubal infertility, ectopic pregnancy and chronic pelvic pain. Gonococcal infections can also increase the risk of HIV transmission. *N. gonorrhoeae* has become resistant to many medications. Currently, the only antimicrobial medications that *N. gonorrhoeae* is not resistant to are broad-spectrum cephalosporins (CDC, 2001).

Chlamydia

There are from three to five million cases of genital chlamydial infections in the U.S. every year (CDC, 2001). Chlamydia infections cost the U.S. over $3.5 billion a year (CDC, 2001). Chlamydia is caused by *C. trachomatis.* Chlamydia infections in females involve the lower genital tract and can cause PID. In males chlamydia causes urethritis, proctitis and epididymitis. Chlamydia can also cause conjunctivitis and pneumonitis syndromes in neonates.

Chlamydia is typically diagnosed by obtaining cultures. However, new diagnostic methods have been developed. There are several new tests that do not require cultures, and they can detect *C. trachomatis* in specimens of the cervix, urethra, or urine. Patient-collected vaginal swabs do not require a pelvic exam. Since *C. trachomatis* has exhibited resistance to several antibiotics, it is important to assess susceptibility prior to treatment (CDC, 2001).

Syphilis

Syphilis is caused by *T. Pallidum* and is diagnosed by visualizing the organism in secretions, tissues or blood (CDC, 2001). Syphilis is transmitted through direct contact with a syphilis sore. Symptoms of syphilis include a small sore that is firm, round and painless. The sore will resolve without treatment in three to six weeks. Symptoms may also include a rash on the palms of the hands, soles of the feet or on other body areas. As syphilis progresses, symptoms may include fever, swollen lymph glands, sore throat, hair loss, headache, weight loss, tiredness and muscle aches.

Advanced or latent symptoms of syphilis will continue if treatment is not sought. Syphilis can cause internal damage even after external symptoms are no longer present. The brain, nerves, eyes, heart, blood vessels, liver, bones and joints may all be damaged by syphilis. Internal damage can progress to paralysis, dementia and death. Early treatment with penicillin can cure syphilis and prevent long-term damage to internal organs. Delayed treatment with antibiotics will prevent further damage; however, it will not reverse any damage that has already occurred (CDC, 2001).

Chancroid

Chancroid is caused by *Haemophilus ducreyi.* This is one of the genital ulcerative STDs. Chancroid is prevalent in Africa and parts of Asia and is a risk factor for HIV transmission. It is suspected that chancroid is underreported in the United States because diagnosis is difficult. *H. ducreyi* is resistant to many antimicrobials; therefore, susceptibility testing is important (CDC, 2001).

Treatment and Prevention

STD screening should be done every year or when symptoms are present. Diagnostic testing may include gram stain, cultures, pap smear or imaging. Laboratory values for ESR and CRP may also be obtained (Behrman, 2000). Over-the-counter medications provide rapid treatment for *Candida vaginitis,* genital warts and pediculosis. However, patients should be cautioned about self-treatment risks of untreated more serious infections. Nurses need to explain the need to report STDs to the health department at the beginning of the visit (Behrman, 2000).

Nurses can encourage prevention during office visits and ER visits or during the course of treatment. Nurses need to encourage maintenance of healthy sex behavior, compliance with medical care, examination of partner and limiting the number of partners. Nurses also need to encour-age the use of condoms and contraception. Teenagers should be encouraged to ask partners about their STD history. Teenagers should be instructed to examine their partner prior to sexual intercourse and abstain from sex if a STD is present or suspected.

HIV related illness and death impacts young people more than any other age group. There is a significant increase in the rate of infection as individuals reach late adolescence to early 20s. The incidence of AIDS in youth from 13 to 25-years-old has increased by 20% (CDC, 2001).

Summary

Total abstinence is the only sure way to avoid contracting HIV or other STDs. However, behavioral sciences have demonstrated that other methods of prevention need to be promoted for teenagers. The consistent use of condoms can be very effective in preventing the transmission of HIV infection. However, adolescents' typical "It won't happen to me" attitude necessitates the precaution of promoting the use of barrier protection. Although the majority of Americans agree to initiating condom advertisements on television, there are some groups that are opposed to this preventive measure. Many scientific studies have documented that sex education does not cause increased sexual activity in the adolescent. This is a topic of continued debate.

EXAM QUESTIONS

CHAPTER 10
Questions 66–70

66. Risk factors that may contribute to early adolescent sexual activity are

    a. good grades, early curfew, and abstain from drugs and alcohol.

    b. involved in sports, delayed puberty, and upper middle class family.

    c. Girl Scout, started dating at 18, and no steady relationships.

    d. behavioral problems, poor parental supervision, and early puberty.

67. Which of the following facts should be included in contraceptive education about implants?

    a. No back up contraceptive method is needed.

    b. Implants should not move after insertion.

    c. Implants are replaced every year.

    d. No barrier method is needed for STD protection.

68. Which of the following statements about pregnancy and STD prevalence in the adolescent population is accurate?

    a. Individuals over 25-years-old are at the greatest risk of STDs.

    b. Providing information about contraception has increased the rate of pregnancy.

    c. European countries have a higher rate of teenage pregnancies and STDs than other industrialized countries.

    d. One out of every 10 adolescent females becomes pregnant every year.

69. An effective communication technique that nurses should use in dealing with adolescents is to

    a. discuss contraception only if the teen is sexually active.

    b. reduce speaking time and ask open-ended questions.

    c. talk about STD facts for at least ten minutes then verify understanding.

    d. ask yes or no questions while taking vital signs.

70. Which of the following is an example of adolescents' problem solving skills?

    a. Lecture about sexual risk factors such as pregnancy and STDs.

    b. Teach adolescents how to avoid condom breakage by teaching how to put one on.

    c. Promote condom use only after a teenager is sexually active.

    d. Explain why contraception is important.

CHAPTER 11

ADOLESCENTS PART II: PSYCHOLOGICAL ASSESSMENTS

CHAPTER OBJECTIVE

After completing this chapter, the reader will be able to identify the risk factors for developing abnormal adolescent psychological behaviors and their potential complications.

LEARNING OBJECTIVES

After studying this chapter, the learner will be able to

1. identify the symptoms of anorexia and bulimia.

2. recognize the symptoms of depression and the factors that put adolescents at risk for developing depression.

3. select the prevalence and risk factors for adolescent suicidal ideation, attempts and incidence.

4. choose the appropriate interventions for adolescents with eating disorders or depression.

5. specify the potential complications that can develop from anorexia and bulimia.

EATING DISORDERS

Introduction

The incidence of anorexia nervosa (AN) and bulimia nervosa have increased over the past two decades. This increase may be partially attributed to improved detection and more liberal diagnostic criteria (Kreipe & Birndorf, 2000). Approximately one out of every 100 adolescent females has anorexia nervosa (Behrman, 2000). There is a peak of incidence at 14-years-old and again at 18-years-old. The increased incidence of anorexia has been noted in all Western countries. Anorexia affects females more often than males with a ratio of 10:1 (Behrman, 2000). Approximately 75% of individuals with eating disorders developed the disorder during adolescence (Kreipe & Birndorf, 2000). Anorexia can develop in teenagers from any socioeconomic level. Although the majority of patients with an eating disorder are white, this diagnosis is also common among a variety of ethnic groups (Kreipe & Birndorf, 2000). Bulimia is more common than anorexia. Studies have shown a genetic link with eating disorders. Adolescents with affected family members are more likely to become anorexic or bulimic (Berhman, 2000).

Eating disorders typically start as innocent dieting, but those with anorexia gradually progress to profound weight loss and emaciation (Behrman, 2000). Adolescents with eating disorders are often very studious and academically successful. Most have been "model children" before the onset of the eating disorder. Adolescents who have eating disorders are classified as restrictive or bulimic. Restrictors severely limit their caloric intake, whereas bulimics engage in binge eating followed by episodes of purging (self-induced vomiting or the use of cathartics). Excoriations on the knuckles of the hand may suggest bulimia (Behrman, 2000).

Symptoms

Patients with eating disorders are usually very honest when answering questions about symptoms. Some physical symptoms of eating disorders are related to malnourishment and hypothalamic dysregulation (Kreipe & Birndorf, 2000). Amenorrhea, cold hands or feet, acrocyanosis, constipation, dry skin or hair loss, headaches, fainting, dizziness, lethargy and anorexia may be seen in patients with anorexia nervosa. A drop in blood pressure, pulse and temperature along with the growth of lanugo-type hair over the upper body represents a physiologic adaptation to starvation (Kreipe & Birndorf, 2000).

Bulimia symptoms include weight gain, bloating, fullness and lethargy. Patients who induce vomiting often experience gastrointestinal pain or dysfunction. Their symptoms may be similar to gastroesophageal reflux, including pain or burning of the throat. Hypovolemia may cause dizziness. Resting bradycardia with orthostatic hypotension may be seen. Patients who binge and purge may have enlarged salivary glands, dental enamel erosion and calluses over their knuckles (Russell's sign). Depression is often seen with eating disorders, so it is important that health care providers screen for suicidal thoughts or intentions (Kreipe & Birndorf, 2000).

A detailed physical examination is important because patients often dress in baggy clothes that hide their cachexia. They may try to increase their weight by attaching weights to their underwear or by drinking large amounts of fluids before getting weighed (Kreipe & Birndorf, 2000).

Anorexia

Anorexia nervosa is a syndrome in which there are not enough calories consumed to maintain a person's weight. Anorexia involves a delusion of being fat and an obsession to be thin. The desire to be thin and the feelings of being fat continue regardless of the amount of weight that is lost. No matter how thin they become, anorexic adolescents still feel fat. They are compelled to lose even more weight. Weight loss is achieved by dieting and excessive exercise. Three-fourths of anorexic patients exercise to lose weight. Vomiting and cathartics are less common methods of weight loss for anorexic patients. Although a goal weight may start at 110 pounds, when that weight is achieved the goal drops to 105 pounds, then to 100 pounds, then to 95 pounds. There is no end because the anorexic feels fat at every weight (Kreipe & Birndorf, 2000). Approximately 40% of patients with anorexia nervosa experience bulimia at sometime during their illness (Kreipe & Birndorf, 2000).

Characteristics of anorexia include:

• Fear of obesity, which does not diminish with weight loss.

• Disturbance in body image or "feeling fat" even when emaciated or underweight.

• Refusal to maintain body weight.

• Three consecutive missed menstrual cycles.

• Excessive physical activity despite emaciation.

• Denial of hunger.

• Preoccupation with food preparation.

• Bizarre eating behaviors.

Bulimia

Bulimia nervosa involves eating a large amount of food during a short period of time. The bulimic feels a lack of control over eating. The binge eating is followed by self-induced vomiting, use of laxatives, fasting or excessive exercise (Kreipe & Birndorf, 2000). The binge episodes occur about two times a week. Bulimia involves eating fast, eating until it hurts, eating without hunger and eating alone. Victims of bulimia often feel disgust, depression or guilt over their eating behaviors. Self-induced vomiting, laxative abuse and diuretic abuse are methods of weight loss. Fasting or exercise may be done to prevent gaining weight, but patients with bulimia are typically normal weight or overweight.

Characteristics of bulimia include:

- Episodes of binge eating (rapidly eating large amounts in less than two hours).

- During the eating binges, there is a fear of not being able to stop eating.

- Self-induced vomiting on a regular basis.

- Regular use of laxatives.

- Rigorous dieting or fasting to counteract binge eating.

- An average of two binge-eating episodes per week for at least three months.

- Self-evaluation is abnormally influenced by body weight and shape.

- A normal weight or slight obesity.

Complications

Anorexia and bulimia cause disturbances in almost every organ system. Sleep disturbances and hypothermia may occur in some patients. Temperatures may drop below 35ºC. Amenorrhea is common, and some females fail to resume menses even when they return to their normal weight. One quarter of anorexic patients may continue to be amenorrheic up to eight years later (Behrman, 2000). However, one study showed that in long-term follow-up 90% of anorexic patients returned to normal menstruation after reaching 90% of their average body weight for height, and fertility resumed at 100% of the average body weight (Kreipe & Birndorf, 2000). Amenorrhea during the disorder does not eliminate the possibility of conception.

A lowered basal metabolic rate may result from malnutrition and carbohydrate deprivation. Mild proteinuria, hematuria and pyuria may occur. These

changes will also resolve with rehydration. Constipation is a common complication of anorexia, and esophagitis is common with bulimia. Decreased gastrointestinal motility may cause perforation, which has been reported following the insertion of a nasogastric tube in patients who refuse to eat (Behrman, 2000). Electrolyte imbalances can results from vomiting, diuretics, laxatives or waterloading (drinking large amounts of water before getting weighed). Studies show that patients with anorexia are remarkably resistant to infection (Behrman, 2000). Adequate protein intake in these otherwise malnourished persons may contribute to a stable immune system.

Bone density may be abnormally low but improves with weight gain. Osteoporosis is caused by low estrogen, and hormone replacement may be a treatment consideration. Bone marrow hypoplasia has also been seen in anorexic patients. This causes leukopenia, anemia and (rarely) thrombocytopenia (Behrman, 2000). Patients with anorexia often have dry skin, and lanugo hair is often seen. Hair loss often occurs with the return of good nutrition. Structural changes may occur in the brain, such as a decreased volume of white and gray matter (Behrman, 2000). An increased volume of cerebrospinal fluid has also been reported. There may be an impairment of concentration and problem solving. EKG abnormalities are common. Bradycardia, arrhythmias and decreased blood pressure occur gradually. A prolonged corrected QT interval, ventricular dysrhythmias and abnormal contractility may occur suddenly and can be fatal (Kreipe & Birndorf, 2000).

The death rate of anorexic patients is approximately 10% (Behrman, 2000). Death is usually caused by severe electrolyte disturbance, cardiac arrhythmia or congestive heart failure during recovery. Death from congestive heart failure may occur if the patient is rehydrated and refed too rapidly. A daily weight gain limited to 0.2–0.4 kg is a safe rate of weight increase. Bradycardia and postural hypotension are common. The pulse rate may drop as low as 20 beats per minute (Behrman, 2000). Heart rate and blood pressure will improve with good nutrition.

Risks for Developing an Eating Disorder

Females are at a greater risk for developing an eating disorder than males are. If there is a family history of eating disorders, there is an increased risk for an adolescent to develop an eating disorder. Individuals with eating disorders are often perfectionists and eager to please other people. They may have difficulty communicating negative emotions, such as anger, sadness or fear (Kreipe & Birndorf, 2000). They may also have low self-esteem and have trouble resolving conflict. Anorexic patients may exhibit excessive dependency, developmental immaturity or isolation. Their families may have difficulty with problem solving, may be intrusive or may be overprotective. Psychiatrists suggest that the onset of anorexia may be a defense against emerging sexuality, a problem in identity development or a mood disorder that may involve manic or depressive symptoms (Behrman, 2000). Adolescents' attempts to gain independence and develop their own identity can be stressful, and this may put them at increased risk. Adolescents often struggle with weight when menstruation begins because there is a natural growth spurt during this time. A history of sexual abuse can precipitate an eating disorder and can also complicate the treatment of the eating disorder (Kreipe & Birndorf, 2000).

Nursing Responsibilities

Communication with adolescents who have eating disorders is difficult for nurses who do not have a good understanding of the disorder (Kreipe & Birndorf, 2000). A good understanding is a must in order to establish trust with the adolescent. Nurses will gain the patient's trust if they focus on the symptoms instead of the diagnosis. Anorexic adolescents may not be able to understand the con-

nection between their symptoms and their diagnosis, and adolescents do not want to hear that they have to gain weight. Tactful communication will facilitate information gathering. Adolescents are often egocentric; therefore, nurses can help best by focusing on symptoms that are directly related to the body (Kreipe & Birndorf, 2000). For example, nurses may explain to the adolescent, "If you take in more energy (calories) by eating more nutritious food, you will feel warmer and less tired." The loss of muscle mass that occurs with significant weight loss can be addressed by explaining how this creates a loss of strength, endurance, flexibility and physical fitness. Because the ability to exercise is important to most anorexic patients, a loss of muscle mass may provide an incentive for patients to improve their nutrition and therefore gain weight.

An adolescent receiving treatment for an eating disorder may be in denial, resist treatment and express anger toward health care providers (Kreipe & Birndorf, 2000). Treatment of eating disorders is difficult because the patients are not always willing to work with the nurse and physician because they do not want to gain weight. Future health problems or complications from anorexia are less important than staying thin.

It is helpful to make the office or facility as adolescent friendly as possible so that the adolescent will feel relaxed and receptive to medical care. Adolescent-oriented screening forms can be used to obtain information about adolescent symptoms. Interviewing adolescents may take more time than other patients, extra time should be allowed whenever possible. Health care providers need to always try to recognize the individual needs of each adolescent and take care to maintain privacy and confidentiality.

Treatment

There are three important aspects of medical care for adolescents with eating disorders. The first is to establish trust with the adolescent. Next is to create a team approach for medical care and most importantly to ensure the return to a normal nutritional and physiologic state as soon as possible (Kreipe & Birndorf, 2000). Early recognition of an eating disorder is essential in restoring a normal eating pattern. The earlier an eating disorder is recognized, the more treatable the condition is. Patients with eating disorders are often seen for physical symptoms caused by the eating disorder; therefore, the nurse or physician may be the first person to recognize that the disorder is present (Kreipe & Birndorf, 2000). There is not much research available regarding the treatment of eating disorders. Current treatments combine psychotherapy (individual and family), behavior modification techniques and nutritional rehabilitation. Pharmacologic therapy, with the use of antidepressants, appears to be helpful for depressed patients with eating disorders. The success rate in short-term follow-up is about 70% (Behrman, 2000).

Mild to Moderate Disorders

For patients with mild to moderate eating disorders treatment begins with an assessment of the weight loss. After establishing trust with the patient, a goal weight should be agreed upon. If the patient is not able to agree on a goal weight or sets an unrealistically low goal weight, this indicates the need for close follow-up (Kreipe & Birndorf, 2000). A dietitian or nurse can assist the patient in creating a healthy meal plan, which provides the appropriate amount of calories needed for weight gain. Especially important is addressing unhealthy food choices and assistance with special diets such as vegetarian diets. The nurse can also provide positive reinforcement whenever possible to encourage the patient to continue good eating habits. An eating journal is recommended to allow health care providers detailed information regarding the patient's eating habits and to evaluate nutritional status (Kreipe & Birndorf, 2000). Follow-up for the compliant patient may be done in one to two month intervals. There is no quick fix. Recovery

may take from six months to over two years (Kreipe & Birndorf, 2000).

Nurses can also teach the patient some warning signs of being too thin. A weight that drops below the goal weight is a concern. Nurses should discuss the physical symptoms that accompany malnourishment so that the patient will be aware to adjust their diet if those symptoms occur. The patient should also watch out for unhealthy eating attitudes such as feeling guilty while eating a meal. Close observation and follow-up may prevent a mild or moderate disorder from becoming a severe disorder (Kreipe & Birndorf, 2000).

Moderate to Severe Disorders

Treatment for patients who have moderate to severe eating disorders should include psychiatric therapy and a dietitian consultation. Nurses need to keep in mind that it does not help to disagree with the patient's perception of fatness (Kreipe & Birndorf, 2000). The subjective feeling of fatness cannot be argued. However, it is helpful for nurses to acknowledge the desire to lose weight but stress that it can be done in a healthy way. Being too thin can be discussed in terms of objective data such as physical symptoms of malnutrition. This approach will help to maintain the patient's trust. Treatment instructions should be based on preventing the physical symptoms, not on gaining weight (Kreipe & Birndorf, 2000). The difference between gaining weight and being too thin may seem like splitting hairs, but in dealing with an anorexic patient, it is an important distinction.

Parents need to understand the seriousness of the disorder and how to adapt new coping mechanisms to assist the adolescent in recovery. Nurses must teach parents to focus on eating to prevent symptoms not to gain weight. Parents should be encouraged to provide three structured healthy meals a day, regardless of whether or not the adolescent is eating the meals (Kreipe & Birndorf, 2000). Parents should understand that adolescents need to be responsible for their own dietary intake and that battles over food are not productive and may even lead to self-induced vomiting. It is best if parents respond to poor eating habits by restricting activity. Restriction of athletic activities can be especially effective because sports and exercise are often a mechanism of weight loss for the adolescent (Kreipe & Birndorf, 2000). Not only does this restriction encourage adolescents to maintain their goal weight, but it also conserves calories. The opposite can be done to reward healthy eating habits. Providing favorite activities such as shopping, movies or sports can be an important method of positive reinforcement for maintaining the goal weight (Kreipe & Birndorf, 2000).

Hospitalization

Hospitalization may be necessary for unsuccessful outpatient treatment of a severe eating disorder. Patients should be hospitalized if they drop below their minimum weight or based on specific physiological changes. A temperature below 36°C, a pulse below 45, fainting or mental status changes all warrant hospitalization (Kreipe & Birndorf, 2000). If the patient has a weight loss of more than 10% in less than two months, or an overall weight loss of more than 15% there is a need for inpatient treatment (Kreipe & Birndorf, 2000). Fluid and electrolyte imbalances may also indicate that the patient is not doing well. If outpatient treatment is unable to break the cycle of the eating disorder, hospitalization may be the only alternative. The goal for inpatient treatment is to break the dysfunctional eating patterns and establish healthy eating behaviors. Weight gain should be gradual (Kreipe & Birndorf, 2000). Rapid weight gain causes a rapid increase in metabolic rate, tachycardia and increased venous pressure. This leads to dyspnea and edema. Individuals who were allowed to eat freely after starvation developed congestive heart failure. This demonstrates that the rehabilitation phase of this disorder can be more dangerous than the starvation phase. Underlying psychiatric issues

should also be addressed. A mental health professional should be consulted for mood disorders or emotional problems.

Summary

The longer the duration of the eating disorder, the worse the prognosis (Kreipe & Birndorf, 2000). Early diagnosis and treatment are very important in preventing long-term complications and a fatal outcome. Adolescents with depression, substance abuse, personality disorder or a history of sexual abuse typically have a poorer prognosis. The primary care physician and office nurse are in an excellent position to recognize and initiate treatment of adolescents with eating disorders. Communication with the adolescent should always focus on health instead of the diagnosis or mental illness (Kreipe & Birndorf, 2000).

DEPRESSION

Changes in mood are a normal part of adolescent development. The challenge for nurses is to distinguish between these normal variations and disorders that require mental health intervention. The belief that major depression in children and adolescents is rare has caused underdiagnosis and delayed treatment for about two-thirds of adolescents with depression (Behrman, 2000). Depression can range from sadness and disappointment to major depressive or bipolar disorders (Son & Kirchner, 2000). Depressed adolescents are at risk for behavioral dysfunctions that range from failure at school to suicide. Therefore, prompt referral to a mental health professional is very important.

The rate of depression in girls and boys increases after puberty. Depression is two to three times higher in girls than in boys. There is another mental health disorder present along with depression 40–70% of the time. The most frequent disorders that are seen in conjunction with depression are anxiety, substance abuse, attention deficit disorder and disruptive behaviors (Behrman, 2000).

Genetics and environment both play a role in major depressive disorders. Adult studies suggest that individuals with a high genetic risk are more vulnerable to environmental stress in comparison with adolescents with low genetic risk. Adolescents with depressed parents are three times more likely to develop lifetime depression (Behrman, 2000). Other parental factors such as marital conflict, poor parenting, or death of a parent can also contribute to depression. It is possible that low-self esteem, self-criticism, hopelessness and social skill deficits increase adolescent risk for depression (Behrman, 2000).

Symptoms of Depression

- Failure at school

- Behavioral problems

- Sadness

- Anger

- Depressed or irritable mood

- Diminished interest or pleasure

- Weight loss or gain or failure to make expected weight gains

- Insomnia or hypersomnia

- Psychomotor agitation or retardation

- Fatigue or loss of energy

- Feelings of worthlessness

- Poor self-esteem

- Excessive or inappropriate guilt

- Diminished ability to think or concentrate

- Suicidal ideation or attempts

Symptoms are less intense with sadness in comparison to major depression, and there is minimal impact on the adolescent's functioning. If symptoms occur every day for two weeks or more, the adolescent may have a major depressive disorder. If symptoms occur within three months of an identifiable stressor, it is considered an adjustment disorder with depressed mood (Behrman, 2000). The average duration of a major depressive disorder is seven to nine months. However, depression may last up to three years. When depression is complicated by other mental disorders, the prognosis is much worse. Anxiety disorders, disruptive disorders, attention-deficit disorders and substance abuse will increase the duration and severity of depression (Son & Kirchner, 2000).

Screening for Depression

Screening for depressive symptoms is recommended as part of a routine adolescent exam. The diagnosis of depressive disorder is based on an adolescent interview and observational information from parents. The American Medical Association's Guidelines for Adolescent Preventive Services recommends a series of questions to screen for mild, moderate, severe or high risk depressive symptoms. Sample questions may include: "What have you done for fun during the past two weeks?" or "Are you happy with the way things are going for you?" If responses are negative, there is a need for follow-up questions to determine the presence of depressive symptoms. Another screening option is the use of a depressive screening questionnaire such as the 21-question Beck Depression Inventory (Behrman, 2000).

Adolescents are at increased risk of depression if there is a family history of depression, previous depressive episodes, family conflict, uncertain sexual orientation, poor school performance, anxiety or substance abuse. Evaluation of depression includes determining the onset, duration, frequency, intensity, severity and presence of other disorders (Son & Kirchner, 2000).

Depression can begin as early as infancy or preschool. In these age groups, depressive behaviors that may be observed are apathy, withdrawal, regression or failure to thrive. School-age children may display low self-esteem and excessive guilt.

They may also experience headaches, stomachaches and irritability. Teachers and parents can provide valuable information. The psychosocial development of adolescents puts them at risk for feelings of hopelessness and despair (Son & Kirchner, 2000).

Treatment

Studies indicate that only one-third of parents who had depressive concerns about their child discussed them with their pediatricians. Of those that did discuss their concerns, only 40% of physicians followed up on the concerns (Son & Kirchner, 2000). This indicates that there are many symptomatic children and adolescents that are not receiving treatment. Managed care further imposes limitations to available treatments and time for assessments. Parental checklist questionnaires can be used to screen six to 12-year-olds when there is not time for complete interview assessments (Son & Kirchner, 2000). Nurses who are familiar with symptoms of depression and know which screening questions to ask can make the difference between an undiagnosed disorder and early recognition and treatment.

There are several treatments for depression. Individual therapy, group therapy or family therapy can be implemented alone or in combination with psychopharmacological treatment. A pediatrician's need to make a mental health referral depends on their previous training and experience with mental health problems. A multidisciplinary approach includes psychotherapy, pharmacotherapy and education of the patient and family (Son & Kirchner, 2000). The cultural stigma of mental health therapy must also be overcome. Early intervention will avoid disruption of normal adolescent development (Behrman, 2000). An extended disruption may impair adolescent functioning even after recovery from the depressive episode. Early identification and treatment cannot be overemphasized. Establishing trust with the adolescent is helpful.

Nurses need to clarify the limits of confidentiality prior to starting an assessment.

The basis of behavior therapy involves changing negative thoughts and feelings that contribute to depression. Studies show that behavior therapy is effective for both short and long-term treatment (Son & Kirchner, 2000). The success of intervention depends on patient and parent education of depressive disorders. Education improves both understanding of the disorder and treatment compliance.

Tricyclic antidepressants have no proven effectiveness for children or adolescents. Tricyclic antidepressants should not be prescribed for adolescents as they are potentially lethal, and there is a very small difference between the therapeutic level and toxic level in adolescents. Selective serotonin reuptake inhibitors (SSRIs) are the first choice of pharmaceutical treatment for depression. They are safe for adolescents and are effective in treating depression (Son & Kirchner, 2000). Adolescents placed on SSRIs should be monitored for new onset suicidal ideation (American Academy of Child and Adolescent Psychiatry [AACAP], 2001). Adverse effects of SSRIs may include mild gastrointestinal upset and sedation. Dosages should be tapered before discontinuing. Discontinuation may cause withdrawal effects of dizziness, nausea, headaches and sensory disturbances (Son & Kirchner, 2000).

Prognosis

A survey of adolescents and young adults with major depression showed that more than one-fifth had attempted suicide. An untreated major depressive episode can last up to seven to nine months. About 40% of these cases will reoccur within two years, and 70% will reoccur within 5 years (Behrman, 2000). The earlier the depression occurs, the more severe it will be. Untreated major depression will persist into adulthood and will cause impaired psychological, social and academic functioning (Behrman, 2000). After recovering from depression, children often experience sequelae. Potential sequelae include poor self-esteem, poor interpersonal relationships or increased risk-taking behaviors. Office nurses can follow an adolescent's progress and screen for sequelae and risk factors at future visits.

SUICIDE

Statistics

Suicide is extremely rare before puberty but becomes increasingly more prevalent throughout adolescence (AACAP, 2001). About 2,000 adolescents commit suicide every year in the U.S. (AACAP, 2001). Approximately two million American adolescents attempt suicide every year. Suicide is the third leading cause of death for individuals from 15 to 24-years-old (Behrman, 2000). It is also the second leading cause of death for white males. There are more suicidal deaths in Alaskan youth, Asian Americans, Native Americans and chronically ill adolescents (Behrman, 2000; AACAP, 2001). Females make more suicide attempts; however, males have more suicidal deaths. This may be related to the more lethal methods used by males compared to females. Males are more likely to commit suicide by hanging, shooting or slashing wrists. Guns are the most prevalent method of suicide (Behrman, 2000).

Risk Factors

Adolescents are at a greater risk of attempting suicide if there is a psychiatric disorder. Mood disorders, depression, anxiety and substance abuse are commonly seen in association with suicide attempts. Suicide attempts are more common for females than males at a ratio of 1.6:1 (AACAP, 2001). Suicide ideation is much more prevalent than suicide attempts. Adolescents who attempt suicide are more likely than those with ideation to have an associated mental condition (AACAP,

2001). Medication overdose is the most common method of attempted suicide.

Approximately 90% of adolescents who commit suicide suffered from a mental disorder at the time of their death (AACAP, 2001). A family history of suicidal behavior, substance abuse, gay or bisexual orientation or serotonin abnormalities are all risk factors for suicidal behavior. Parent-child conflicts, exposure to suicides and exposure to violence make adolescents more prone to suicide (Behrman, 2000). A lack of social support or a lack of suicide prevention programs contribute to an increased risk. The availability of a lethal method is an important risk factor. Adolescents who frequently engage in high-risk behaviors are considered high risk for suicide (Behrman, 2000). Typical high-risk behaviors may include not wearing a seat belt, carrying a gun, frequent physical fights, tobacco use or IV drug use. Suicidal ideation is considered high-risk if the adolescent has a plan for attempting suicide. Suicide often occurs following a stressful event such as a disciplinary crisis, a disappointment or rejection. The three most serious risk factors are prior suicide attempts, mood disorders and substance abuse (Behrman, 2000). Adolescents who attempted suicide with a lethal method and those who still wish to die are at an extremely high risk for further attempts (AACAP, 2001).

Treatment

It is difficult to tell the difference between benign and serious suicidal behavior. Assessment involves evaluation of the suicidal behavior, prior attempts, the risk for repeat attempts and the underlying diagnosis (AACAP, 2001). Assessment information should be obtained from several different sources including the adolescent, the parents, teachers and peers. Suicide scale questionnaires may accompany evaluations but should not take the place of a thorough assessment (AACAP, 2001). It is helpful if the nurse is able to establish a rapport with the adolescent and family in order to stress upon them the importance of treatment.

Treatment involves consultation with a psychiatrist and should be adapted to meet individual needs. There may be a need for inpatient or outpatient treatment. Outpatient treatment has been associated with very poor compliance (AACAP, 2001). Hospitalization can be effective; however, adolescents often do not follow-up with outpatient treatment when discharged from an inpatient facility. Discharge of an adolescent after a suicide attempt requires the support of family members to provide supervision and a secure environment (AACAP, 2001). Firearms, drugs, alcohol and medication should be removed from the home prior to discharge. Also, it is best to schedule a follow-up appointment for a complete evaluation prior to discharging the patient. Nurses can provide the family with community resource information, including a 24-hour hotline for suicide prevention. Most cities have community prevention programs available; however, the effectiveness of such programs is not known (Behrman, 2000). After an adolescent attends the first outpatient appointment, there is a greater chance of compliance.

Psychopharmacology should specifically meet the needs of the adolescent. Lithium reduces the rate of suicide and suicide attempts in adults. However, discontinuing lithium creates an increased risk of suicide. As discussed with use for depression SSRIs are safe for adolescents and are effective in treating depression. Selective serotonin reuptake inhibitors (SSRIs) reduce both suicide ideation and attempts in adults who are not depressed. Adolescents placed on SSRIs should be monitored for new onset suicidal ideation (AACAP, 2001). Tricyclic antidepressants should not be prescribed for adolescents as they are potentially lethal, and there is a very small difference between the therapeutic and toxic levels in adolescents.

Prevention

Restricting adolescent access to firearms is an important preventive method. There has been a reduction in suicides following an increase in the legal drinking age. Suicide awareness programs for schools have not been found to be very effective. A more effective approach is to focus on clinical symptoms of depression. Self-completion questionnaires can be used to determine high-risk adolescents, but once identified, high-risk adolescents should be followed up with a thorough assessment. Studies show that adolescents who are at risk for suicide will answer honestly to direct questioning about ideation. After a suicide, the relatives and friends can be referred for grief counseling or support groups to facilitate grieving and reduce feelings of guilt and depression (AACAP, 2001). Addressing feelings of guilt and depression experienced by the adolescent's friends is an important aspect of further suicidal ideation prevention.

EXAM QUESTIONS

CHAPTER 11
Questions 71–78

71. Symptoms of anorexia and bulimia include

    a. arthritis, diarrhea and sinusitis.

    b. amenorrhea, constipation and dizziness.

    c. back pain, menorrhagia and polyuria.

    a. dysmenorrhea, hyperthermia and pyuria.

72. Symptoms of depression in adolescents include

    a. becoming grade conscious and reading more.

    b. making new friends and signing up for band.

    c. failing grades and lack of interest in activities.

    d. helping the teacher and joining Girl Scouts.

73. Potential complications that can develop in the anorexic or bulimic patient are

    a. retinopathy, hyperthyroidism, carcinoma.

    b. cirrhosis, uterine fibroids, stridor.

    c. diabetes mellitus, hyperpnea, dermatitis.

    d. hypothermia, osteoporosis, cardiac arrhythmias.

74. Appropriate nursing interventions for adolescents with an eating disorder include

    a. instructing the patient to eat at least 60 grams of fat per day.

    b. explaining why the patient should eat and gain weight.

    c. keeping treatments focused on symptom relief.

    d. reassuring the patient it is okay to eat more as long as she exercises more.

75. What is the prevalence of adolescent suicidal behavior?

    a. Guns are the least prevalent method of successful adolescent suicides.

    b. About 2 million American adolescents attempt suicide every year.

    c. Males attempt suicide more often, but females are more successful.

    d. There are about 1,000 successful adolescent suicides in the U.S. every year.

76. Anorexia nervosa affects 1 out of every

    a. 10 adolescent females.

    b. 100 adolescent females.

    c. 500 adolescent females.

    d. 1,000 adolescent females.

77. Two risk factors for developing depression are

    a. hyperactivity and attending social events weekly.

    b. nervousness and laughing a lot with friends and family.

    c. fearfulness and shyness around strangers.

    d. anxiousness and drinking alcohol with friends.

78. Which of the following is a correct statement regarding the treatment and prevention of eating disorders?

    a. An adolescent with a weight loss of 10% can be treated at home.

    b. Early diagnosis and treatment are essential in preventing long-term complications.

    c. Treatment goals include weight gain as rapidly as possible.

    d. A history of substance abuse has no effect on the severity of an eating disorder.

CHAPTER 12

ADOLESCENTS PART III: DRUGS AND VIOLENCE

CHAPTER OBJECTIVE

After completing this chapter, the reader will be able to identify the prevalence of adolescent violence and drug use and the potential long-term adverse drug effects on adolescents.

LEARNING OBJECTIVES

After studying this chapter, the learner will be able to

- identify the prevalence of adolescent violence.

- select the accurate description of drug use prevalence in adolescents.

- recognize symptoms of drug use in the adolescent patient.

- choose the correct toxic effects of abusive drug use in the adolescent patient.

- identify the importance of gun safety and the behavioral factors that put adolescents at high-risk for gun violence.

- specify effective methods that may be used in the prevention of drug use and violence.

DRUG USE AND ABUSE

Introduction

Drug use in the U.S. has been on the rise since 1960. Drug use increased from 4 million users in 1962 to 87.7 million users in 1999 (U.S. Department of Justice: Drug Enforcement Administration [DEA], 2001). One out of every 10 adolescents aged 12 to 17 used drugs in 1999 (10.9%) (DEA, 2001). Even more concerning is the increase in drug potency. Drugs are far more potent and accessible today than they were 30–40 years ago. The content of THC (the active ingredient in marijuana) for example has increased from 1.5–7.6% (DEA, 2001). Heroin purity has also increased. In the past, heroin purity levels ranged from one to ten percent. Now the average purity in the U.S. is 35% (DEA, 2001). Purity of heroin in South America ranges from 70–80% (DEA, 2001). Drug use has increased among teenagers and children as young as 13-years-old (DEA, 2001). Marijuana use among high school seniors has increased from 41–55% in 1999.

More disturbing news involves studies of adolescent attitudes about drugs. According to the Partnership for a Drug-Free America nearly 50% of kids today believe that marijuana is not harmful. There are too many mixed messages in our society (Strasburger, 2000). Adolescents are told not to drink alcohol or take drugs, yet alcohol is the most common food or drink shown on prime time TV.

Alcohol is in 93% of the movies that are popular with teenagers, and it is rarely condemned in the movies (Strasburger, 2000). Even movies made for young children have multiple scenes that depict the use of cigarettes or alcohol. Teenagers need a life skills training approach to learn how to say no to drugs (Strasburger, 2000). The "Just say no" approach does not teach skills and often does not even teach how to say no.

Drug use effects everyone. Society suffers from a less productive workforce, increased incidence of on-the-job errors and 110 billion dollars per year in drug related expenses. Another negative drug related social effect is violence. Approximately 75% of the adult males in New York City that were arrested for a violent crime tested positive for drug use (DEA, 2001). Even smaller cities such as Ft. Lauderdale, Florida and Albuquerque, New Mexico have drug use rates at 64% of all adult males arrested for violent crimes. Drug abuse causes violence within families as well as violent crimes. Up to one-half of all domestic violence is related to drug use. Crimes and physical abuse are the visible effects of drug abuse; emotional abuse and financial problems further increase the devastating effects of drug abuse.

Gateway Drugs

The progression of adolescent drug use is predictable. Adolescents generally begin with tobacco or alcohol, then move on to marijuana. Inhalants are also popular among adolescents. These drugs are called gateway drugs because they are typically a stepping stone toward the use of other drugs. Many adolescents will experiment with gateway drugs and never try other drugs, but several will go beyond the gateway drugs and experiment with other abusive drugs (Panzarine, 2000).

Alcohol

Adolescent use of alcohol has increased in the past decade. Alcohol contributes to 8,000 adolescent deaths every year (Behrman, 2000). There are an additional 45,000 injuries related to alcohol each year (Behrman, 2000). Alcohol is also involved in an estimated 5,000 suicides or homicides per year (Behrman, 2000).

A typical progression of alcohol use begins with drinking beer, then wine and eventually hard liquor. If an adult male of average height and weight consumes four ounces of hard liquor on an empty stomach, his plasma ethanol level will be approximately 65 mg/dL; a female of average size will have a level of 80 mg/dL. The legal definition of intoxication in most states is 100 mg/dL (0.08% or 0.10%) (Behrman, 2000). Alcohol is a central nervous system (CNS) depressant. It is absorbed into the stomach rapidly, and its effects are enhanced when used with tranquilizers. The effects of alcohol are euphoria, grogginess, talkativeness, impaired short-term memory and increased pain threshold. Other physical effects of alcohol include diuresis, erosive gastritis, vomiting and abdominal pain. Alcohol intoxication can cause vasodilation and hypothermia. High serum levels of alcohol can cause respiratory depression.

Alcohol levels greater than 200 mg/dL put an adolescent at risk of death, and levels greater than 500 mg/dL are considered lethal. If the level of CNS depression is greater than the reported amount of alcohol consumption, head trauma or other drug ingestion should be considered. Artificial ventilation can be provided until the liver eliminates enough alcohol from the body to improve respirations. It may take up to 20 hours to reduce the blood level of alcohol from 400 mg/dL to zero (Behrman, 2000). Dialysis may be considered for extremely high alcohol levels.

Adolescents who have been drunk more than six times in the last year; have had problems with school, friends or the police; or have driven while under the influence of alcohol are considered problem drinkers (Behrman, 2000). A positive family history of alcohol use is significant. Studies of families, twins and adoptions have shown a connection between genetics and alcoholism (Behrman, 2000). Alcohol use not only threatens the intellectual development of adolescents, but teenagers who drink and drive also put the lives of others at risk. Nurses can help to recognize alcohol use in adolescents and need to take every opportunity to do preventive teaching for teenagers and their parents.

Tobacco

Tobacco use is the most preventable cause of death or illness in the U.S. (Moolchan, Ernst & Henningfield, 2000). Approximately 85% of smokers began smoking before the age of 21 (Behrman, 2000). One study indicated that nearly 25% of twelfth graders and 18% of tenth graders smoked cigarettes on a daily basis in 1997 (Behrman, 2000). Predictions indicate that 75% of teenage smokers will continue smoking in adulthood (Moolchan et al., 2000). White Americans and Native Americans are most likely to become smokers. Smoking is least prevalent among African Americans and Asian Americans (Moolchan et al., 2000). Studies also show a genetic link to nicotine addiction (Moolchan, 2000). The earlier the onset of smoking, the greater the addiction (Moolchan, et al., 2000). By 17-years-old 50% of teenagers that smoke would already like to quit smoking (Moolchan et al., 2000). Because nicotine is a gateway drug, adolescents who smoke are likely to experiment with stronger drugs.

Nicotine is absorbed by the lungs, skin and gastrointestinal tract as well as the nasal and buccal mucosa. The average cigarette contains 10 mg of nicotine. The average intake of nicotine from one cigarette is from 1.0–3 mg. Nicotine effects the brain within 20 seconds (Behrman, 2000). Relaxation, pleasure, peer pressure, self-image, curiosity, stress and boredom are some of the reasons adolescents smoke. Self-assertiveness and rebellion are additional reasons why teenagers start smoking. The use of nicotine to self-medicate is also suggested as a motivation for adolescent smoking. Nicotine has a similar effect on attention deficit hyperactivity disorder (ADHD) as some medications.

Smoking causes a chronic cough, phlegm production and wheezing. Smoking has adverse effects on pregnancy including low birth weight, potential teratogenic effects and increased fetal morbidity and mortality. Tobacco has adverse effects on the heart, circulation and lungs (including emphysema and lung cancer). Smokers who take estrogen (such as birth control pills) are at an increased risk of myocardial infarction.

Adolescent smoking continues to increase despite efforts to reduce adolescent access to tobacco. Adolescent nicotine dependence is a gradual process. Smoking in the teenage years begins with a trial of cigarette use, followed by occasional use, then eventually daily use. Initiating smoking cessation prior to daily use has the greatest success rate (Moolchan et al., 2000). Cessation for occasional smokers has a success rate of 46% compared to daily smokers' success rates of 6–12% (Moolchan et al., 2000).

Preventive measures can be directed toward teenagers that are at high-risk of nicotine addiction. Strong predictors of teenagers who will smoke are those who drink, are sexually active, have a significant other who smokes, believe that teachers and friends will not mind, are uncertain about smoking in the future, have parents who smoke or have family conflicts. Studies show a link between some psychiatric disorders and smoking. Individuals with depression, schizophrenia, anxiety, ADHD and substance abuse are more likely to smoke cigarettes.

There have not been enough studies to evaluate the effectiveness or safety of adolescent smoking cessation replacement therapies (Moolchan et al., 2000). Nicotine nasal spray is not recommended for adolescent use. A combination of antidepressants and nicotine replacement therapies have been successful in adults and may be indicated for highly addicted teenagers or teenagers with a psychiatric disorder. Counseling is also important for adolescents who are trying to quit smoking (Behrman, 2000).

Adult smoking cessation programs must be adapted for adolescents. Smoking cessation programs for adolescents have a low success rate. Recruiting and retaining adolescents for these programs is difficult. It is difficult for teenagers to perceive the positive long-term effects of not smoking compared to the immediate positive effect of continued smoking. If an adolescent's mother smokes or if the adolescent is depressed, studies show that smoking cessation is much more challenging (Moolchan et al., 2000). Peer facilitated groups may improve compliance of adolescent programs. Adolescent tobacco-related studies are needed to improve smoking cessation programs.

Marijuana

Marijuana is another popular substance used by adolescents. It is the most common illicit drug in America (DEA, 2001). Marijuana is also referred to as THC, pot, weed, hash, mary jane, reefer or grass. Marijuana joints and blunts may be laced with other drugs such as PCP. Cultivation advancements have resulted in a higher potency. Potency has risen from 3.2% in 1977 to 12.8% in 1997 (DEA, 2001). One study showed that 49.7% of high school seniors reported using marijuana at least once (DEA, 2001). Fifty percent of 13-year-olds reported that they knew where to purchase marijuana (DEA, 2001). It is readily available in small and large cities in the United States. Marijuana-related emergency room visits have increased from 15,706 in 1990 to 87,150 in 1999 (DEA, 2001). This increase in visits is attributed to the increased potency of marijuana. Marijuana is frequently grown on public land in remote areas so that the owners can avoid prosecution.

Marijuana is rapidly absorbed through the nose and mouth. There is a peak effect at about 10 minutes following inhalation and one hour following ingestion (Behrman, 2000). There is a significant variation in content; however, on average one marijuana cigarette or "joint" contains about one gram of marijuana or 20 mg of delta-9-THC. About 300 mg of marijuana is equivalent to 70 gm of alcohol (Behrman, 2000).

The desired effects of marijuana are euphoria and elation. It may also cause short-term memory loss, loss of fine motor coordination, prolonged reaction time and mental clouding. Loss of critical judgment, distorted time perception, visual hallucinations, impaired concentration, fantasies and paranoia are other potential effects (Behrman, 2000). Some physical effects include dry mouth, red eyes, hypothermia, tachycardia and transient hypertension. Marijuana has an antiemetic effect followed by a stimulated appetite.

Studies have shown a reduction in testosterone levels and spermatogenesis following six months of marijuana use. Marijuana contains toxins and other cancer causing chemicals that are stored in the fat cells of users for up to several months. Some marijuana effects are similar to nicotine use such as bronchitis, emphysema and bronchial asthma. Long-term use increases the risk for respiratory and reproductive problems. There is also a risk of immune problems. There is no scientific evidence of physiologic dependency with marijuana use (Behrman, 2000).

Inhalants

Inhalants are used by adolescents because they have a rapid effect, are readily available and are inexpensive. A survey in 1998 showed that 2.2% of fourth graders and 2.7% of sixth graders admitted to monthly use of inhalants (DEA, 2001). There were an estimated 991,000 new inhalant users in 1998 (DEA, 2001). Approximately 62% of new users were between 12 and 17-years-old (DEA, 2001).

There are over 1,000 household products that may be inhaled. Some popular inhalants are glue, gasoline, hair spray, air fresheners, lighter fluid and paint products (DEA, 2001). Inhalants may be sniffed from an open container or huffed from a paper or plastic bag. The capillaries of the lungs allow rapid absorption and blood levels rise quickly. The effects on the brain are almost as intense as intravenous drug use (DEA, 2001). Inhalants cause psychoactive effects similar to alcohol. There is a loss of inhibition, followed by depression. Users may experience a distortion of time and space perception. They may experience relaxation and pleasant hallucinations for up to two hours after use. Inhalants are used as music enhancers and aphrodisiacs.

Adverse effects include lack of coordination, disorientation, headaches, syncope, lightheadedness, nausea, vomiting, slurred speech, hypotension, flushing, tachycardia, bronchial irritation and increased intraocular pressure. Inhalant users build up a tolerance for the inhalants, and continued use leads to addiction. Euphoria may be followed by violent excitement and possibly coma (Behrman, 2000). Complications and fatalities may occur in relation to suffocation from plastic bags used for inhalation or location of use such as rooftops. Cerebral, pulmonary and myocardial effects may be severe (Behrman, 2000). High concentrations of solvents or aerosol sprays can cause heart failure and death. Potential long-term, irreversible effects are damage to the central nervous system, liver, kidneys, bone marrow or hearing (DEA, 2001).

Diagnosis is difficult because the effects are very brief. Treatment involves supportive measures. Withdrawal symptoms are not typically seen. There may be a rash around the nose and mouth and an odor of paint or solvents on the clothes, skin and breath (DEA, 2001).

Hallucinogen

Lysergic Acid Diethylamide (LSD)

In 1997, approximately 15% of high school seniors had used a hallucinogen (Behrman, 2000). LSD is the most popular hallucinogen. It made a come back in the 1990s. It is currently consumed at a lower dose than in previous years, which may explain the increased use among teenagers. The lower potency also correlates with fewer LSD-related emergency room visits. LSD may be sold as a small tablet called microdots or on sugar cubes or squares of gelatin (window panes) or as blotter paper (small sheets of paper soaked with LSD) (DEA, 2001). There are more than 80 street names associated with LSD — acid, blotter, cid and trips are a few. Distribution often occurs at all-night parties or raves.

The onset of action is from 30–60 minutes and the peak action is between two to four hours. Higher doses may last up to 12 hours. The most common physical effects are dizziness, dilated pupils, nausea, goose bumps, perspiration, flushing, increased blood sugar, elevated temperature or lowered temperature and tachycardia (Behrman, 2000; DEA, 2001). Psychological effects may include delusional ideation, body distortion, visual changes, mood changes, impaired depth and time perception, suspiciousness or toxic psychosis. With LSD use, the ability to perceive danger is impaired. A "bad trip" occurs when the user becomes terrified or panicky. After LSD use, the user may experience anxiety or depression. The user may also experience flashbacks, days or months after the last dose. Complications such as hyperthermia, seizures or hypertension should be treated with supportive measures. LSD is not associated with withdrawal symptoms (Behrman, 2000).

Opiates

Heroin

The use of opiates has dropped since the 1980s. However, in recent years students have begun snorting or smoking rather than injecting opiates. Smoking has less social stigma and less risk of HIV and hepatitis. The Drug Enforcement Administration (DEA) considers heroin a serious concern because it is more available, less expensive and can cause devastating effects. In the past, the purity of heroin ranged from one to ten percent. Today the purity rate in South America may be as high as 98% (DEA, 2001). The average purity in the U.S. is 41% (DEA, 2001). A study of major U.S. cities showed that opiate related deaths rose from 2,868 in 1992 to 4,327 in 1998 (DEA, 2001). The increase in reported deaths is associated with the increased purity of heroin (DEA, 2001). Approximately 80% of new heroin users in 1998 were under 26-years-old (DEA, 2001).

Heroin causes euphoria and analgesia. The desired effect of heroin occurs about 30 minutes after snorting the drug; if given subcutaneously (skin-popping), the effect is achieved within minutes. If heroin is injected intravenously (mainlining), it has an immediate effect (Behrman, 2000). Black tar heroin is manufactured in Mexico. This type of heroin ranges from 20–80% purity and is usually dissolved then injected (DEA, 2001). Tolerance develops over time.

Some adverse effects of heroin are constipation, constricted pupils, hypothermia, nausea, vasodilation, respiratory depression, pulmonary edema and loss of libido. Overdose syndrome is an acute reaction and is the leading cause of death among drug users. Symptoms of heroin overdose include slow shallow breathing, cyanosis, clammy skin, stupor, convulsions, coma and possible death (DEA, 2001; Behrman, 2000). Pulmonary edema can also be fatal. Intravenous naloxone causes dilation of the pupils and can hasten the diagnosis. Supportive measures will include oxygenation and ventilation as needed (Behrman, 2000).

Track marks or smaller discreet scars may be seen. Amateur tattoos may be used in unusual places in attempts to conceal track marks. Abscesses are common following the use of non-sterile techniques. Cerebral microabscesses or endocarditis may also occur. Female users may resort to prostitution to support the habit, increasing the risk of STDs and pregnancy. Heroin is occasionally swallowed in a condom or balloon for concealment. If the balloon breaks the sudden overdose can be fatal. Heroin can be detected in the urine up to 48 hours after administration (Behrman, 2000).

Withdrawal begins eight hours after use in the addicted user. Dilated pupils, lacrimation, yawning, insomnia, cramping, hyperactive bowel sounds and diarrhea may occur. There may also be tachycardia and hypertension. Grand mal seizures are rare in adolescents. Diazepam is effective for detoxification. Methadone may also be given, although safe use in adolescents has not been established (Behrman, 2000).

Stimulants

Cocaine

In 1999, cocaine was used by 3.7 million Americans (DEA, 2001). Approximately 1.5 million Americans use cocaine on a regular basis (DEA, 2001). Studies show that cocaine experimentation is occurring at much younger ages than in the past. Cocaine use starting in eighth, tenth and twelfth grades has nearly doubled since 1991 (DEA, 2001). Cocaine is easy to obtain in any major city.

Cocaine can be snorted, injected or smoked. It is the most potent natural stimulant. Crack cocaine is a very addictive smokable form of cocaine. Crack is absorbed rapidly from the nasal mucosa. The half-life of crack cocaine is about one hour. There are a variety of dilutents added to or substituted for crack. Smoking cocaine or "freebasing" in pipes or cigarettes has become very popular (Behrman, 2000). Accidental burns are a potential complication. The user feels high in less than 10 seconds. Smoking cocaine is more addicting than snorting cocaine. The effects are felt quickly and do not last a long time (DEA, 2001). As tolerance occurs, the user will increase the dose or change the route of administration or both.

Cocaine produces euphoria, increases motor activity, reduces fatigue and may cause paranoid ideation. Smokers may suffer from coughing, shortness of breath, chest pain, lung trauma and bleeding. Dilated pupils, tachycardia, hypertension, hyperthermia, dizziness, paresthesias and seizures may occur. There is increased sexual promiscuity and risk of STDs with cocaine use. Lethal doses are possible, especially when injected with other drugs such as heroin. This is referred to as a "speedball" (Behrman, 2000). Withdrawal symptoms are not associated with cocaine. Pregnant adolescents using cocaine may have low birthweight infants, premature delivery, or newborns with congenital malformations or developmental disorders. Intensive supportive therapy may be required for acute intoxication (Behrman, 2000).

MDMA (3, 4-methylenedioxymethamphetamine)

MDMA, "X" or Ecstasy is a synthetic drug. It is a Schedule I stimulant with hallucinogenic properties. MDMA is a chemical variation of amphetamine or methamphetamine. Nationwide emergency room treatment for MDMA rose from 70 cases in 1993 to 2,850 cases in 1999 (DEA, 2001). It is taken in tablet or capsule form and lasts from four to six hours. The doses range is from 50–150 mg. Doses are sometimes taken "piggy-back," which is a series of doses over a period of a few hours. Piggyback dosing causes an increased risk for adverse effects (DEA, 2001).

The desired effects are euphoria, heightened sensual awareness, increased psychic and emotional energy. MDMA produces positive feelings and empathy. It eliminates anxiety and causes extreme elation. MDMA is an appetite suppressant and allows users to stay awake for up to three days

(DEA, 2001). These effects often lead to exhaustion and dehydration. MDMA is most often seen at all night rave or techno parties, nightclubs or concerts (DEA, 2001).

MDMA is rarely taken with alcohol because alcohol can decrease the effects of MDMA. Adverse effects are nausea, hallucinations, chills, sweating, hypothermia, tremors, muscle cramping, jaw clenching, teeth grinding and blurred vision. After effects may include anxiety, panic attacks, paranoia and depression. In severe cases there may be a loss of consciousness, seizures, extreme heat stroke, heart failure and occasionally death (Behrman, 2000; DEA, 2001). New research has shown that MDMA use causes permanent brain damage, which leads to visual and verbal memory loss (DEA, 2001). The extent of memory loss is dose-related. Other long-term effects may include depression, anxiety, memory loss, learning problems, emotional disorders and difficulty sleeping. Studies show that memory loss is present for at least two weeks after MDMA use. Animal studies document that brain damage from MDMA can last up to seven years (DEA, 2001).

Methamphetamine

Methamphetamine is a potent stimulant. It is the second most frequently reported illicit drug used by high school seniors. Only marijuana is used more often. Methamphetamine use is increasing rapidly (DEA, 2001). Mexico-based meth traffickers have expanded, and there has been an increase in the number of U.S. laboratories. This is a dangerous, unpredictable and sometimes lethal drug. Methamphetamine-related emergency room visits increased from 4,900 in 1991 to over 17,000 in 1994 (DEA, 2001). There was a drop in emergency-related incidence in 1995 and 1996 that was probably related to a shortage of methamphetamine. Reports of methamphetamine incidence rose again in 1997 to 17,154 (DEA, 2001). One survey indicates that 4.8% of high school seniors have used methamphetamine at least once (DEA, 2001).

Methamphetamine is also known as ice, meth, speed or crystal. It is popular among adolescents because it is potent and absorbs quickly. Methamphetamine can be taken by injecting, snorting, smoking or swallowing. It can also be absorbed by mucous membranes such as the vaginal mucosa (Behrman, 2000). Smoking meth is known as a "cool smoke," where as smoking crack is a "hot smoke" (DEA, 2001). The effects of methamphetamine last longer than the effects of crack, and the effects are dose-related.

Adverse effects may include increased heart rate, blood pressure, temperature and respirations. Methamphetamine use often results in violent behaviors. It causes dilated pupils, hyperactivity, euphoria, increased energy and tremors. Chronic use may cause cerebrovascular damage and psychosis. High doses can slow cardiac conduction, cause hypertension, hyperpyrexia and seizures. Increased nervousness, irritability and paranoia may be seen. There may be psychotic ideation with a potential for violence (Behrman, 2000). Withdrawal from high doses can cause depression. Chronic use can cause a schizophrenic like psychosis. Symptoms include picking at the skin, paranoia, auditory and visual hallucinations. The most dangerous stage of methamphetamine use is called tweaking (DEA, 2001). After three to fifteen days of no sleep, the user becomes irritable and paranoid. There is an intense craving for more meth, but the user is unable to obtain a satisfactory high. The user becomes frustrated and potentially violent (DEA, 2001).

There are withdrawal symptoms when amphetamine use is discontinued. There is an initial crash phase with depression, agitation and drug craving. The intermediate phase involves a loss of physical and mental energy, a decreased interest in the environment and the inability to feel pleasure. In the last phase, there is a return of drug craving in relation to specific situations or objects. Haloperidol or droperidol can be given to treat agitation or delusions. Phenothiazines are contraindicated as they may cause a rapid drop in blood pressure or seizures. Additional supportive measures may include a cooling blanket for hyperthermia and lorazepam or diazepam for treatment of hypertension or arrhythmias (Behrman, 2000).

Methylphenidate (Ritalin®)

Ritalin is a Schedule II stimulant that has effects similar to cocaine and amphetamines (DEA, 2001). It is prescribed to treat ADHD. Adolescents and young adults use Ritalin for its stimulant effects of appetite suppression, wakefulness, increased attentiveness (for long nights of studying) and euphoria (DEA, 2001). Tablets are taken orally, or they are crushed and snorted. Some addicts dissolve the tablets in water and inject the mixture. Because there are some insoluble fibers in these tablets, injected doses can cause blockage of small blood vessels. These blockages can cause damage to the lungs and retina of the eye. Increased heart rate and blood pressure are dose-related (DEA, 2001). Ritalin may also cause severe psychological dependence.

Depressants

Flunitrazepam (Rohypnol)

Flunitrazepam is also known as roofies. It is a benzodiazepine that is about ten times more potent than diazepam (DEA, 2001). It has never been approved for medical use in the U.S.; although it is legally prescribed in over 50 other countries. In Mexico, it is used a great deal to treat insomnia and as a pre-anesthetic. Flunitrazepam is a Schedule IV drug in the U.S. (DEA, 2001). Flunitrazepam causes sedation, muscle relaxation, reduced anxiety, and it is an anticonvulsant. The effects occur in approximately 15–20 minutes, and they last about four to six hours. Residual effects may be seen up to 12 hours after administration. Because of its partial amnesia effects, flunitrazepam is sometimes used to commit sexual assault and has become known as the date-rape drug (DEA, 2001).

It is unknown how many flunitrazepam-facilitated rapes have occurred in the U.S. In order to detect the ingestion of flunitrazepam, urine samples need to be collected within 72 hours (DEA, 2001). Amnesia induced by flunitrazepam makes early suspicion and detection unlikely. Victims are often uncertain of the events and frequently delay reporting a sexual assault.

Flunitrazepam is used by gang members and students at rave parties to produce profound intoxication, increase the high of heroin and modulate the effects of cocaine. It is usually taken orally and may be mixed with alcohol to increase the alcohol's effects. It may also be crushed and snorted (DEA, 2001).

Adverse effects of flunitrazepam are drowsiness, dizziness, loss of motor control, lack of coordination, slurred speech, confusion and gastrointestinal problems. Adverse effects may last more than 12 hours. Large doses can cause respiratory depression. Flunitrazepam will impair reaction time and driving skills. Dependence develops with use and withdrawal symptoms do occur (DEA, 2001).

Gamma-Hydroxybutyrate (GHB)

Gamma Hydroxybutyrate (GHB) is known as liquid X, Georgia homeboy, Goop, gamma-oh and grievous bodily harm. It is a CNS depressant that is abused for its euphoric and hallucinogenic effects. It also has an alleged ability to release growth hormone and stimulate muscle growth. GHB was believed to be safe until the medical community became aware that it could cause health problems (DEA, 2001).

Some GHB effects include drowsiness, dizziness, nausea, unconsciousness, seizures, severe respiratory depression and coma. GHB comes in a liquid form or as a white powder. It can be taken orally and is frequently used with alcohol. High school and college students use GHB at rave parties for its intoxicating effects. Body builders also abuse GHB for its alleged effects on muscle growth. GHB is also used to incapacitate women during sexual assault. In 1990, the Food and Drug Administration (FDA) decided GHB was unsafe and illicit except under FDA-approved, physician-supervised protocols. In March 2000, GHB was classified as a Schedule I controlled substance (DEA, 2001).

Anesthetics

Ketamine

Ketamine hydrochloride, known as special k or "k," is used for human and veterinary general anesthesia. It is a Schedule III drug in the U.S. The effects are similar to PCP, and there are visual effects similar to LSD (DEA, 2001). The hallucinations are short, lasting less than an hour. However, ketamine can affect the senses, judgment and coordination for up to 18 to 24 hours (DEA, 2001). It may be snorted, added to alcohol or smoked in combination with marijuana. The use of Ketamine is increasing and is often used by teenagers at rave parties (DEA, 2001).

Phencyclidine (PCP)

Phencyclidine is known as PCP, sternyl, angel dust, super grass, killer weed, rocket fuel, hog, peace pill or sheets. It is easily made in home laboratories. PCP can be used as a tablet, liquid or powder and may be taken alone or sprinkled on cigarettes or joints. PCP is one of the most dangerous abusive drugs.

Two to three minutes after smoking 1–5 mg the user will experience euphoria, nystagmus, ataxia and emotional liability (Behrman, 2000). There may be numbness, slurred speech, exaggerated gait, blank stare, rapid eye movements and loss of coordination. Hallucinations, distorted body image, panic attacks, mood disorders and amnesia may occur. Adverse effects are cramps, diarrhea and hematemesis. Toxic psychosis, disorientation, hypersalivation and abusive language may occur after doses of 5–15 mg. The effects may last for several hours (Behrman, 2000). The psychoses may appear to be schizophrenia.

Oral ingestion of 15 mg or more can result in a coma within one hour. The coma may be intermittent with periods of wakefulness and irregular, involuntary clonus. Plasma concentrations between 40 and 200 mg/dL cause hypotension, seizures and arrhythmias. These adverse effects can be fatal. There is no respiratory depression and no response to naloxone. A urinalysis can confirm the diagnosis. Treatment should include protection from injury. Diazepam can be given for agitation, if the user is not comatose. Hydration and other supportive measures should be provided (Behrman, 2000).

Other

Steroids

During the past decade there was an increase in anabolic steroid abuse (DEA, 2001). Weight lifters, body builders, long distance runners, cyclists and others began using steroids. The use of steroids by adolescents remains alarmingly high. Even adolescent females have begun using steroids to improve athletic ability. Anabolic steroids were placed into the Schedule III class of drugs because of the increasing abuse and potential for long-term adverse effects (DEA, 2001). Adverse effects include elevated blood pressure, increased cholesterol levels, severe acne, premature balding and reduced sexual function. Males may experience testicular atrophy and abnormal breast development. Females may experience a masculinizing effect with an increase in body hair, a deeper voice, smaller breasts and fewer menstrual cycles. Some of these effects are not reversible (DEA, 2001). In adolescents, steroid abuse may result in stunted growth (DEA, 2001).

Nursing Responsibilities

Nurses can be alert for symptoms of drug use (see *Table 12-1*) and make rehab referrals as needed. Nurses can utilize teachable moments to engage youth in drug-related conversations. Nurses need to assess the adolescent's current knowledge about drug use and respond with informed safety and preventative statements. Nurses can provide information regarding the short and long-term adverse effects of drug use. Adolescents should be asked what their friends think about drug use and should also be asked how easy it is for kids to buy drugs at school. Nurses should ask adolescents their opinion about why kids smoke or do drugs. Teenagers should be asked if they know what can happen as a result of drug use. In addition to talking to teenagers, nurses need to take every opportunity to teach parents about the signs of drug use. Parents need to know how adolescent curiosity can lead to experimentation — even in well-behaved children.

The goals of treatment for drug abuse are age-specific counseling, parental support and family counseling. Nurses can help by identifying adolescents who at a greater risk for drug use and providing information before a drug problem begins (see *Table 12-2*).

Substance Abuse Resources

- National Drug and Alcohol Treatment Referral Routing Service, U.S. Department of Health and Human Services Center for Substance Abuse Treatment, 1-800-662-4357.

- National Clearinghouse for Alcohol and Drug Information, 1-800-729-6686, or PREVLINE: http://www.health.org

- www.drugfreeamerica.org

- www.kidsource.com

- www.parentsoup.com

- National Institute on Drug Abuse at: www.nida.nih.gov

TABLE 12-1
Signs of Drug Use in the Adolescent

- Problems in school

- Less interest in hobbies

- Less interest in physical appearance

- Change in friends

- Withdrawal from family

- Lying about activities

- Rebelliousness, hostility or irritability

- Frequently borrows money or money is found missing

- Depression or mood swings

- Anxiety

- Confusion or hallucinations

- Headaches and decreased coordination

- Dilated or constricted pupils

- Red eyes, runny nose or sore throat

- Blackouts or slurred speech

- Decreased appetite or weight loss

- Problems sleeping, fatigue, or restlessness

- Track marks

- Tattoos in unusual places

Source: Panzarine, S. (2000). Sex, drugs, and rock 'n' roll: Experimenting and taking risks. In S. Panzarine (Eds.), *A Parent's Guide to the Teen Years: Raising Your 11 to 14-Year-Old in the Age of Chat Rooms and Navel Rings* (87–120). New York, NY: Facts on File, Inc.

- Office of National Drug Control Policy at: www.whitehousedrugpolicy.gov

- Substance Abuse and Mental Health Services Administration at: www.samhas.gov

Conclusion

Adolescent health can be improved by preventive and anticipatory guidance. Prevention of drug and alcohol use should be incorporated into routine adolescent care. Facilitating optimal health for ado-lescents includes supporting them in successfully navigating schoolwork, job issues, personal issues and family problems (Behrman, 2000).

ADOLESCENTS AND VIOLENCE

Statistics

Accidental gun injuries kill about 400 children every year (Jackman, Farah, Kellermann & Simon, 2001). Another 3,000 children sustain gun injuries annually (Jackman et al., 2001). Eighty percent of shooting incidents involve males, and the incidents usually occur in the child's home with friends or siblings (Jackman et al., 2001). About 40% of American households contain at least one gun. The lack of parent education about securing firearms continues to be a problem. Many parents are unrealistic about their children's behavior around guns (Jackman et al., 2001).

Out of every five people arrested for a violent crime, one of them is an adolescent (Scott, 1999). Males commit violent acts six times more often than females do (Scott, 1999). After 13 years of age, the adolescent homicide rate increases yearly (Scott, 1999). Black adolescents are arrested five times more often than white adolescents (Scott, 1999). The racial differences are associated with lower socioeconomic status. A family history of violence, drug use and psychiatric disorders increase the incidence of youth violence.

Risk Factors

History of Violence

Having a past history of violence puts an adolescent at a much greater risk of future violence. Violent teenagers tend to commit a variety of illegal acts rather than repeating the same act many times (Scott, 1999). The number of violent acts rather than the type of violent acts are predictive of

---

TABLE 12-2
Characteristics of an Adolescents at Risk for Drug Use

• Vulnerable to peer pressure

• Low income family

• Parental drug use

• Family conflicts

• Peer rejection

• Academic problems

• Learning or physically disabled

• Low self esteem

• Gang member

Source: Sutherland, J. (2001). Craving to rave: The agony of ecstasy abuse. *NurseWeek, 1*(2), 10–11.

---

continued violence into adulthood. Committing violent acts at an early age also increases future risk factors. About 45% of youths who are violent before the age of 11, will continue to commit violent acts into their twenties (Scott, 1999).

Aggressive or Abuse Parents

Having aggressive parents is a risk factor for adolescent violence. Children who have had a father in jail or are victims of child abuse are at a greater risk of committing violent crimes (Scott, 1999). Adolescents who have been repeatedly exposed to violent events are more likely to have impaired relationships, act aggressive toward peers and become violent (Scott, 1999).

Psychiatric Conditions

There are several psychiatric conditions that may predispose an adolescent to violent behavior. The most common of these is conduct disorder (Scott, 1999). ADHD is often noted in juvenile delinquents. Problems in school, impulsiveness, hyperactivity and poor attention span are common characteristics of violent youth. Major depressive disorders may present with irritability, mood disorders and antisocial behaviors.

Several convicted youths have met the criteria for post-traumatic stress disorder. Often these youth become emotionally numb towards violence. They have an "I don't care" attitude and have little empathy for their victims.

Alcohol and Drugs

Substance abuse can contribute to violence. Alcohol, LSD and PCP are often associated with violent behavior (Scott, 1999). About one third of all juveniles in detention tested positive for at least one drug (Scott, 1999). More than 40% of juveniles who committed murder acknowledged being under the influence of alcohol or drugs at the time (Scott, 1999). Adolescents who sell drugs are at an even higher risk for committing violent crimes than those who use drugs. Drug dealers are also much more likely to carry weapons (Scott, 1999).

Sexual Violence

Studies show that half of the adult sex offenders committed their first sexual offense during adolescence, and about 30% of sexual abuse cases involve juvenile offenders (Scott, 1999). A typical adolescent sexual abuser is 14-years-old, white, male and lives with both parents (Scott, 1999). The victim is usually seven or eight-years-old, and is usually not related to the abuser (Scott, 1999). The abuser usually repeats the abuse on the same victim; although there may be as many as seven different victims. Some abusers have more than 30 victims (Scott, 1999).

Sexual abuse begins with deviant sexual fantasies. There are usually acts of aggression in the fantasies. The adolescent has a feeling of power when committing the abuse (Scott, 1999). The sexual abuse becomes associated with sexual arousal, which leads to further abusive episodes. Sexual abusers find ways to minimize or rationalize their behavior. Adolescent sex offenders are much more likely to commit both sexual and violent acts as an adult than an adolescent who engages in violence without sexual activity. Early signs may involve sadistic behaviors toward children or animals. Many adult sex offenders have a history of being sexually abused as a child (Scott, 1999).

Homicides

Homicide is the second leading cause of death among teenagers (Strasburger, 2000). Most adolescent homicides are committed by males. Boys typically are friends or acquaintances with the person they have killed (Scott, 1999). There is usually a history of a violent father, seizures, suicidal ideation or a psychiatrically ill mother (Scott, 1999). Gang membership, educational struggles and drug abuse are all possible characteristics of an adolescent who has or may commit a homicide. There are also three situational patterns of homicide in the adolescent. The first is when an adolescent has psychotic symptoms or behavior. The second pattern involves an interpersonal conflict with the victim, and a third is when the homicide occurred during some other criminal event such as a robbery.

Gangs

Gang participation is a major factor in adolescent violence. A gang consists of three or more individuals with an identified leader. A gang usually lays claim to a specific territory, uses specific symbols and engages in violent behaviors. Gangs have extended beyond inner cities to small communities and suburbs. Gang violence is frequently related to territory competition or gang status. Gang culture is based on three things (1) reputation, (2) respect and (3) retaliation or revenge (Scott, 1999). Reputation is based on respect. To obtain respect, members must show disrespect to other gangs. Showing disrespect may involve hand signs, graffiti or staring down. If a gang member does not show disrespect to other gangs, then that member may be beaten by members of his own gang. If he does show disrespect to another gang,

he will become a victim of retaliation. Retaliation is often shown by drive-by shootings or other acts of violence. Murder in response to a stare is extreme; however, this is the expected behavior in gang culture (Scott, 1999). Becoming a gang member is a no win situation for an adolescent. Scott (1999) suggests caution in labeling youth psychosis based on "normal" gang behaviors.

Teenagers Who Carry Guns

An alarming number of adolescents are carrying weapons. One national survey found that one out of every five high school students had carried a weapon the previous month, and one out of ten carry a weapon to school (Scott, 1999). The most common weapons carried are knives and razors. Black males are more likely than other males to carry a gun. Among inner city adolescents, one out of every three males carries a gun on the street. During the past 15 years, the number of gun homicides by youth has tripled (Scott, 1999). Many adolescents carry a gun for protection.

Even more alarming than the possession of guns is a change in the belief systems of violent adolescents. Nearly one third of incarcerated youth agreed that it is okay to shoot someone if that is what it takes to get what you want (Scott, 1999). A 16-year-old killed someone and then stated, "Murder is not weak, it is gutsy and daring" (Strasburger, 2000).

Many youths acquire their gun from a friend or family member before the age of fifteen (Scott, 1999). Children are more likely to carry a weapon if they are male, living with one parent, abuse alcohol, have destroyed school property or believe that other students carry weapons to school (Scott, 1999).

Guns in the Home

The unrealistic expectations of parents in relation to guns were revealed in a study done by Jackman et al. This study was done to determine how boys behave when they find a handgun. The study compared the boys' behavior to the parents' prediction of the boys' behavior upon finding a real gun (Jackman et al., 2001).

Before the study began, parents rated their child's interest in guns. Then each boy and one friend went into a room where a real gun was hidden in a drawer (Jackman et al., 2001). There were toys on the counter, and the boys were instructed not to open any cabinets. They were allowed to exit for questions. There were two brightly colored water guns in one drawer and a real .380 caliber handgun in another drawer. The handgun was rigged to show a light behind a one way mirror if the trigger was pulled with enough force to fire the gun (Jackman et al., 2001). The boys were observed to see (1) if they found the gun, (2) if they told an adult they found the gun, (3) if they handled or shot the gun or (4) if they believed it was a real gun (Jackman, et al., 2001). Twenty-nine groups of boys participated. The average age was 9.8 years. Seventy-five percent of the boys discovered the real gun. Sixty-three percent of those that discovered the gun, handled the gun, and about 33% of the boys that handled the gun pulled the trigger (Jackman et al., 2001). Approximately half of the boys who found the gun thought that it was a toy or were unsure if it was real (Jackman et al., 2001).

Parents' predictions were incorrect. Boys who were predicted to have a low interest in guns were as likely to handle the gun as those who had a high interest in guns. Even though more than 90% of the boys who handled the gun had previously received gun safety instructions, they still handled the gun or pulled the trigger (Jackman et al., 2001). Thirty-five percent of the boys who handled the gun and 33% of the boys who pulled the trigger were from gun-owning families (Jackman et al., 2001). After the study, each boy's knowledge of guns was assessed and they all received counseling about gun safety.

This study indicates that many 8 to 12-year-old boys will handle a gun if they find one — even if they have been taught not to (Jackman et al., 2001). Kids from gun-owning families were as likely to pull the trigger as those from nongun-owning families. Surveys show as many as 61% of gun-owning parents store at least one gun unlocked and/or loaded. In a sample of gun-owning parents, 23% stated that they would trust their 4 to 12-year-old child with a loaded gun (Jackman et al., 2001). Studies show that guns kept in the home kill a family member 43 times more often than they kill an intruder (Strasburger, 2000).

Prevention

Nurses can help reduce local violence by leading anti-violence programs (Steger, 2000). Nurses can help to identify kids who have problems and suggest or plan interventions before violent acts occur (Steger, 2000). Most school shootings have not been committed by adolescents who are disadvantaged or students without goals. Most shootings have been committed by smart teenagers from middle class, two parent homes with no prior history of drug use. It may be difficult to distinguish typical teenage angst from a truly troubled teen; however, there are six indicators of violence that may help. Every teenager may have one or two of these indicators, but if three or more are noted, the teenager should be referred for counseling. There are six "Vs" of violence to look for (Steger, 2000).

Venting A child may ventilate anger in several ways such as angry outbursts, frequent mood swings, cruelty to animals, fascination with weapons or violence.

Vocalizing A teenager may threaten to hurt himself or others.

Vandalizing Teenagers may intentionally damage property including their own.

Victimizing The teenager may see himself as a victim, even if he is not. The teenager may blame others for his own problems, never taking responsibility for his own actions. He may spend a lot of time alone.

Vying The teenager may be involved in gang activity. He may act out in class or wear outlandish clothing. He may purposefully get expelled or suspended.

Viewing Teenagers who have witnessed abuse of others are more likely to be violent.

Nurses can be instrumental in initiating parenting classes on time management or stress reduction to help reduce aggression or violence in the home. Support groups for teenagers and adults can help with anger management. Youth should be encouraged to join scout troops or 4H clubs. These groups help to build self-esteem and promote respect and diversity. Local programs on gun safety and drug abuse prevention can be very helpful.

Nurses can also help by encouraging congressman to support youth programs for violence prevention. Legislators in North Carolina are considering a bill that would require employers to give employees four hours off every month to attend school functions or volunteer at their child's school. The Safe School Act is a federal law that requires schools to expel students for one year if they bring weapons to school. Nurses might also suggest anger management programs in the schools and courses on improving communication.

Gun Prevention

There are three "Es" of injury control that will decrease the risk of handgun injury (Jackman et al., 2001). "Education," "Enforcement" of safety regulations, and "Engineering" gun safety features. The American Academy of Pediatrics states, "Even the most well-behaved children are curious and will naturally explore their environment. It is safest to have no guns in the home" (Jackman et al., 2001). Parents should be continually reminded that guns kept in the home should always be inaccessible to children.

If parents must have a gun, it should be kept unloaded, locked and inaccessible to children. Nurses need to teach kids never to touch a real gun and to tell an adult if they find one. If parents think teaching gun safety to children replaces keeping the gun locked, then teaching may do more harm than good (Jackman et al., 2001). Some states have laws that hold adults legally responsible for injuries caused by their firearms (Jackman et al., 2001). Most handguns lack safety features to prevent unintentional discharge. Nurses need to support safer handguns. Handguns are involved in 85% of all firearm injuries and fatalities (Jackman et al., 2001). A survey showed that 80% of gun owners are in favor of mandatory child proofing all new guns sold in the U.S. (Jackman et al., 2001). It is the responsibility of adults to ensure that children are safe from guns. Firearms must be inaccessible to children.

Nurse Responsibilities

Office nurses can encourage gun safety through parent teaching, posters and flyers. Emergency room and trauma care nurses can take every opportunity to talk about gun risks and safety during teachable moments throughout their bedside care. During a dressing change, a bed bath or ambulation nurses can take the opportunity to initiate conversations. Nurses can start by asking youths their opinion on gun control or other topical issues. The adolescent's knowledge should be assessed, and nurses need to be prepared to correct misconceptions. Interactive communication should be used, and nurses should keep their comments brief, to a minute or less. Nurses should not be afraid to say "I don't know the answer, but I will find out." Then they need to make sure to follow-up later on. When assessing teenagers for further risk of violence, nurses should ask not only about previous arrests but also about how many violent acts the teenager has gotten away with.

Treatment

Issues of confidentiality need to be addressed by health care providers before they interview an adolescent. Confidentiality is important. In situations when the teenager is threatening another youth, the nurse or physician should notify the police.

Treatment should address any underlying psychological disorder. Treatment of adolescents should be individualized to match the adolescents' needs. Violent adolescents seldom benefit from individual or group therapy. Family therapy that includes behavioral training for parents has produced better outcomes in aggressive children. This type of therapy has not been as successful with violent teenagers. For adolescents who are in a correctional facility, cognitive behavioral approaches have been effective; however, these methods are not typically effective once the individual is released from the facility (Scott, 1999). The best recommendation involves a multisystem therapy where case management interacts in the home, school, neighborhood and with peers. The use of medication should be accompanied by psychiatric treatment.

Conclusion

Guns in the home are much more likely to kill a family member that an intruder (Strasburger, 2000). Children and adolescents have a natural curiosity about guns, and even the best-behaved child might handle a gun if it is found unattended. Nurses can assist in the identification of adolescents who are high risk for committing violent acts. These adolescents could receive preventive personal or family counseling before violent behaviors occur. Nurses are also capable of having a strong voice in promoting stricter gun laws and regulations.

EXAM QUESTIONS

CHAPTER 12
Questions 79–87

79. The annual incidence of gun mortality and morbidity in the U.S. is

    a. 600 children die and about 5,000 children are injured.

    b. 400 children die and about 3,000 children are injured.

    c. 200 children die and about 2,000 children are injured.

    d. 100 children die and about 1,000 children are injured.

80. Which of the following is an accurate description of drug use prevalence in adolescents?

    a. In 1999, there were less than 50 million drug users in the U.S.

    b. In 1999, there were more than 80 million drug users in the U.S.

    c. In 1999, there were less than 80 million drug users in the U.S.

    d. In 1999, there were more than 100 million drug users in the U.S.

81. Which of the following are referred to as "gateway" drugs?

    a. heroin and methamphetamines

    b. tobacco and alcohol

    C. LSD and cocaine

    D. GHB and PCP

82. Which of the following statements about adolescent marijuana use is accurate?

    a. Since marijuana is not proven to be addictive, it is a safe drug to use.

    b. Marijuana is used to reduce nausea in cancer patients; therefore, it is a safe recreational drug.

    c. Long-term use of marijuana can cause the development of emphysema or cancer.

    d. Marijuana had the same potency in 1992 that it did in 1977.

83. Which of the following environmental and behavioral factors put adolescents at high risk for violence?

    a. Adolescent substance abuse is not associated with increased adolescent violence.

    b. ADHD, depression and impulsiveness increase an adolescent's risk for violent behaviors.

    c. Becoming a gang member reduces an adolescent's risk for gun violence.

    d. Abusive parents are not associated with increased adolescent violence.

84. Which of the following methods may be effective in the prevention of violence?

    a. Teach children that it is okay to handle a gun if it looks like a toy.

    b. Teach children that it is okay to handle a gun if it is not loaded.

    c. Teach parents that guns should always be locked up.

    d. Teach parents that guns should be kept unloaded and locked.

85. Which of the following is an accurate statement regarding tobacco use?

    a. Less than 50% of teenage smokers will become adult smokers.

    b. More than 80% of smokers started smoking before the age of 21.

    c. African and Asian Americans are most likely to become smokers.

    d. Smoking cessation success for daily smokers is 20–50%.

86. According to a 1998 survey, in which grade did 2.2% of adolescents use inhalation substances monthly?

    a. third grade

    b. fourth grade

    c. fifth grade

    d. sixth grade

87. Which of the following is an accurate statement regarding adolescent violence?

    a. Violent teenagers never make verbal threats of violence.

    b. Witnessing abuse has no effect on a teenager's risk for becoming violent.

    c. A teenager who feels like a victim and is a loner is at risk for becoming violent.

    d. Intentional property damage is considered normal adolescent behavior, not a risk factor.

CHAPTER 13

THE CHRONICALLY ILL CHILD AND PALLIATIVE CARE

CHAPTER OBJECTIVE

After completing this chapter, the reader will be able to recognize pediatric palliative care goals and the appropriate nursing interventions for the chronically ill child in relation to palliative care. The reader will also gain comfort and instruction on dealing with the parents of the chronically ill child in relation to palliative care.

LEARNING OBJECTIVES

After studying this chapter, the learner will be able to

1. select the definition and goals of pediatric palliative care.

2. indicate the importance of parental support and collaboration in dealing with a dying child.

3. recognize the differences between adults and children with regard to chronic illness and palliative care.

INTRODUCTION

Although advances in medical technology have resulted in decreased pediatric mortality, these medical advances have also resulted in an increased incidence of chronically ill children. Chronically ill children often require prolonged hospitalization, multiple repeat hospitaliza-tions, home health care or placement in a long-term care facility (Curley & Moloney-Harmon, 2001). In 1988 there were up to 17,000 children who required some type of extended technical support (Curley & Moloney-Harmon, 2001).

Despite the overall decline in pediatric deaths, some pediatric deaths are unavoidable (Behrman, 2000). In contrast to nurses who care for adult patients, pediatric nurses rarely encounter death in their patient population (Behrman, 2000). This limited experience for pediatric health care providers causes discomfort and intense emotional responses in nurses caring for terminally ill children. The lack of experience with pediatric deaths can also cause nurses to have feelings of insufficiency when caring for a dying child. A common reaction for health care providers is to become emotionally and physically distant from the dying child (Sahler, Frager, Levetown, Cohn & Lipson, 2000).

The death of a child is a monumental threat to families; it means the loss of an entire lifetime (Behrman, 2000). Effective palliative nursing care and communication can offer comfort and emotional healing to patients and families when there is no curative care left to offer (Behrman, 2000).

CHRONIC ILLNESS

The Patient

Chronic illness during childhood can adversely affect all stages of development. It influences the cognitive, social, emotional and physical development of children. Chronically ill children are at risk of losing their motivation for developmental progress.

During infancy, repeat hospitalizations can prevent parental attachment and delay the development of trust. Illness prevents toddlers and preschoolers from becoming independent. By school age, parents recognize that their chronically ill child lacks social skills and often displays aggressive and self-destructive behaviors. School is often stressful for these children because their academic and social progress has been frequently interrupted. Peers are rarely supportive and are often unkind to a chronically ill child. Adolescents may experience an increased dependency on families while their peers are becoming more independent. Adolescents may also have to accept illness induced limitations on their social, educational and vocational plans (Curley & Moloney-Harmon, 2001). Frequent exclusion from activities, feelings of inferiority, and nonacceptance negatively effects the child's emotional well being (Curley & Moloney-Harmon, 2001).

Hospitalized children are faced with multiple challenges. These children face separation from family, home, school and other familiar environments while hospitalized (Curley & Moloney-Harmon, 2001). Children who are ventilator dependent, who have significant neurological impairment or who suffer neuromuscular disease with respiratory complications may require extended care. Extended care may include ventilator support, parenteral nutrition, IV medications, or other respiratory or nutritional supplements and treatments (Curley & Moloney-Harmon, 2001). Separation from their home and other familiar environments in addition to feeling sick, dyspneic or painful can be very stressful for pediatric patients. Caregivers are frequently changing and there may be disorientation from medications, anesthesia or surgery. These children and their families are often in need of increased emotional and social support (Curley & Moloney-Harmon, 2001).

Chronic illness affects family life in many ways. There is an increase in obligations, commitments and financial stress. A chronically ill child may cause anxiety and stress in social situations where others are unsure of how to interact with the ill child. The family must learn to adjust to changes in normal life routines in order to accommodate the diagnosis and care of a chronically ill child. Parents often have feelings of guilt, blame, and grief because of their child's illness. Hospitalizations bring additional stress and sadness. When parents can master the guilt and grief there will be enhanced family well-being and improved self-esteem of the chronically ill child (Curley & Moloney-Harmon, 2001). Therefore, nursing support of parents can indirectly promote the well-being of the pediatric patient.

To help support pediatric patients, it is recommended that parents stay with their hospitalized children who are less than six years old. Distractions and activities are helpful. An opportunity to act out fears and painful procedures through play helps children cope with their illness. Music and art therapy can be very useful in helping children express their concerns.

For the medical technology dependent child, prolonged hospitalization requires the assistance of a multidisciplinary team. The multidisciplinary team including a child life specialist, social worker, and psychologist provide services that benefit the child and the child's family (Curley & Moloney-Harmon, 2001). Ongoing evaluations and needs assessments are important in order to optimize psychosocial and cognitive development of the pediatric patient. The best interest of the child should guide all care plan decisions. Regression is a common response to hospitalization, and nurses can help to minimize this response by providing an environment conducive to growth and development. Nurses who are able to respond to the specific emotional needs of a chronically ill child are helping the child to adapt and continue developmental progression. Minimizing physical and emotional pain requires ongoing assessments and treatment adjustments. Nurses who develop partnerships with both the child and the child's parents are providing support and developing a trusting relationship.

Parents of a Chronically Ill Child

When a child is first diagnosed with a chronic illness, parents may want to inform their child of the diagnosis themselves. However, parents may want the nurse or physician present to answer any questions the child may have. Parents have a need to feel in control and a need to protect their child. Nurses should warn parents to be prepared to deal with their child's anger about the chronic illness. Children over ten years of age are supported best by providing accurate factual information (Behrman, 2000). Children often take clues regarding acceptable or expected behavior from their parents. Efforts to offer some realistic hope can help with the gradual acceptance of a chronic illness. Including the child in discussions from the beginning is a good start toward continued open communication with the child as the illness progresses.

Some parents do not want to discuss disease progression or prognosis with their child. Sometimes parents act as filters when passing information on to their sick child. It may not be a conscious effort to keep secrets but rather a desire to protect their child from bad news. Nurses need to explain to parents that children are intuitive and will be relieved to discuss the sadness of their illness. Nurses may also consider providing age

appropriate information to the patient and parents together to promote open communication between them. If nurses keep the information as non-technical as possible and remain as hopeful as is realistically possible, parents may be more accepting of including their child in the conversation. Nurses can use simple drawings to help explain information to the child and parents. Gradual introduction of technical information can promote understanding by both the parents and the pediatric patient. Utilization of basic communication techniques will help nurses gain confidence (see *Figure 13-1*). Later, nurses can offer additional sources of information such as books, videos or internet printouts. Directing parents to appropriate associations, such as the National Cystic Fibrosis Foundation, can also be helpful. Appendix B contains a list of associations and web sites that parents can be referred to.

Parents of a chronically ill child are often seen as demanding by nursing staff. They may even seem uncooperative. Some parents may have specific requests and desire a lot of information. These parents may have particular preferences about care delivery. Parents often try to maintain their normal home routine while in the hospital (Curley & Moloney-Harmon, 2001). Some aspects of routine care can be negotiated with nurses to ease the family's transition to hospitalization. These changes in routine care can be incorporated into the care plan of the chronically ill child. Daily communication with the family by hospital staff is essential. Nurses may be on the receiving end of anger, blame, or guilt from emotional parents. Nurses should take advantage of teachable moments during patient care to incorporate end-of-life care education to the chronically ill child and the child's parents. Pediatric nurses must find a balance between the care of a physiologically unstable patient and the expectations and demands of the parents (Curley & Moloney-Harmon, 2001). Parents should be encouraged to meet their own needs, even if that

---

FIGURE 13-1
Communicate with Confidence

- Ask open-ended questions
- Use simple drawings
- Use non-technical terms
- Communicate daily
- Be an active, engaged listener
- Assess current knowledge base and skill level

- Provide age appropriate information
- Offer additional resources
- Listen to concerns
- Be patient, repeat information as needed
- Take advantage of teachable moments
- Repeat back information to clarify understanding

---

means leaving their child alone in the hospital for brief periods of time (Behrman, 2000).

Approximately 70–90% of illness episodes for the chronically ill child are managed at home. This indicates that parents are knowledgeable and skillful in caring for their child. Parents are capable of assessments and making some decisions about their child's care (Curley & Moloney-Harmon, 2001). Parents should be given information about their child's illness and any end-of-life issues that may need to be addressed in the future. Parents need to be made aware of home care assistance and respite care options in their area. Internet printouts, educational books, or videotapes are all helpful. These learning aids help parents to digest information at their own pace. If these types of learning aids are provided to parents, periodic follow-ups are essential to see if there are any questions regarding the provided material. Parents should be encouraged to explore parent support groups. These support groups can be a great source of comfort for parents.

Case Report 1

Haddad (2000) described an example of parents trying to protect their child from his terminal diagnosis. The parents of the terminally ill child did not want anyone to tell their child how sick he was. Knowing that the parents are adamant that their son not be told he is dying may put the nurse in a difficult situation when the child figures it out on his own. How should the nurse respond to the child when he asks, "Am I really going to get any better?" (Haddad, 2000).

There is definitely a need to provide the child with an immediate response of some sort, and it may be safest initially for the nurse to answer with a question encouraging the child to express his concerns. The nurse might simply ask, "What do you think?" (Haddad, 2000). Asking open-ended questions will encourage the child to talk about how he feels. The child may already know the answer and just need to opportunity to talk about it.

It would be important then for the nurse to follow up with the parents and teach them how intuitive and aware their young child is. The child can sense his parents' distress and pick up easily on mixed messages. The nurse should tell the parents how important it is for the child to be able to express his concerns. The child needs to know that he is loved and will be missed when he is gone. The child needs reassurance from his parents about heaven or death. What the child might imagine is often far worse than the truth. If the nurse were to disrespect the parents' wishes and tell the child that he is dying, the nurse would lose the parents' trust. The nurse-parent alliance and their collaboration is important in providing optimal care to the child.

The parents may not want to tell their child that he is dying because they are unable to deal with their own grief (Haddad, 2000). The nurse can help the parents grieve by being an engaged active listener. Giving the parents an opportunity to express their grief will help them to work through the grieving process. Helping the parents often results in helping the child.

The parents may think that they are protecting their child from the bad news, but once they see the harm in not telling their child, they may change their minds. The nurse needs to remember that the parents have a need to protect their child and to feel in control of their child's care. Discussing the issue with the parents will allow them to remain in control, and they may wish to be the ones to tell their child once they agree that he should be told.

It is always best for the child to be involved in the treatment plans or palliative care plans (Haddad, 2000). The nurse who has established a relationship with the parents and has gained their trust is more likely to have an impact on the parents' decisions to discuss death with their dying child.

PALLIATIVE CARE

Definition and Goals

Palliative care is defined by the World Health Organization as "The active total care of patients whose disease is not responsive to curative treatment." Control of pain, physical symptoms, psychological, social and spiritual problems are included (Wallace, 2000). Although many pediatric disorders are not curable, most of them are not immediately fatal. Many children live for years with no possibility of a cure. There is no fine line between life-prolonging treatment and palliative care for the pediatric patient. With cystic fibrosis for example, previous palliative care has resulted in a prolonged life expectancy for up to several decades. Since much of the care for chronic illnesses involves treatment with no hope for cure, it is nearly impossible to determine where pallia-

tive care begins for some chronic conditions (Sahler et al., 2000). However, the goals of therapy may change focus if continued treatment becomes too burdensome for the patient, or if there is a significant change in the patient's quality of life. Care for chronically ill children should focus then on the patient's quality of life. This is much different from the all or nothing approach of adult palliative or hospice care.

The main goal of pediatric palliative care is to enhance the quality of life for the terminally ill child. Palliative care treats the symptoms that detract from the child's quality of life. It also strives to keep families functional and intact. Pediatric palliative care should address the psychological, social and spiritual problems of the terminally ill child and the family (American Academy of Pediatrics [AAP], 2000). As the disease progresses, the desire for certain interventions may change. Medical technology is used only when the benefits outweigh the burdens. Many chronically ill children live with handicaps or disabilities for years before they die (Behrman, 2000). Because of the variety of crisis and exacerbations, palliative care may be involved for unpredictable and intermittent periods of time followed by a return to baseline.

Respect for the family's wishes is an important aspect of pediatric palliative care. Pediatric palliative care may also include education, grief and family counseling, peer support, music therapy, child life intervention, and appropriate respite care (AAP, 2000). Respite care may be available for hours, days or on a schedule.

The palliative care multidisciplinary team may include the patient, family, teacher, nurses, physicians, chaplains, bereavement counselors, social workers, and consultants. Physical, emotional, psychosocial and spiritual issues should be addressed. The child should participate as much as possible based on age and degree of illness (AAP, 2000).

The AAP states, "The goal is to add life to the child's years, not simply years to the child's life."

Implementation of Pediatric Palliative Care

Palliative care should be discussed early in the disease process and should be carried out throughout the chronic illness of a child. When the child and parents find that the burdens of continued life-prolonging treatment outweigh the benefits, palliative care may focus on comfort measures and quality of life. Because a child with a chronic illness may experience a gradual and unpredictable decline in health, early palliative care plans will provide guidance for nurses and other members of the health care team. Early planning allows plenty of time for preparation and a gradual adjustment to the inevitable demise. The quality of life and irreversibility of the disease process for the individual pediatric patient should be considered while making palliative care choices. Palliative care should be a multi-phase, dynamic process throughout the last few months, weeks or years of disease progression. There will be ongoing assessment of the burdens of living and the appropriateness of continued treatment. End-of-life preferences are subjective, and patient wishes can vary a great deal. With advanced planning and professional guidance, patients' needs are more likely to be met during their last weeks or months of life (Wallace, 2000).

What began as comfort care provided to some chronically ill children has resulted in prolonging life by several years. This was the case for many cystic fibrosis patients who received treatment for respiratory distress; their relief of symptoms resulted in several years of prolonged life. This underlies the most significant difference between pediatric palliative care and adult palliative care. The distinction between comfort care and curative care for pediatric patients is less clearly defined. The uncertainty in pediatric disease progression and the all or nothing treatment philosophy of some hospice programs often eliminates the eligibility for many children (Sahler et al., 2000). As a result, many terminally ill children are cared for in acute care hospital settings.

Health care professionals should address their terminal patient's concerns, and efforts should be made to ensure that a patient's last days or months are spent in as much comfort as possible and in compliance with the patient's wishes. Hospice providers have found that a dying patient's most common concerns are fear of pain, loss of control and indignity. Time should be taken to discuss physical limitations and how the pediatric patient and family may be able to alter or adjust their life styles to accommodate the ill child's changing needs. An explanation of the different types of pain medication available should be presented to the parents and the child. When appropriate, nurses can inform pediatric patients and/or parents of their rights to determine when to discontinue life-prolonging therapies. Improving palliative care services and assisting with family and patient decision making will help maintain a terminally ill child's dignity, relieve suffering and enhance the death experience (Wallace, 2000). Maintaining cleanliness and privacy and continuing to speak to the dying child are some ways to maintain comfort and dignity.

Improving palliative care in a hospital setting involves making adjustments for the ill child and family, such as more liberal visitation, minimizing testing and monitoring and respecting the family's privacy. A hospice philosophy can be attained in a hospital setting when the focus of care changes to comfort and quality of life (Behrman, 2000). Nurses can continue to manage new symptoms as they occur and discontinue the use of equipment that is no longer needed. Frequent attendance at the bedside will prevent the perception that the dying child is being abandoned (Wallace, 2000). Pain control is important for both the child and the parents. Parents will also benefit from participating in the physical care of their child. Parents should be allowed to assist in their child's care in any way that they are able in order to provide them with a sense of closeness to their child (Curley & Moloney-Harmon, 2001). When appropriate, a discussion regarding plans for funeral arrangements should be broached with the parents.

Case Report 2

The life span for children with chronic illnesses has improved a great deal with palliative type care. A 21-year-old cystic fibrosis patient was admitted to the pediatric intensive care unit (PICU) with exacerbation of her disease process. She was well known to the staff from multiple previous admissions. She was admitted to the PICU because the other units were full. This young woman's condition had been deteriorating for some time. She was very noncompliant, rarely following the instructions of the doctors or nurses.

It appeared to the nurses that the patient was getting even sicker, and they felt certain that this might be the last admission for this patient. The nurses knew from past conversations that the patient was not interested in a No-Code status, but given her current status, the nurses felt it was appropriate to again discuss palliative care and hospice with the patient and her mother. Once again, the patient adamantly refused to consider palliative care and a No-Code status. She was well aware of her chronic condition, she knew that she had outlived her doctor's predictions, and she knew that CPR would not be useful in prolonging her life. She may have been in denial regarding her imminent death, or she may have just felt comforted knowing that she would be cared for completely until the very end.

This cystic fibrosis patient did not return home. She died a few weeks after admission. The nurses would have liked for the patient to discuss the options of palliative care and going home with a home health nurse, but as the patient requested they

kept her a full code until there was no response to resuscitation efforts (Hart, 2001). This is another example of the subjectivity involved with palliative care and dying.

Palliative Care and the Parents

Sometimes parents blame themselves for their child's illness, and they often search for miracle cures. Parents can benefit from nurses who are attentive, engaged listeners. Parents need to know what palliative care options are available to their child. Information about home health care, hospice and support groups should be provided to parents. Parents should be encouraged to discuss their thoughts about their child's death. It should be determined whether parents have a strong preference for being at home, or whether they prefer the support of hospital staff (Behrman, 2000). Nurses can help to address misconceptions and differences about pain control versus terminal sedation (Behrman, 2000). Regular meetings between care givers and parents will keep the parents informed and help to ease their anxiety. Nurses need to listen to parents' concerns and have parents repeat information back to ensure accurate understanding (Behrman, 2000).

Processing bad news takes time. With each discussion, the parents will understand more information than they did during previous conversations. When there are no more curative options available, the parents should be approached with care options that are available. Comfort measures should be brought to light instead of continuing to discuss care that is no longer an option. To reduce the risk of misunderstandings, nurses need to use specific terms when speaking to parents. Comfort measures should be presented as positively as possible and tactful discussions about a No-Code status may be appropriate. Instead of bluntly asking parents for a No CPR status, nurses need to help parents understand their child's condition. This can be accomplished by explaining the lack of benefits for performing procedures such as CPR and intubation.

The moment of a child's death will be remembered in great detail by the parents and family. Parents and siblings should be encouraged to talk to the dying child up until death, even if the child is unresponsive (Behrman, 2000). Some chronically ill children seem to die only after their parents have been able to "let go" or accept the fact that the child is dying. The family should be allowed to hold their child for as long as they need to. If the child is an infant and the parents have not been allowed to hold their baby since birth, they should be provided with the opportunity to do so before or immediately after their infant dies. Nurses may sit quietly with the family or provide them with some private time. The physician should discuss the topic of autopsy if needed. Genetic counseling may also be suggested.

Siblings are at risk during illness and after death. They may feel like their needs are not being met and may even feel guilt over their own good health. Siblings should be encouraged to maintain their normal routines (Behrman, 2000). Siblings who are involved with the care of their sick brother or sister will adjust easier to the death of their sibling than those who were not involved. The siblings' fears need to be acknowledged. The nurse needs to be open and honest and should offer them some ways to help in the care of their sick sibling. Parents should be encouraged to involve siblings in palliative care plans. Parents need to be encouraged to include sibling participation at the funeral. This provides siblings with closure and assists them with their own grieving process (Behrman, 2000).

There are several methods of palliative care that will continue to provoke debate. Terminal sedation is one of those methods, and it is not always black and white when extended to children with incurable diseases. Continued discussion and public awareness of all of the socially and legally acceptable palliative care options need to be

increased (Wallace, 2000). When aggressive interventions are discontinued, the patient's comfort and dignity are the primary focus of care (Curley & Moloney-Harmon, 2001).

The Medicare model of hospice is restricted to patients with a life expectancy of six months or less. Because the timing of a child's death is so difficult to predict, this model omits many pediatric patients. Also, some hospice programs require the cessation of all life-prolonging therapies, and this may not be appropriate for some pediatric patients (AAP, 2000). Palliative and respite care programs are needed to manage the care of chronically or terminally ill children. Palliative care should be initiated at the time of diagnosis. Medicare and insurance companies should accommodate the need for palliative care services for pediatric patients. There is a need for increased support and research for pediatric palliative care.

Case Report 3

A twelve-year-old boy with end stage leukemia suffered several relapses and several courses of treatment. He suffered miserably through each course of treatment that he received. He was admitted with yet another relapse and sat drawn, thin and sad in his mother's lap. His small-for-a-12-year-old body slumped against her chest. His nurse walked in to begin his next series of treatments and stopped cold when she heard him say to his mother, "I can't do this anymore."

The nurse quickly discovered a task that she needed to do and left the room to allow time for mother and son to discuss the patient's newly expressed feelings. A short time later when the boy was resting in bed, the nurse asked the mother into the hall where she broached the topic of palliative care. After additional discussions with the boy's parents, the boy, the physician and home health nurses, the boy's nurse finalized the discharge planning. A palliative care plan was developed with the boy and his family. This palliative care plan would allow the boy's family to continue his care in his own home with comfort and dignity (Stafford, 2001).

Nursing Responsibilities

Studies have shown that pediatric nurses rarely discuss death or palliative care with their patients or their patients' parents. The American Nurses Association and the American Association of Critical-Care Nurses regard palliative care teaching a nursing role (Puopolo, 1999). Developing effective communication skills can increase nurses' confidence and comfort in discussing pediatric palliative care. Nurses have a unique opportunity to utilize teachable moments throughout the course of bedside care (Puopolo, 1999).

Nurses will find it helpful to get to know the pediatric patient's values and beliefs either through conversation with the child or family members. It is important for nurses to be careful to assess their own personal beliefs and to remain as neutral and nonjudgmental as possible while discussing palliative care. Nurses who are familiar with end-of-life issues will be more confident in providing information (Puopolo, 1999). Nurses should learn about the hospice programs in their area. Palliative care homes run by volunteers are available in some areas.

When talking about palliative care plans, nurses need to coach the patient or parents in their consideration of palliative care options. Medical terms should be clearly defined and the patient's and parents' comments need to be repeated to clarify understanding. Nurses should ask open-ended questions to learn about a patient's preferences. Information about the disease process needs to be provided to the patient and parents, and the nurse must make sure the patient and parents have a good understanding of treatment options (Puopolo, 1999). Palliative care wishes need to be shared with the patient's physician so that orders can be written and followed through (Puopolo, 1999).

Although it is extremely difficult to predict time of death, nurses may be able to recognize clues that a terminally ill child is entering the final stages of illness. Medical professionals have thoroughly documented the difficulties in predicting the time of death. Prognosticating the terminal phase in pediatric patients may be even more difficult. However, families often wish to know how long their children will live. The family caregiver has become a vital member of the health care team, so it makes sense for nurses to support the caregiver as much as possible (Wallace, 2000). Family members who wish to maintain a bedside vigil must deal with career and household responsibilities as well as with the stress of witnessing the impending death. Health care professionals should understand how difficult uncertainty is and interpret any signs that indicate the time remaining. However, health care professionals should avoid giving actual estimates as to the time of death. Predictions are often not accurate. It is best for the health care team members to explain that it is difficult to estimate how much time is left. However, nurses may encourage relative visits or funeral planning when they suspect that death is imminent. The pediatric patient and family should be consulted regarding all plans for end-of-life care, and time of death predictions can help to facilitate family participation (Behrman, 2000).

There are grading systems for survival predictions in adults. Although these systems are not created for pediatric patients, they may be useful to nurses who lack experience and comfort with palliative care. Some authors suggest using the Palliative Performance Scale (PPS) grading system and the Palliative Prognostic Index (PPI) for survival prediction in terminally ill cancer patients. The PPI ranges from 0 to 15. Higher scores indicate a poorer condition. When a patient has a PPI of more than 6.0, the patient's survival is predicted to be three weeks or less. PPI is defined by several factors including the PPS, oral intake, edema, dyspnea at rest, and delirium. This tool could help health care professionals guide their patients through palliative care decisions by giving families a calculated estimate of impending death (Wallace, 2000).

Asking pediatric patients about their desires for death is not an easy task. Even health care professionals who deal with death everyday find it difficult to discuss this topic. For health care professionals, discussing death may mean facing a long list of questions. It may involve dealing with a patient's grief and acknowledging that there is no further curative treatment to offer. Health care professionals cannot prevent grief, but they can provide much needed support during end-stage illness (Wallace, 2000).

EXAM QUESTIONS

CHAPTER 13
Questions 88–94

88. Providing information and support to the parents of a dying child will ultimately help the

    a. child.

    b. nurse.

    c. hospital.

    d. doctor.

89. What is one difference between adult and pediatric chronic illness and palliative care?

    a. Only adults can receive analgesics during end-of-life care.

    b. Long-term chronic illness in a pediatric patient often has no distinct change to palliative care.

    c. Pediatric patients do not usually know that they are dying, but adults always know.

    d. Palliative care for children is left up to the parents and is not a nursing concern.

90. At what age should parents be encouraged to stay with their hospitalized child?

    a. <12 years old

    b. <10 years old

    c. <8 years old

    d. <6 years old

91. About what percentage of illness episodes are managed at home for the chronically ill child?

    a. 10%

    b. 30%

    c. 50%

    d. 70%

92. Nurses can help parents through the grieving process by

    a. being available as an active, engaged listener.

    b. taking parents to a separate room to grieve alone.

    c. trying not to worry them with details.

    d. providing medical information only when they ask questions.

93. Which statement regarding pediatric palliative care is accurate?

    a. Pediatric palliative care involves all or none curative treatments.

    b. Pediatric palliative care is approached in the same way as adult palliative care.

    c. Pediatric palliative care is instituted at diagnosis and never changes.

    d. Pediatric palliative care should focus primarily on quality of life.

94. Which of the following statements is accurate with regard to the siblings of a dying child?

    a. Siblings generally do not have a need to talk about the child's death or illness.

    b. Siblings of a dying child rarely feel guilty over their own good health.

    c. Siblings should be allowed to participate with care of the dying child.

    d. Siblings' parents should not involve them in the palliative care plan.

CARE OF THE DYING CHILD

CHAPTER OBJECTIVE

After completing this chapter, the reader will be able to recognize pediatric palliative care pain management goals and the appropriate nursing interventions for the dying child in relation to pain control. The reader will also gain comfort and instruction on communicating about death with the dying patient.

LEARNING OBJECTIVES

After studying this chapter, the learner will be able to

1. choose the appropriate pain control options for a terminal pediatric patient.

2. specify the additional symptoms typically seen during the terminal phase of illness and their appropriate treatment measures.

3. recognize the comparison of comfort measures versus terminal sedation.

PAIN CONTROL AND SYMPTOM MANAGEMENT

Pain control is a very important aspect of care for the chronically ill and terminal pediatric patient. Pain management applies to all patients regardless of their prognosis (Sahler et al., 2000).

Multiple Symptoms

Dying patients often have many symptoms in addition to pain. Dyspnea, secretions, anxiety, nausea, vomiting and sleep disturbances are commonly seen. Seizures and irritability may occur and can be treated with medication. Feeding and hydration issues require evaluation of the risks and benefits of artificial feedings. Constipation and diarrhea are also symptoms that should be controlled for optimal patient comfort. Decubitus ulcers and pruritus can be avoided with proper skin care, position changes and good hygiene. Reducing exposure to soap and increasing the use of lotions can help to control itchy skin. A primary source of pain and discomfort can be reduced by omitting or limiting tests and procedures when they are no longer necessary. Antiemetics, antidepressants, or sedatives should be offered as indicated by the patient's complaints or symptoms.

Secretions typically accumulate when the patient is approaching death. This may result in noisy respirations and is sometimes referred to as the "death rattle." By this point in time, patients are usually unconscious; therefore, the noisy respirations are usually more distressing for the family than the patient. Anticholinergics may be helpful in reducing secretions, and thus the noisy respirations, but parents may just need reassurance. If the patient is in distress and if dyspnea is present, treatment with opioids can provide relief.

Nonpharmacologic Therapies

Nonpharmacologic pain control methods such as biofeedback, relaxation and music therapy should be considered. For young children, having a parent with them is an important pain control measure. Parents should be taught about guided imagery, distraction, biofeedback, and behavior modification. Nurses can assist parents with distraction by suggesting activities such as massage or reading a story (Sahler et al., 2000). There are many alternative therapies available today; although, most of them are unproven. Some of these therapies are inexpensive and may provide relief of symptoms; other therapies may be expensive, painful and even dangerous. Discussions about the use of alternative methods should be encouraged in a nonjudgmental way so that parents can learn about the safety or dangers of alternative therapies.

Pain Control

The pediatric patient and parents need to be educated about pain control options that are available. Both pharmacologic and nonpharmacologic methods of pain control need to be explained (Behrman, 2000). The nurse must be realistic about what is appropriate for each individual patient. Anesthetic blocks can be suggested for severe regional pain. A TENS unit or patient controlled analgesia (PCA) may be appropriate for older children. Patient controlled analgesia allows patients some control over their pain management along with continuous pain control. The least invasive route possible should be used. Regularly scheduled pain medication is more appropriate than intermittent medication for chronic or terminal pain. Pain status must be reassessed frequently, and the treatment should be changed as needed (Behrman, 2000).

Nurses should provide continuous pain assessment and monitoring of pain relief. Nurses should also anticipate adverse effects of pain medications and initiate preventive measures. Pain medication can be scheduled with around-the-clock dosing, with breakthrough dosing as needed. Frequent titration of dosing may be needed until pain relief is achieved. Adjunctive mediations can be administered as needed for anxiety or sleep disturbance. If analgesics are unsuccessful, the nurse needs to consult with parents, the patient and other health professionals about pain management. Opioids are the first choice for moderate or severe pain. The most common side effects of opioids are constipation and pruritus. Self reported pain is the most accurate assessment method. Numeric pain scales can be used for pain level assessment in children over seven years of age. Picture pain scales are appropriate for pain level assessment in children age six and under. Changes in vital signs may not be accurate indicators of pain in children with chronic illnesses.

The goal of palliative care is to make the most of the time a child has left. There is no goal to hasten death. However, when symptoms such as pain or dyspnea are progressive, the patient may require higher doses of analgesics and sedatives in order to achieve the same relief attained previously. With increased doses of medication, the patient may become less responsive, and parents may blame the medication instead of the disease process. The American Academy of Pediatrics suggests this misplaced blame comes from the phrase "terminal sedation" (AAP, 2000). Terminal sedation sounds like a method used to hasten death; when in fact it represents a pain free death — not the cause of death. The goals of palliative care remain the same regardless of the label. Dying pain free with dignity is the primary goal for all terminally ill children and adults. The American Academy of Pediatrics does not support either physician-assisted suicide or euthanasia for children (AAP, 2000).

Refractory or persistent pain often occurs with disease progression and may require added pain control measures. Making the decision to administer high doses of analgesics and sedatives is a difficult decision. The patient, family and health care providers should make this decision together with the child's best interest in mind.

PEDIATRIC DEATH

Causes of pediatric death include cancer, metabolic disorders, and neurodegenerative disorders (Behrman, 2000). In 1997, 43,000 infants and 27,000 children died in the U.S. Almost two-thirds of infant deaths occur during the first month of life. Most of these deaths are attributed to congenital abnormalities or perinatal complications. Only about 20% of deaths during the first year of life are acute and unexpected. Approximately 45% of toddler and school age deaths are related to trauma, and almost 80% of adolescent deaths are related to accidents, homicide and suicide (Sahler et al., 2000). The high rate of accidental and preventable deaths of adolescents creates increased guilt and blame complicating decisions about continuing or discontinuing life support.

Children are expected to outlive their parents; however, despite advancements in technology, some children will sustain extensive irreversible brain damage that results in brain death. Before 1960, death was defined as the absence of breathing and circulation. Currently in the U.S., the diagnosis of death is determined by irreversible cessation of breathing and circulation or irreversible cessation of neurological functions (brain death). Brain death is the absence of cerebral and brain stem functions. (Spinal reflexes may persist after brain death.) To be legally dead, it must be determined that the entire brain is irreversibly damaged (Curley & Moloney-Harmon, 2001). When a patient's condition is terminal, brain death is not required to withhold or withdraw life support. In 1987, the first guidelines for pediatric brain death were published (see *Figure 14-1*) (Curley &

Moloney-Harmon, 2001). The cause of a coma is an important factor in determining the reversibility of the patient's condition. Sometimes a coma is caused by a treatable condition. Some reversible causes of coma are metabolic disorders, sedatives, paralytics, hypothermia, hypotension, and surgically treatable lesions.

Case Report 4

C. Van Der Woude is a nurse who recalls how incredibly brave parents can be in the face of losing a child. A young couple found out at 19 weeks gestation that their baby was anecephalic. Their obstetrician suggested that they terminate the pregnancy knowing that without brain and skull formation the baby's condition was not compatible with life. The couple refused to terminate the pregnancy. At full-term the couple came to the hospital for delivery. The nurse and physician discussed the baby care prior to delivery. The baby would receive care but no resuscitation. The birth was very emotional; the baby was perfectly formed from the bridge of the nose down. His skull was absent, and soft brain tissue was visible. The baby had a heart rate and irregular respirations. His vital signs were stabilized, and he was bathed and dressed. A sterile moist dressing was applied to the exposed brain tissue. The dressing was covered with a hat that came down to the infant's nose. The mother cradled him tearfully and requested to take him home. The nurse taught the parents how to care for the baby and told them what to do when he died. The baby died at home one week later. The parents expressed how grateful they were to have been able to spend some time with their son (Van Der Woude, 1999). Many parents might have chosen to terminate the pregnancy. Delivery and care for an infant with such a deformity took great courage and strength. This case demonstrates the intensity and infinite love that parents can give regardless of adversity.

FIGURE 14-1

Guidelines for the Determination of Brain Death in Children

Physical Examination*	1. Coma
	2. Absence of brainstem function
	   a. Midposition of fully dilated pupils, nonreactive to light
	   b. Absence of spontaneous eye movements, inducing by oculocephalic and oculovestibular testing
	   c. Absence of bulbar musculature
	   d. Apnea
	3. Flaccid tone, absence of spontaneous or induced movements†

Observation period (for patient age)	1. Seven days to 2 months: two examinations separated by at least 48 hours 2. Two months to 1 year: two examinations separated by at least 24 hours 3. Over 1 year: observation period of at least 12 hours when irreversible cause known
Laboratory testing	1. Seven days to 2 months: two EEGs separated by at least 48 hours 2. Two months to 1 year: two EEGs separated by at least 24 hours 3. Over 1 year: laboratory testing not required when irreversible cause is known

Data from Task Force for the Determination of Brain Death in Children: Guidelines for the determination of brain death in children. *Neurology, 37*:1007, 1987.

* The physical examination should remain unchanged during the entire observation and laboratory testing periods. Severe hypothermia and hypotension must be excluded.

† Spinal cord reflexes may be present.

EEG, Electroencephalogram

Reprinted with permission from W. B. Saunders, Critical Care Nursing of Infants and Children, (2001).

Talking About Death

Children under two years of age have little awareness of death. Children ages three to five years old think that death is temporary and reversible, like sleep. Children in these age groups often think that when someone dies they go to heaven, where they continue to live with physical actions and thoughts (Curley & Moloney-Harmon, 2001). Children who cannot comprehend the future beyond a few days are not able to comprehend death. In order to have an accurate perception of death, children must be able to understand that all things inevitably die; that people cannot come back to life; people do not talk, eat or move when they are dead; and that there is a cause of death (Behrman, 2000).

Between the ages of six and eight children begin to understand that people die and that they themselves will eventually die too. They also begin to understand that death is not reversible. The cause of death is the last concept that children are able to understand. Death is linked to violence, illness or old age; it is considered dangerous, scary, or mean (Curley & Moloney-Harmon, 2001). Children ages 10 to 12 recognize that death is universal and final. They also understand that all living things will die. Dying is associated with pain and suffering. Death is fearful and is associated with feeling sad and lonely (Curley & Moloney-Harmon, 2001). Adolescent attitudes of invincibility may delay the teenager's acceptance of terminal illness (Behrman, 2000). Adolescents understand death as adults do. Death is final, but it is also very personal. Adolescents are often fearful about death (Curley & Moloney-Harmon, 2001).

Children's Concerns

Children with chronic illnesses typically have advanced understanding of their disease and of the concept of death. Terminally ill children come to know that they are dying even though no one tells them so (Behrman, 2000). If they are given the opportunity, children do want to talk about death (Sahler et al., 2000). Sometimes when patients ask if they are going to die, they really just want to know if it is okay to talk about death (Sahler et al., 2000). A child's questions about death may be a test to see who is telling the truth and who is receptive to discuss death. Children sometimes just want answers to their concerns: "Who will feed my dog?" or "Is it nice in heaven?"

When children do ask about death, they primarily want to be reassured that they are loved and will not be alone (Behrman, 2000). Children fear separation from their parents and other loved ones when they die. This fear can be eased with reassurances of relatives who are waiting for the child in heaven, religious figures, or spiritual connections (Behrman, 2000). Like adults, children find comfort in knowing that their life had meaning. Questions like "Will you keep my pictures in the album after I die?" give children a sense of meaning to their life.

Even though they know they are dying, some children do not talk about it to family or health care professionals (Curley & Moloney-Harmon, 2001). Some children are too ill to have discussions about death (Curley & Moloney-Harmon, 2001). Even

when it is difficult to tell if the child can hear or understand, nurses can continue to talk to an unconscious patient. This gives parents permission to continue interacting with their dying child (Curley & Moloney-Harmon, 2001).

Parental Concerns

Adults usually believe that either the children do not know that they are dying or they think that children do not want to talk about dying (Curley & Moloney-Harmon, 2001). However, when adults put off answering questions about death, it gives the child the message that it is not okay to talk about dying. Parents sometimes do not realize that children are able to interpret mixed messages. They are aware of inconsistent verbal and nonverbal communication (Curley & Moloney-Harmon, 2001). Children understand the significance of whispering voices and tearful anxious parents (Curley & Moloney-Harmon, 2001). Parents should know that children cannot be protected from the reality of their illness. Trying to insist that everything will be all right causes distrust and eliminates the opportunity for children to express fears and concerns or feelings of guilt regarding their illness. Children should be reassured that they have done nothing wrong and are not responsible for their illness or the illness of a sibling (AAP, 2000). Children should be encouraged to talk about their feelings. They may express anger, sadness, fear, isolation, and guilt.

Nursing Interventions

Thoughtful sincere responses will help to decrease the child's concerns. Nurses should never be flippant in their responses to the child. Instead, nurses should be prepared to provide sensitive and satisfying answers to the child's questions. Nurses should thoughtfully answer only what the child asks. Nurses must learn how to respond to the child's feelings of hopelessness. The best way for nurses to gain comfort talking to a dying child is by doing it.

It is difficult to know when is a good time to initiate a conversation about death; however, avoiding it may encourage the child's silence. Honest communication is supportive and promotes personal growth. Nurses can watch for clues that indicate a child's interest in talking about death. Thoughts of death are evident in a child's play and art. Another clue that a child is thinking about death is the child's lack of future plans. The child begins to avoid talking about topics that involve the future. The child may also become anxious with increased acting out or withdrawing from others (Curley & Moloney-Harmon, 2001). A child who is alert and able to talk should be encouraged to discuss feelings, especially if an aggressive treatment is planned.

Fear of abandonment is a major concern of the pediatric patient and parents throughout the child's illness. Nurses can help to reassure the child and family that the medical team will provide support throughout the course of the illness. The parents must be allowed to complete any family, religious or cultural rituals at the time of death (AAP, 2000). Many children remain alert and active until very late in their course of illness, and their desire to talk about death varies a great deal. Many children with chronic illness are living into adolescence and young adulthood. Nurses and physicians can help these children communicate their desires for treatment or treatment withdrawal. Communicating with children about death is most effective when their cognitive and developmental levels are taken into consideration. When nurses share information with their pediatric patients, it lessens the patients' feelings of isolation and abandonment.

Parents and Grief

The death of a child is a very stressful and traumatic event. Childhood deaths are viewed as unnatural and particularly tragic. Parental grief can be especially severe. Grieving is promoted when parents are able to hold their child either during or following the child's death. Appropriate support by nurses can assist parents in their grieving process (Curley & Moloney-Harmon, 2001). It requires time and patience to listen to parents after the death of their child; they may have questions or misconceptions and may also need help with funeral arrangements (Behrman, 2000).

Siblings should be told of their brother or sister's death as soon as possible in a clear and truthful way. Parents should also share their feelings of sadness with their living children. There are books that may assist in helping siblings understand death. Support groups are also very beneficial in assisting with bereavement (Curley & Moloney-Harmon, 2001). Nurses can provide information about support groups such as The Compassionate Friends, Candlelighters or Lamplighters.

Grief is complex and very individualized. The death of a child involves intense feelings of sadness for many years. Parents are supported when nurses acknowledge that nothing can replace their child. Parents also need to know that although their memories of the child will last forever, the pain and grief will subside over time. The child's physician may arrange to meet with the family after the child's death to review the autopsy results and answer questions. Divorce is not necessarily higher for bereaved couples; however, physicians may make counseling referrals if needed.

Support for Nurses

All deaths provoke a response of some kind, but caring for dying children is an especially difficult task. Not all nurses are able to handle the emotional strain and stress of palliative care. Sometimes personal issues interfere with the ability to handle emotional situations at work. Nurses should try to recognize their own needs and seek needed support or relief from co-workers. Nurses may benefit from institutional support such as psychologist sessions for staff and remembrance ceremonies (AAP, 2000).

Some nurses may feel a great deal of frustration and sadness when their hard work and dedicated care cannot prevent the death of a child (Behrman, 2000). Professionals may feel confident that they did everything they could, or they may feel they should have done more. Nurses may feel powerless or vulnerable (Sahler et al., 2000). Providing end-of-life care is emotionally challenging, and the death of a child is even more likely to create emotional responses than the death of an adult.

Case Report 5

One registered nurse found comfort in providing parental support (Walsh, 1999). A five-year-old boy fighting a relapse of leukemia was very stoic. He never joked around. He was especially guarded around nurses, always weary of their torturous treatments. One day while bathing the boy, the nurse started talking about his illness. She told him it was not his fault that he was sick. She acknowledged how lousy he felt and how rotten it was that he was sick. The nurse explained that some things just happen and it is nobody's fault. Later, his mom thanked the nurse for expressing feelings that she was having trouble talking about. One day after much vomiting and diarrhea the nurse took the boy's blanket home to wash it. She was working the next morning and knew she would be able to return it early. When she returned she sensed that something was wrong. She quickly learned from her co-workers that the boy had died during the night (Walsh, 1999). The blanket went with the boy to the funeral home, and at the funeral the mother introduced all his nurses to her family and friends.

Even though the nurse never found a way to get close to the boy, she knew he had all the love and support that he needed from his parents. The nurse was comforted by the fact that she was able to provide support to the parents, which in turn enabled them to have more energy and freedom to support their son (Walsh, 1999). This case illustrates the importance of the nursing role in providing support to the parents of an ill or dying child.

CONCLUSION

The ultimate goal of pediatric palliative care is to provide humane care to sick children and to improve bereavement outcomes for their families. End-of-life care factors for nurses to keep in mind are age appropriate communication, pain and symptom management, caregiver distress, and focusing on patient oriented goals. Nurses can assist patients and families to achieve closure by listening to their concerns. Nurses and patients will benefit from effective communication.

Time of death is difficult to predict. If palliative care is not initiated until close to the time of death, many children will not be able to benefit from it. Also, if palliative care is incorporated into patient care from the onset of the disease process, distinguishing between palliative or curative treatments will not be an issue. For instance, mechanical ventilation may be seen as curative and life-prolonging, but it also serves to reduce dyspnea—thus improving the child's quality of life.

The American Academy of Pediatrics supports the introduction of palliative care at the time of diagnosis, with continued support throughout the course of the illness. Professional and public education will increase the awareness of pediatric palliative care and the need for palliative care programs (AAP, 2000). Health care professionals can further support pediatric palliative care by participating in research studies and by improving palliative care processes.

CHAPTER 14
Questions 95–100

95. Which of the following is an additional symptom typically seen during the terminal phase of illness?

   a. dry mouth
   b. facial swelling
   c. nausea
   d. oily skin

96. Which of the following is an appropriate pharmacologic pain control method for an older child who is terminally ill?

   a. aspirin
   b. biofeedback
   c. patient controlled analgesia
   d. Compazine

97. Nurses should teach parents that terminal sedation

   a. is given to hasten the death of a child.
   b. represents a pain free death, not the cause of death.
   c. involves opioid dosages that are increased regularly regardless of symptoms.
   d. involves opioids at one specific dose throughout end-stage illness.

98. The age at which children begin to understand that everyone will die and that death is irreversible is

   a. before the age of 5.
   b. after the age of 6.
   c. not until age 12.
   d. at the age of 15.

99. A common parental misbelief about a dying child is that children

   a. want to talk about death.
   b. are able to interpret adult mixed messages.
   c. should be protected from the reality of their illness.
   d. often know that they are dying.

100. The best way for nurses to gain comfort in talking to a dying child is to

   a. read as much as possible about the process of death.
   b. watch other nurses talk to dying patients.
   c. talk to dying patients themselves.
   d. attend inservice classes on death and dying.

   This concludes the final examination. An answer key will be sent with your certificate so that you can determine which of your answers were correct and incorrect.

APPENDIX A

Recommended Childhood Immunization Schedule
United States, 2002

Legend	
range of recommended ages	
catch-up vaccination	
preadolescent assessment	

Vaccine ▶ / Age ▼	Birth	1 mo	2 mos	4 mos	6 mos	12 mos	15 mos	18 mos	24 mos	4-6 yrs	11-12 yrs	13-18 yrs
Hepatitis B[1]	Hep B #1 (only if mother HBsAg (-))	Hep B #2			Hep B #3						Hep B series	
Diphtheria, Tetanus, Pertussis[2]			DTaP	DTaP	DTaP		DTaP			DTaP	Td	
Haemophilus influenzae Type b[3]			Hib	Hib	Hib	Hib						
Inactivated Polio[4]			IPV	IPV	IPV					IPV		
Measles, Mumps, Rubella[5]						MMR #1				MMR #2	MMR #2	
Varicella[6]						Varicella				Varicella	Varicella	
Pneumococcal[7]			PCV	PCV	PCV	PCV			PCV	PPV		
Hepatitis A[8]									Hepatitis A series			
Influenza[9]					Influenza (yearly)							

Vaccines below this line are for selected populations

This schedule indicates the recommended ages for routine administration of currently licensed childhood vaccines, as of December 1, 2001, for children through age 18 years. Any dose not given at the recommended age should be given at any subsequent visit when indicated and feasible. ▨ Indicates age groups that warrant special effort to administer those vaccines not previously given. Additional vaccines may be licensed and recommended during the year. Licensed combination vaccines may be used whenever any components of the combination are indicated and the vaccine's other components are not contraindicated. Providers should consult the manufacturers' package inserts for detailed recommendations.

Approved by the Advisory Committee on Immunization Practices (www.cdc.gov/nip/acip) the American Academy of Pediatrics (www.aap.org), and the American Academy of Family Physicians (www.aafp.org).

Footnotes: Recommended Childhood Immunization Schedule
United States, 2002

1. Hepatitis B vaccine (Hep B). All infants should receive the first dose of hepatitis B vaccine soon after birth and before hospital discharge; the first dose may also be given by age 2 months if the infant's mother is HBsAg-negative. Only monovalent hepatitis B vaccine can be used for the birth dose. Monovalent or combination vaccine containing Hep B may be used to complete the series; four doses of vaccine may be administered if combination vaccine is used. The second dose should be given at least 4 weeks after the first dose, except for Hib-containing vaccine which cannot be administered before age 6 weeks. The third dose should be given at least 16 weeks after the first dose and at least 8 weeks after the second dose. The last dose in the vaccination series (third or fourth dose) should not be administered before age 6 months.

Infants born to HBsAg-positive mothers should receive hepatitis B vaccine and 0.5 mL hepatitis B immune globulin (HBIG) within 12 hours of birth at separate sites. The second dose is recommended at age 1-2 months and the vaccination series should be completed (third or fourth dose) at age 6 months.

Infants born to mothers whose HBsAg status is unknown should receive the first dose of the hepatitis B vaccine series within 12 hours of birth. Maternal blood should be drawn at the time of delivery to determine the mother's HBsAg status; if the HBsAg test is positive, the infant should receive HBIG as soon as possible (no later than age 1 week).

2. Diphtheria and tetanus toxoids and acellular pertussis vaccine (DTaP). The fourth dose of DTaP may be administered as early as age 12 months, provided 6 months have elapsed since the third dose and the child is unlikely to return at age 15-18 months. **Tetanus and diphtheria toxoids (Td)** is recommended at age 11-12 years if at least 5 years have elapsed since the last dose of tetanus and diphtheria toxoid-containing vaccine. Subsequent routine Td boosters are recommended every 10 years.

3. *Haemophilus influenzae* type b (Hib) conjugate vaccine. Three Hib conjugate vaccines are licensed for infant use. If PRP-OMP (PedvaxHIB® or ComVax® [Merck]) is administered at ages 2 and 4 months, a dose at age 6 months is not required. DTaP/Hib combination products should not be used for primary immunization in infants at age 2, 4 or 6 months, but can be used as boosters following any Hib vaccine.

4. Inactivated poliovirus vaccine (IPV). An all-IPV schedule is recommended for routine childhood poliovirus vaccination in the United States. All children should receive four doses of IPV at age 2 months, 4 months, 6-18 months, and 4-6 years.

5. Measles, mumps, and rubella vaccine (MMR). The second dose of MMR is recommended routinely at age 4-6 years but may be administered during any visit, provided at least 4 weeks have elapsed since the first dose and that both doses are administered beginning at or after age 12 months. Those who have not previously received the second dose should complete the schedule by the visit at age 11-12 years.

6. Varicella vaccine. Varicella vaccine is recommended at any visit at or after age 12 months for susceptible children (i.e. those who lack a reliable history of chickenpox). Susceptible persons aged ≥ 13 years should receive two doses, given at least 4 weeks apart.

7. Pneumococcal vaccine. The heptavalent **pneumococcal conjugate vaccine (PCV)** is recommended for all children aged 2-23 months and for certain children aged 24-59 months. **Pneumococcal polysaccharide vaccine (PPV)** is recommended in addition to PCV for certain high-risk groups. See *MMWR* 2000;49(RR-9);1-37.

8. Hepatitis A vaccine. Hepatitis A vaccine is recommended for use in selected states and regions, and for certain high-risk groups; consult your local public health authority. See *MMWR* 1999;48(RR-12);1-37.

9. Influenza vaccine. Influenza vaccine is recommended annually for children age ≥ 6 months with certain risk factors (including but not limited to asthma, cardiac disease, sickle cell disease, HIV and diabetes; see *MMWR* 2001;50(RR-4);1-44), and can be administered to all others wishing to obtain immunity. Children aged ≤12 years should receive vaccine in a dosage appropriate for their age (0.25 mL if age 6-35 months or 0.5 mL if aged ≥ 3 years). Children aged ≤ 8 years who are receiving influenza vaccine for the first time should receive two doses separated by at least 4 weeks.

Additional information about vaccines, vaccine supply, and contraindications for immunization, is available at www.cdc.gov/nip or at the National Immunization Hotline, 800-232-2522 (English) or 800-232-0233 (Spanish).

APPENDIX B

HELPFUL WEB SITES

Emergency Medical Services for Children Program (EMS-C)
www.ems-c.org

Kids Health
www.ama-assn.org/KidsHealth

Mayo Health O@sis
www.mayohealth.org/mayo/common/htm/pregpg2.htm

National Library of Medicine
www.nlm.nih.gov/databases/freemedl.html

American Academy of Pediatrics
www.aap.org

Pediatrics in Review
www.pedsinreview.org

Medical Matrix
www.medmatrix.org/index.asp

Pedbase Mini-Textbook
www.icondata.com/health/pedbase/index.htm

Pediatrics
www.pediatrics.org

Virtual Children's Hospital from the University of Iowa
http://vch.vh.org/

American Academy of Child and Adolescent Psychiatry
www.aacap.org/web/aacap/

Adolescent Preventive Services (GAPSP)
www.ama-assn.org/adolhth/recomend/monogrfl.htm

Allergy, Asthma and Immunology Online
http://allergy.mcg.edu/

American Academy of Allergy, Asthma and Immunology
www.aaaai.org/

Asthma Management Handbook 1998
http://hna.ffh.vic.gov.au/asthma/amh/amhcont.htm

JAMA Asthma Information Center
www.ama-assn.org/special/asthma/

Congenital Heart Disease Information and Resources
www.tchin.org/

Pediatric Critical Care Medicine
http://PedsCCM.wustl.edu/

Pediatric Neuro-Oncology
www.med.miami.edu/neurosurgery/start_intro.htm

Camp Cancer (For Kids)
http://netpressence.com/camp-cancer/

OncoLink at the University of Pennsylvania
www.oncolink.upenn.edu/specialty/ped_onc/

Children with Diabetes
www.childrenwithdiabetes.com

Diabetes Online Self-Assessment
www.campsweeney.org/selftest.html

NICU-NET Mailing List
http://neonatal.peds.washington.edu/NICU-
    WEB/subscribe.stm

Down Syndrome: Health Issues
http://www.ds-health.com

ImmunoFacts.com
www.immunofacts.com/

Centers for Disease Control and Prevention
www.cdc.gov/

Pediatric AIDS Foundation
www.pedaids.org/

Immunization Action Coalition
www.immunize.org/

National Immunization Program
www.cdc.gov/nip/

Pediatric Orthopedic Cases
http://gait.aidi.udel.edu/res695/homepage/pd_ortho
    /educate/clincase/clcasehp.htm

American Academy of Neurology
www.aan.com/

Children and Medicine from the United States
    Pharmacopeia
www.usp.org/did/children/

Agency for Toxic Substances and Disease Registry
    ToxFAQs
http://atsdrl.atsdr.cdc.gov:8080/toxfaq.html

Preventive Pediatrics, Bright Futures
www.brightfutures.org/

Burn Prevention Tips from Shriners
www.shrinershq.org/Hospitals/BurnTips/index.html

National Committee to Prevent Child Abuse
www.childabuse.org/

The Arc of the US, (Association for Retarded
    Citizens of the US)
http://TheArc.org/

Compassionate Friends
www.compassionatefriends.org/

Convonation (For Kids with Disabilities)
www.maniax.com/

Patient Education Pamphlets—American Academy
    of Dermatology
www.aad.org/P_Frameset.html

Sports Parents
www.sportsparents.com/

National Clearinghouse for Alcohol and Drug
    Information
http://www.health.org

www.drugfreeamerica.org

www.kidsource.com

www.parentsoup.com

National Institute on Drug Abuse
www.nida.nih.gov

Office of National Drug Control Policy
www.whitehousedrugpolicy.gov

Substance Abuse and Mental Health Services
    Administration
www.samhas.gov

APPENDIX C

SAMPLE ADOLESCENT ASSESSMENT FORMS

Early Adolescence Visits (11, 12, 13, 14 Years)	ID#:		Date:
Name:		DOB:	Sex:
Parent Name:		Phone:	

Wt. (___%)	Ht. (___%)	BMI	T	P	R	BP

Questions for Parent

● How is _____ doing in school? What does he do after school?

● What has _____ been taught in school or at home? about drugs, sex, and other health objects?

● Have you clearly stated rules about how you want _____ to act?

Questions for Adolescent

* Who is your best friend? What do you and your friends do for fun?

* Tell me some of the things you're really good at.

* Do your friends try to pressure you to do things that you don't want to do? How do you handle that?

* How much time each week do you spend watching television or playing video games?

* Has anyone talked with you about what to expect as your body develops?

* Have you started dating? Do you have any worries or questions about sex?

* Who do you live with? How do you get along with your family?

School Performance

* How are you doing in school? How often do you miss school?

* What activities or sports are you involved in?

Family's Questions

● What questions or concerns would you like to discuss today?

Interval History

Medications:

Allergies:

Recent injury/illness:

Special health care needs:

Visits to other health care providers, facilities:

Changes/stressors in family or home:

Physical Exam

	Normal		Normal
General	[ ]	Neurologic	[ ]
Skin (acne)	[ ]	Reflexes	[ ]
Head	[ ]	Signs of abuse	[ ]
Eyes	[ ]	Tanner stage	[ ]
Ears	[ ]	*Females*	
Nose/throat	[ ]	Condyloma/lesions	[ ]
Mouth	[ ]	Instruction in breast	[ ]
Teeth	[ ]	self-exam	
Neck	[ ]	*Males*	
Lungs	[ ]	Gynecomastia	[ ]
Heart	[ ]	Hernias, condyloma/	[ ]
Abdomen	[ ]	lesions	
Back (scoliosis)	[ ]	Testicular cancer	[ ]
Extremities	[ ]	Instruction in testicular	[ ]
Feet	[ ]	self-exam	

If abnormal, please explain:

Early Adolescence Visits (11, 12, 13, 14, Years)	**Date:**
Name:	

Anticipatory Guidance

Healthy habits

* ※ [ ] Adequate sleep, exercise
* ※ [ ] Athletic conditioning, fluids
* ※ [ ] Weight training, changes
* [ ] Limit TV
* [ ] Seat belts, helmets, sunscreen
* [ ] Protective sports gear
* [ ] Smoke-free environment
* ※ [ ] Weapons
* [ ] Learn to swim
* [ ] Challenges, self-confidence
* [ ] Listen to friends/adults
* ※ [ ] Stress, nervousness, sadness
* [ ] Three meals a day, nutritious snacks
* [ ] Family meals
* [ ] Food choices (fruits, vegetables, grains)
* [ ] Iron, calcium
* [ ] Sugar, high-fat foods
* ※ [ ] Weight management
* [ ] Brush teeth
* [ ] Fluoride, dental sealants
* [ ] Dental emergency care
* ※ [ ] See dentist
* [ ] Body changes
* [ ] Sexual feelings normal
* [ ] How to say no, abstinence
* [ ] Birth control, safer sex
* [ ] Cigarettes, spit tobacco
* [ ] Diet pills, steroids
* [ ] Alcohol , drugs
* [ ] Peer counseling

Social competence

* ※ [ ] Family time
* [ ] Respect parents' limits/consequences
* [ ] Social activities, groups, sports
* [ ] Peers, sibling relationships
* ※ [ ] Peer pressure, peer refusal

Responsibility

* [ ] Respect others
* [ ] Ethical role model
* [ ] Rules, chores, responsibilities
* [ ] New skills, talents, interests

School achievement

* [ ] School transitions
* [ ] Attendance, homework
* [ ] Frustrations, dropping out
* ※ [ ] School activities
* [ ] Future plans, college, career

Community interaction

* ※ [ ] Religious, cultural, volunteer activities
* [ ] Social responsibility
* [ ] Referrals

Screening

PPD (once at 14-16)

If risk: Vision R _____ L _____

  Hearing R _____ L _____

PPD Hyperlipidemia

Hematocrit or hemoglobin (females)

If sexually active:

Annual pelvic exam (females) Gonorrhea, chlamydia

Syphilis, HIV Urine dipstick for leukocytes ___

Immunizations

Immunizations up to

  Side effects discussed? [ ]

Hepatitis B # [ ]

Tetanus and diptheria toxoids [ ]

Measles, munps, rubella # [ ]

Varicella # [ ]

Summary

● Summarize visit.

● Arrange continuing care

_____

Referral	**Phone Numbers**	
Health Insurance	_____	[ ]
SSI	_____	[ ]
WIC	_____	[ ]
Food Stamps	_____	[ ]
Social Services	_____	[ ]
Housing	_____	[ ]

Other:

Notes:

Signature:

Provider Form – BACK

Bright Futures is sponsored by **MCHB**, **HRSA**, and, in part, supported by unrestricted educational grants from **Pfizer Pediatric Health.** Bright Futures material is produced by **NCEMCH** and is not copyrighted.

Middle Adolescence Visits (15, 16, 17 Years)	ID#:	Date:
Name:	DOB:	Sex:
Parent Name:	Phone:	

Wt. (___%)	Ht. (___%)	BMI	T	P	R	BP

Questions for Adolescent

* What do you do for fun? Is it easy or hard for you to make friends?
* Do you ever feel really down and depressed? Who do you talk to about these feelings?
* How do you feel about the way you look? About your weight? What kind of exercise do you get?
* Do you work? How many hours per week?
* Do you smoke cigarettes, drink alcohol, or use drugs? How often?
* Do you date? Do you have a steady partner? Are you happy?
* Have you begun having sex? Do you use birth control? What kind?
* Are the rules in your family clear and reasonable?

School Performance

* Is school work difficult for you? How often do you miss school?
* What activities or sports are you involved in?

Questions for Parent (if present)

● What about _____ makes you proud?
● Do you feel _____'s school work matches his/her future goals or your goals for him/her?
● Have you talked with _____ about sexuality and your values about sex?
● What are some of your family's traditions?

Family's Questions

● What questions or concerns would you like to discuss today?

Interval History

Medications:

Allergies:

Recent injury/illness:

Special health care needs:

Visits to other health care providers, facilities:

Changes/stressors in family or home:

Physical Exam

	Normal		Normal
General	[ ]	Neurologic	[ ]
Skin (acne)	[ ]	Reflexes	[ ]
Head	[ ]	Signs of abuse	[ ]
Eyes	[ ]	Tanner stage	[ ]
Ears	[ ]	*Females*	
Nose/throat	[ ]	Condyloma/lesions	[ ]
Mouth	[ ]	Instruction in breast	[ ]
Teeth	[ ]	self-exam	
Neck	[ ]	*Males*	
Lungs	[ ]	Gynecomastia	[ ]
Heart	[ ]	Hernias, condyloma/	[ ]
Abdomen	[ ]	lesions	
Back (scoliosis)	[ ]	Testicular cancer	[ ]
Extremities	[ ]	Instruction in testicular	[ ]
Feet	[ ]	self-exam	

If abnormal, please explain:

Middle Adolescence Visits (15, 16, 17 Years)	Date:
Name:	

Anticipatory Guidance

Healthy habits

[ ] Adequate sleep, exercise
[ ] Athletic conditioning, fluids
[ ] Weight training, changes
[ ] Diet pills, steroids
* [ ] Limit TV
[ ] Seat belts, speed limits
[ ] Protective helmets, mouthguards, gear
* [ ] Sunscreen, tanning salons
[ ] Smoke detectors
[ ] Job safety, emergencies
[ ] Cigarettes, spit tobacco
[ ] Alcohol, drugs, weapons
[ ] Learn to swim
* [ ] Self-protection
* [ ] Handle anger, conflict resolution
[ ] Self-confidence, strengths
* [ ] Trust feelings, listen to friends/adults
[ ] Stress, depression, hopelessness

[ ] Goals (challenging, reasonable)
[ ] Three meals a day, nutritious snacks
[ ] Family meals
[ ] Sugar, high-fat foods
* [ ] Food choices (fruit, vegetables, grains)

[ ] Weight management
[ ] Brush teeth
[ ] Dental emergency care
* [ ] See dentist
[ ] Normal sexual feelings
[ ] How to say no, abstinence
* [ ] Birth control, STDs, safer sex
[ ] Limit sex partners, use condoms correctly
[ ] Support friends, peer counseling

Social competence

[ ] Family time
[ ] Social activities, groups, sports
* [ ] Respect parents' limits/consequences
[ ] Peer pressure, peer refusal

Responsiilities

* [ ] Respect others
[ ] Rules, chores, responsibilities
[ ] New skills, talents, interests

School achievement

[ ] Attendance, homework
* [ ] Frustrations, dropping out
[ ] School activities
* [ ] Future plans, college, career

Community interaction

[ ] Referrals
[ ] Religious, cultural, volunteer activities
[ ] Social responsibility

Screening

PPD (once at 14-16)
Assess hyperlipidemia risk

If risk: Vision   R _____   L _____

      Hearing   R _____   L _____

PPD   Hyperlipidemia
Hematocrit or hemoglobin (females)

If sexually active:

Annual pelvic exam (females)   Gonorrhea, chlamydia
Syphilis, HIV   Urine dipstick for leukocytes ___

Immunizations

Immunizations up to

                               Side effects discussed? [ ]

Tetanus and diptheria toxoids   [ ]

Summary

● Summarize visit.
● Arrange continuing care

Referral	Phone Numbers	
Health Insurance	_____	[ ]
SSI	_____	[ ]
WIC	_____	[ ]
Food Stamps	_____	[ ]
Social Services	_____	[ ]
WIC	_____	[ ]
Housing	_____	[ ]
Other:		

Notes:

Signature:

Provider Form – BACK

APPENDIX D

Normal Heart, Respiratory Rates, and Blood Pressure in Children

Age	*Normal Heart Rates in Children* Awake HR (beats/min)	Sleeping HR (beats/min)	Normal Respiratory Rates in Children (breaths/min)	*Normal Blood Pressures in Children* Systolic Pressure (mmHg)	Diastolic Pressure (mmHg)
Neonate	100–180	80–160	30–60	60–90	20–60
Infant	100–160	75–160	30–60	87–105	53–66
Toddler	80–110	60–90	24–40	95–105	53°66
Preschooler	70–110	60–90	22–34	95–110	56–70
School-age child	65–110	60–90	18–30	97–112	57–71
Adolescent	60–90	50–90	12–16	112–128	66–80

Estimated systolic blood pressure norms (for infants and children beyond 1 year of age): 50th percentile systolic blood pressure = 90 mmHg + (2 x age in years): 5th percentile systolic blood pressure = 70 mmHg + (2 x age in years)

Source: Curley, M. & Moloney-Harmon, P. (2001). *Critical care nursing of infants and children.* Philadelphia: W.B. Saunders.

GLOSSARY

After drop: Rewarming a near-drowning victim may cause an initial drop in temperature this "after drop" is caused by the return of colder blood from the extremities to the warmer central core.

Airway remodeling: Reorganization of airway tissues.

Anergia: Lack of energy or a reduced reaction to antigens.

Aphonia: Losing the voice, or inability to speak.

Atopy: Genetically predisposed or hypersensitive to common environmental antigens.

Aura: A sensation or feeling that a seizure is going to begin.

Autograft: A tissue graft taken from the body and placed somewhere else on the same body.

Autonomic: Self-controlling or independent.

Barotrauma: Injury to an enclosed area, such as the lungs, that was caused by pressure.

Biosynthetic-collagen dressings: A dressing created from a chemical compound of collagen.

Bronchiolitis obliterans: Bronchial inflammation and growth of connective tissue that results in occlusion, often caused from viral infections in children under two years old.

Brudzinski sign: Flexion of the neck causes flexion of the hip and knee.

Buccal: Toward the cheek or pertaining to the cheek.

Cachexia: Very poor health and malnutrition.

Chadwick's sign: A dark blue or purplish-red discoloration and congestion of the vaginal mucosa. A sign of pregnancy.

Clonic: Pertaining to clonus.

Clonus: Rapid muscle contraction and relaxation. A continuous rhythmic tremor.

Comminuted: Crushed into small pieces.

Cylindrical bronchiectasia: Chronic bronchial dilation involving whole sections of the bronchi.

Decerebrate posturing: Muscular rigidity with extension of all four limbs. This occurs following brain injury usually in response to external stimuli.

Diving reflex: Bradycardia and slowing of systems in aquatic mammals during submersion.

Dyspnea: Difficulty breathing or shortness of breath.

Epididymitis: Swelling or inflammation of the epididymis.

Epiphyseal: Pertaining to the epiphysis.

Epiphysis: The end of a long bone, which is developed from a secondary ossification center. During growth it is separated from the shaft by the epiphyseal cartilage.

Eschar: Necrotic tissue that sloughs off of a burn wound.

Focal: Pertaining to a focus.

Focal seizure: A seizure that originates from one area of the brain and is manifest by movement of one area of the body.

Free radicals: An atom that carries an unpaired electron.

Fulminant: A sudden and severe occurrence.

Generalized seizure: A seizure that involves all body parts.

Goodell's sign: A softened cervix, a sign of pregnancy.

Human cadaver allografts: A tissue graft from a deceased person.

Hypercapnia: Too much carbon dioxide in the blood. Also known as hypercarbia.

Hypercarbia: An elevated amount of carbon dioxide in the blood.

Hyperpnea: Abnormal increase in the rate and depth of respirations.

Idiopathic: No known cause or occurred spontaneously.

Intraosseous infusion: The infusion of fluids into bone marrow.

Kernig's sign: A symptom of meningitis. Patients can not completely extend their leg while in a sitting position.

Laminar flow room: A room with a highly filtered air flow that greatly reduces the entry of airborne bacteria.

Lividity: The discoloration of dependent body parts from increased blood flow to the parts.

Lymphadenitis: Inflammation of lymph nodes.

Macerate: To soften by getting soaking wet.

Metaphyseal: Pertaining to metaphysis.

Metaphysis: The wide end of a long bone, connected to the epiphyseal disk.

Molar pregnancy: A nonviable intrauterine tumor growth, which is usually benign.

Morbidity: A diseased condition. The prevalence of disease in a population.

Mortality: The mortality rate means the death rate.

Multifocal: Arising from many different foci.

Myoclonic: Relating to myoclonus.

Myoclonus: Shocklike contractions of one or more muscles. May affect one or more areas of the body at one time.

Obtunded: A decreased level of alertness.

Occiput: The base of the skull.

Oliguria: Reduced urinary output, usually less than 400 mL/24 hours.

Organic: Substances that are derived from living organisms. Chemical substances containing carbon atoms.

Pediculosis: Infestation of Lice (*Pediculus humanus*). *P. capitis,* infestation of lice on the head.

Porcine xenografts: A graft that is transplanted from pig skin.

Postictal state: The condition of a patient following the end of a seizure. Typically experienced as exhaustion or sleep.

Postmortem lividity: The discoloration of dependent parts caused by the accumulation of blood that occurs after death.

Proctitis: Rectal inflammation.

Pyuria: Pus in the urine.

Rales: Crackling breath sounds that indicates the presence of fluid in the lungs.

Rhonchi: Course breath sounds.

Russell's sign: Calluses or sores over knuckles.

Sequelae: The residual effects of a disease, injury or illness.

Spirometry: A method of measuring lung capacity.

Steeple sign: A radiographic finding of the nasopharynx that indicates a swollen epiglottis.

Stridor: A high pitched sound that occurs during inspiration when there is a partially obstructed airway.

Subglottic edema: Edematous swelling below the epiglottis.

Teratogenic: Producing congenital anomalies.

Teratogenic effects: Adverse fetal effects that occur inutero.

Tinnitus: Ringing in the ears, may also be described as clicking, buzzing or roaring.

Todd's paresis: A condition of hemiplegia or monoplegia that lasts for a few minutes, hours or days, after epileptic attack.

Tonic: Increased tone or rigidity

Tracheal stenosis: Abnormal narrowing of the trachea.

Trigger: An allergen that elicits an allergic response.

BIBLIOGRAPHY

Abott, M., Hoffinger, S., Nguyen, D. & Weintraub, D. (2001). Scooter injuries: A new pediatric morbidity. *Pediatrics, 108.* [Available online: http://www.pediatrics.org/cgi/content/full/108/1/e2.] Accessed July 1, 2001.

Agran, P., Winn, D., Anderson, C., Trent, R. & Walton-Haynes, L., (2001). Rates of pediatric and adolescent injuries by year of age. *Pediatrics.* [Available online: http://www.pediatrics.org/cgi/content/full/108/3/e45.] Accessed September 3, 2001.

American Academy of Child and Adolescent Psychiatry (AACAP). (2001). Practice parameter for the assessment and treatment of children and adolescents with suicidal behavior. *Journal of the American Academy of Child and Adolescent Psychiatry, 40*(7). [Available online: http://mdconsult.com/das/article/bod...&sp=119 117273&sid=67971830/N/233294/1.htm1.] Accessed November 3, 2001.

American Academy of Pediatrics (AAP). (2000). Palliative care for children. *American Academy of Pediatrics, 106.* [Available online: http://home.mdconsult.com/das/article/bod...&sp=11461135&sid=73060292/N/184162/1.html]. Accessed December 3, 2001.

American Academy of Pediatrics (AAP) & American Heart Association (AHA). (2001). *Pediatric advanced life support.* American Heart Association, 8-1/8-8.

American Academy of Pediatrics (AAP) & American Pain Society Task Force on Pain in Infants, Children, and Adolescents (APSTFPICA), (2001). The assessment and management of acute pain in infants, children and adolescents. *Pediatrics, 108*(3), 793–797.

American Academy of Pediatrics (AAP) Committee on Community Health Services. (1999). The pediatrician's role in community pediatrics. *Pediatrics, 103*(6), 1304–1305.

Anda, R., Felitti, V., Chapman, D., Croft, J., Williamson, D., Santelli, J., Dietz, P. & Marks, J. (2001). Abused boys, battered mothers, and male involvement in teen pregnancy. *Pediatrics, 107.* [Available online: http://www.pediatrics.org/cgi/content/full/107/2/e19.] Accessed February 2, 2001.

Aquilino, M. & Bragadottir, H. (2000). Adolescent pregnancy: Teen perspectives on prevention. *American Journal of Maternal Child Nursing, 25,* 192–197.

Barkin, S., & Gelberg, L. (1999). Sink or swim—Clinicians don't often counsel on drowning prevention. *Pediatrics, 104,* 1217–1219. [Available online: http://home.medconsult.com/das/citation/bo...p=11123621&sid=53558213/N/11123 621/ /1.htm.] Accessed August 12, 2001.

Behrman, R. (2000). *Nelsons textbook of pediatrics* (16th ed.). [Available online: http://home.medconsult.com/das/book/body/18153049/view/873.] Accessed September 18, 2001.

Behrman, R. (2000). Directions for preventive pediatrics, in *Nelsons Textbook of Pediatrics,* (16th ed.). [Available online: http://home.med-consult.com/das/book/body/0/873/42.html.] Accessed December 3, 2001.

Bernardo, L., Henker, R. & O'Connor, J. (2000). Treatment of trauma-associated hypothermia in children: Evidence-based practice. *American Journal of Critical Care, 9*(4), 227–236.

Bethea, L. (1999). Primary prevention of child abuse. *American Family Physician, 59*(6). [Available online: http://home.medconsult.com/das/artricle/bod...&sp=10686679&sid=50639722/N/214060/1.html.] Accessed July 25, 2001.

Cameron, M., Sponseller, P. & Rossberg, M. (2000). Pediatric analgesia and sedation for the management of orthopedic conditions. *The American Journal of Orthopedics,* September, 665–672.

Camfield, P. & Camfield, C. (2000). *Advances in the diagnosis and management of pediatric seizure disorders in the twentieth century, 136*(6). [Available online: http://home.mdconsult.com/das/article/bod...&sp=11403811&sid=62176971/N/178518/1.html.] Accessed October 2, 2001.

Cardello, L., Ray, E. & Pettey, G. (1995). The relationship of perceived physician communicator style to patient satisfaction. *Communication Reports, 8,* 27–37.

Carpenter, S., Clyman, R., Davidson, A. & Steiner, J. (2001). The association of foster care or kinship care with adolescent sexual behavior and first pregnancy. *Pediatrics, 108.* [Available online: http://www.pediatrics.org/cgi/content/full/108/3/e46.] Accessed September 3, 2001.

Causey, A., Tilelli, J. & Swanson, M. (2000). Predicting discharge in uncomplicated near-drowning. *American Journal of Emergency Medicine, 18,* 9–11. [Available online: http://home.medconsult.com/das/article/bod...&sp=11187136&sid=53539743/N/166650/1.htm.] Accessed August 12, 2001.

Center For Disease Control (CDC). (2001). *Bacterial sexually transmitted diseases (STDs).* [Available online: http://www.cdc.gov/ncidod/dastlr/gcdir/Index.html.] Accessed November 13, 2001.

Chameides, L. & Hazinski, M. (1997–1999). *Pediatric advanced life support by the American Heart Association.* Recognition of respiratory failure and shock. (p.2.8). Emergency Cardiovascular Care Programs.

Christian, C., Taylor, A., Hertle, R. & Duhaime, A. (1999). Retinal hemorrhages caused by accidental household trauma. *Journal of Pediatrics, 135* (1). [Available online: http://home.mdconsult.com/das/article/bod...&sp=10799399&sid=50639722/N/147315/1.html.] Accessed July 25, 2001.

Committee on Child Abuse and Neglect & Committee on Children with Disabilities. (2001). Assessment of maltreatment of children with disabilities. *Pediatrics, 108*(2), 508–512.

Committee on Psychosocial Aspects of Child and Family Health & Committee on Adolescence. (2001). Sexuality education for children and adolescents. *Pediatrics, 108,* 498–502.

Curley, M. & Moloney-Harmon, P. (2001). *Critical care nursing of infants and children* (2nd ed.) (pp. 41–45, 722–723). Philadelphia: W.B. Saunders.

Davis, A. (2001). Adolescent contraception and the clinician: An emphasis on counseling and communication. *Clinical Obstetrics and Gynecology, 44*(1), 114–121.

Deitch, E. & Rutan, R. (2000). The challenges of children: The first 48 hours. *Journal of Burn Care and Rehabilitation, 21,* 423–431.

DiIorio, C., Resnicow, K., Dudley, W., Thomas, S., Wang, D. & Van Marter, D. (2000). Social cognitive factors associated with mother-adolescent communication about sex. *Journal of Health Communication, 5,* 41–51.

Doniger, A., Adams, S., Utter, C. & Riley, H. (2001). Impact evaluation of the "Not me, not now" abstinence-oriented, adolescent pregnancy prevention communications program, Monroe County, New York. *Journal of Health Communication, 6,* 45–60.

Dorland's Illustrated Medical Dictionary, 29th ed. (2000). Philadelphia: W.B. Saunders Company.

Duffner, P. & Baumann, R. (1999). A synopsis of the American Academy of Pediatrics' practice parameters on the evaluation and treatment of children with febrile seizures. *Pediatrics in Review, 20*(8). [Available online: http://home.mdconsult.com/das/article/bod...&sp=10880231&sid=62176971/N/148531/1html.] Accessed October 2, 2001.

Ehde D., Patterson D., Wiechman, S. & Wilson L. (2000). Post-traumatic stress symptoms and distress one year after burn injury. *Journal of Burn Care and Rehabilitation, 21,* 105–111.

First Contraceptive Patch Approved by FDA. [Available online: http://home.mdconsult.com/das/stat/view/15313993/drug?nid=66488&sid=75418772.] Accessed November 21, 2001.

Franck, L., Greenberg, C. & Stevens, B. (2000). Pain assessment in infants and children. *Pediatric Clinics of North America, 47.* [Available online: http://mdconsult.com/das/article/bod...&sp=11302391&sid=67971830/N/175965/1.html.] Accessed November 3, 2001.

Grobler, S., Myburgh, C. & Poggenpoel, M. (1999). Adolescent interpersonal communications patterns [Abstract]. *Curatinois, 22,* 35–40.

Hacker, K., Yared, A., Strunk, N. & Horst, L. (2000). Listening to youth: Teen perspectives on pregnancy prevention. *Journal of Adolescent Health, 26,* 279–288.

Haddad, A. (2000). Ethics in action. *RN, 63(11),* 21–23.

Hart, D. (2001). *Personal communications,* December 11, 2001.

Hopkins, J. (2000). *Harriet Lane handbook* (15th ed.). [Available online: http://home.medconsult.com/dad/book/body/0/871/29.html.] Accessed July 24, 2001.

Jackman, G., Farah, M., Kellermann, A. & Simon, H. (2001). Seeing is believing: What do boys do when they find a real gun? *Pediatrics, 107*(6). [Available online: http://home.medconsult.com/das/article/bod...&sp=11856592&sid=50353734/N/225621/1.html.] Accessed July 24, 2001.

Jain, A. (1999). Emergency department evaluation of child abuse. *Emergency Medicine Clinics of North America, 17*(3). [Available online: http://home.medconsult.com/das/article/bod...&sp=10923095&sid=50639722/N/151490/1.html.] Accessed July 25, 2001.

Kairys, S., & Committee on Child Abuse and Neglect & American Academy of Pediatrics. (2001). Distinguishing sudden infant death syndrome from child abuse fatalities. *Pediatrics, 107*(2). [Available online: http://home.mdconsult.com/das/article/bod...&sp=11544529&sid=50639722/N/209398/1.html]. Accessed July 25, 2001.

Kemp, J. & Kemp, J. (2001). Management of asthma in children. *American Family Physician, 63.* [Available online: http://home.mdconsult.com/das/article/bod...&sp=11570014&sid58198870/N/217318/1.html.] Accessed September 8, 2001.

Kirby, D. (1999). Reflections on two decades of research on teen sexual behavior and pregnancy. *Journal of School Health, 69,* 80–94.

Klassen, T. (1999). Croup a current perspective. *Pediatric Clinics of North America, 46,* 1167–1178. [Available online: http://home.mdconsult.com/das/article.] Accessed September 5, 2001.

Knudsen F. (2000). Progress in epilepsy research febrile seizures: Treatment and prognosis. *Epilepsia 41*(1), 2–9.

Kreipe, R. & Birndorf, S. (2000). Eating disorders in adolescents and young adults. *Medical Clinics of North America, 84*(4). [Available online: http://home.mdconsult.com/das/article/bod...&sp=11371428&sid=67971830/N/181512/1.html.] Accessed November 3, 2001.

Larsen, G. (2000). Differences between adult and childhood asthma. *Journal of Allergy and Clinical Immunology, 106.* [Available online: http://home.mdconsult.com/das/article/bod...&sp=11566714&sid=58198870/N/188188/1.html.] Accessed September 8, 2001.

Lindberg, L., Sonenstein, F., Ku, L. & Levine, G. (1997). Young men's experience with condom breakage. *Family Planning Perspectives, 29,* 128–131 & 140.

Lizana, J., Garcia, E., Marina, L., Lopez, M., Gonzalez, M. & Hoyos, A. (2000). Seizure recurrence after a first unprovoked seizure in childhood: A prospective study. *Epilepsia, 41*(8), 1005–1013.

Malhotra, A. & Krilov L. (2001). *Viral Croup. Pediatrics in Review, 22.* [Available online: http://hone.mdconsult.com/das/article.] Accessed September 5, 2001.

Martinez, F. (1999). Meeting needs of infants and young children with asthma: New developments in nebulized corticosteroid therapy. *Journal of Allergy and Clinical Immunology, 104.* [Available online: http://home.mdconsult.com/das/article/bod...&sp=11079899&sid=58198870/N/154236/1.html.] Accessed September 20, 2001.

Maytal, J., Krauss, J., Novak, G., Nagelberg, J. & Patel, M. (2000). The role of brain computed tomography in evaluating children with new onset of seizures in the emergency department. *Epilepsia, 41*(8), 950–954.

Maytal J., Steele R., Eviatar, L. & Novak, G. (2000). The value of early postictal EEG in children with complex febrile seizures. *Epilepsia, 4*(2), 219–221.

McAbee, G. & Wark, J. (2000). A practical approach to uncomplicated seizures in children. *American Family Physician, 62*(5). [Available online: http://home.mdconsult.com/das/article/bod...&sp=11498968&sid=62176971/N/216818/1.html.] Accessed October 2, 2001.

McQuaid, D., Barton, J. & Campbell, A. (2000). Body image issues for children and adolescents with burns. *Journal of Burn Care and Rehabilitation, 21,* 194–198.

Meckstroth, K. & Darney, P. (2000). Implantable contraception. *Obstetrics and Gynecology Clinics, 27*(4). [Available online: http://home.mdconsult.com/das/article/bod...&sp=11532116&sid=67971830/N/196568/1.html.] Accessed November 3, 2001.

Meyers-Paal, R., Blakeney, P., Robert, R., Murphy L., Chinkes, D., Meyer, W., Desai, M. & Herdndon, D. (2000). Physical and psychologic rehabilitation outcome for pediatric patients who suffer 80% or more TBSA, 70% or more third degree burns. *Journal of Burn Care and Rehabilitation, 21,* 43–49.

Miller, K. & Whitaker, D. (2001). Predictors of mother-adolescent discussions about condoms: Implications for providers who serve youth. *Pediatrics, 108,* e28. [Available online: http://www.pediatrics.org/cgi/content/full/108/2/e28.] Accessed August 2, 2001.

Moolchan, E., Ernst, M. & Henningfield, J. (2000). A review of tobacco smoking in adolescents: Treatment implications. *Journal of the American Academy of Child and Adolescent Psychiatry, 39*(6). [Available online: http://mdconsult.com/das/article/bod...&sp=11 376609&sid=67971830/N/221738/1.html.] Accessed November 3, 2001.

Naspitz, C. & Tinkelman, D. (2001). Barriers to measuring and achieving optimal outcomes in pediatric asthma. *Journal of Allergy and Clinical Immunology, 107.* [Available online: http://home.mdconsult.com/das/article/bod...&s p=11877681&sid=58198530/N/219326/1.html.] Accessed September 8, 2001.

Orlowski, J. & Szpilman, D. (2001). Drowning: Rescue, resuscitation and reanimation. *Pediatric Clinics of North America, 48.* [Available online: http://home.medconsult.com/das/article/bud...&s p=11856796&sid=53558213/N/225372/1.htm.] Accessed August 12, 2001.

Ortho-McNeil. (2001). *The first birth control pathch receives FDA approval.* [Available online: http://www.ortho-mcneil.com/news/archive/pr/news_evra.htm.] Accessed December 17, 2001.

Panzarine, S. (2000). Sex, drugs, and rock 'n' roll: Experimenting and taking risks. In S. Panzarine (Ed.), *A parent's guide to the teen years: Raising your 11 to 14-year-old in the age of chat rooms and navel rings* (pp. 87–120). New York: Facts on File, Inc.

Poirier, M. & Wadsworth, M. (2000). Sports-related concussions. *Pediatric Emergency Care, 16*(4), 278–283.

Polaneczky, M. & O'Conner, K. (1999). Pregnancy in the adolescent patient. *Pediatric Clinics of North America, 46.* [Available online: http://home.mdconsult.com/das/article/bod...&s p=10872211&sid=67971830/N/148583/1.html.] Accessed November 3, 2001.

Ponitz, K., Mortimer, J. & Berman, B. (2000). Establishing a pediatric hopitalist program at an academic medical center. *Clinical Pediatrics,* April, 221–227.

Proctor, M. & Cantu, R. (2000). Head and neck injuries in young athletes. *Clinics in Sports Medicine, 19*(4). [Available online: http://home.mdconsult.com/das/article/bod...&s p=11491717&sid=67971830/N/188807/1.html.] Accessed November 3, 2001.

Puopolo, A. (1999). Gaining confidence to talk about end-of-life care. *Nursing99,* July, 49–51.

Quan, L. (1999). Near-drowning *Pediatrics in Review, 20,* 255–259. [Available online: http://home.medconsult.com/das/article/bod...&s p=10880221&sid=53539743/N/148523/1.htm.] Accessed August 12, 2001.

Rivara, F. (1999). Pediatric injury control in 1999: Where do we go from here? *Pediatrics, 103*(4). [Available online: http://home.mdconsult.com/das/article/bod...&sp=10684197&sid=6797183 0/N/141364/1.html.] Accessed November 3, 2001.

Roback, M. (2000). America's tragedy: Pediatric trauma. *Emergency Medical Services, 29*(4), 61–5.

Robinson, J. & Stivers, T. (2001). Achieving activity transitions in physician-patient encounters from history taking to physical examination. *Human Communication Research, 27,* 253–298.

Rogers, M. (1992). *Textbook of pediatric intensive care.* Baltimore: Lippincott Williams & Wilkins.

Sachdeva, R. (1999). Near Drowning. *Critical Care Clinics, 15,* 281–296. [Available online: http://home.medconsult.com/das/article/bod...&sp=10717808&sid=53539743/N/143476/1.htm.] Accessed August 12, 2001.

Sahler, O., Frager, G., Levetown, M., Cohn, F. & Lipson, M. (2000). Medical education about end-of-life care in the pediatric setting: Principles, challenges, and opportunities. *Pediatrics, 105.* [Available online: http://home.medconsult.com/das/article/bod...&sp=1254188&sid=73060292/N/174292/1.html]. Accessed December, 3, 2001.

Sapir, D., Yael, L., Harel, S. & Kramer, U. (2000). Unprovoked seizure after complex febrile convulsions. *Brain and Development, 22,* 484–486.

Scott, C. (1999). Juvenile violence. *Psychiatric Clinics of North America, 22*(1). [Available online: http://home.mdconsult.com/das/article/bod...&sp=10583530&sid=67971830/N/137780/1.html.] Accessed November 3, 2001.

Sheth, R., Hobb,s G. & Mullett, M. (1999). Neonatal seizures: Incidence, onset and etiology by gestational age. *Journal of Perinatology, 19*(1), 40–43.

Slugg-Moore, A. (1999). Emergency contraceptive options. *RN, 62*(12), 43–45.

Smith, S. & Strunk, R. (1999). Acute asthma in the pediatric emergency department. *Pediatric Clinics of North America, 46,* 1145–1165. [Available online: http://home.mdconsult.com/das/article/bod...&sp=11158354&sid=58198870/N/158861/1.html.] Accessed September 8, 2001.

Son, S. & Kirchner, J. (2000). Depression in children and adolescents. *American Family Physician, 62*(10). [Available online: http://home.mdconsult.com/das/article/bod...&sp=11551847&sid=67971830/N/11551847/1.html.] Accessed November 3, 2001.

Spratto, G. & Woods, A. (2002). *PDR, Nurse's Drug Handbook.* Montvale, NJ: Medical Economics Company.

Stafford, S. (2001). *Personal communication.* December 9, 2001.

Steger, S. (2000). Killed in school. *RN, 63*(4), 37–38.

Strasburger, V. (2000). Getting teenagers to say no to sex, drugs, and violence in the new millennium. *Medical Clinics of North America, 84*(4). [Available online: http://home.mdconsult.com/das/article/bod...&sp=11371417&sid=62572545/N/181501/1.html.] Accessed October 4, 2001.

Sutherland, J. (2001). Craving to rave: The agony of ecstasy abuse. *Nurse Week, 1*(2), 10–11.

Szefler, S. (2000). The changing faces of asthma. *Journal of Allergy and Clinical Immunology, 106.* [Available online: http://home.mdconsult.com/das/article/bod...&sp=11566712&sid=58198870/N/188181/1.html.] Accessed September 8, 2001.

Szefler, S. (2001). Challenges in assessing out-comes for pediatric asthma. *Journal of Allergy and Clinical Immunology, 107.* [Available online: http://home.mdconsult.com/das/article/bod...&sp=11877678&sid=58198870/N/219323/1.html]. Accessed September 8, 2001.

Tasman. (1997). *Psychiatry* (1st ed.). [Available online: http://home.mdcosult.com/das/book/body/0/885/568.html.] Accessed September 20, 2001.

Tepas, J., Ramenofsky, M., Mollitt, D. et al. (1988). The pediatric trauma score as a predictor of injury severity: An objective assessment. *J Trauma, 28,* 427. [Available online: http://lww.com].

The Merck Manual. (2001a). Introduction. Chapter 255. [Available online: http://www.merck.com/pubs/mmanual/secton19/chapter255/255a.htm.] Accessed June 20, 2001.

The Merck Manual. (2001b). Injuries. [Available online: http://www.merk.com/pubs/mmanual/section19/chapter263/263a.htm.] Accessed June 20, 2001.

The Merck Manual. (2001c). Child abuse and neglect. [Available online: http://www.merck.com/pubs/mmanual/section19/chapter264/264a.htm.] Accessed June 20, 2001.

Trussell, J., Koenig, J., Ellertson, C. & Stewart, F. (1997). Preventing unintended pregnancy: The cost-effectiveness of three methods of emergency contraception. *American Journal of Public Health 1997,* 87(6):932–937.

U.S. Department of Justice: Drug Enforcement Administration. (2001). *Drug use in the United States.* [Available online: http://www.usdoj.gov/dea/concern/use.htm.] Accessed November 11, 2001.

Van Der Woude, C. (1999). Meeting Peter. *Nursing99, 29 (12),* 64.

Wallace, N. (2000). At home in my own bed. *Kalamazoo Medicine, 90(1),* 8–10.

Walsh, L. (1999). Hearing the need: Lessons from the bedside. *Nursing99,* April, 48–51.

Weibelhaus, P., Hansen, S. & Hill, H. (2001). Helping patients survive inhalation injuries. *RN, 64*(10).

Werner H. (2001). Status asthmaticus in children, a review. *The American College of Chest Physicians, 119.* [Available online: http://home.mdconsult.com/das/article/bod...&sp=11859322&sid=58198870/N/226998/1.html.] Accessed September 8, 2001.

Whaley, L. & Wong, D. (1999). *Nursing care of infants and children.* St. Louis: The Mosby Company.

Whitaker, D., Miller, K., May, D. & Levin, M. (1999). Teenage partners' communication about sexual risk and condom use: The importance of parent-teenager discussions. *Family Planning Perspectives, 31,* 117–121.

Wittenberg, E., Goldie, S. & Graham, J. (2001). Predictors of hazardous child seating behavior in fatal motor vehicle crashes: 1990 to 1998. *Pediatrics, 108*(2), 438–442.

Wong, D., Hockenberry-Eaton, M., Wilson, D., Winkelstein, M. & Schwartz, M. (2001). *Wong's essentials of pediatric nursing* (p. 1301). St. Louis: Mosby Inc.

INDEX

PRETEST KEY

Pediatric Nursing: Routine to Emergent Care

1.	d	Chapter 1
2.	b	Chapter 2
3.	a	Chapter 3
4.	b	Chapter 4
5.	a	Chapter 4
6.	c	Chapter 5
7.	c	Chapter 5
8.	d	Chapter 6
9.	d	Chapter 6
10.	b	Chapter 7
11.	d	Chapter 7
12.	a	Chapter 8
13.	d.	Chapter 8
14.	a	Chapter 9
15.	c	Chapter 9
16.	c	Chapter 10
17.	c	Chapter 11
18.	c	Chapter 12
19.	b	Chapter 13
20.	b	Chapter 13

Notes

Notes

Western Schools® offers over 1,000 hours to suit all your interests – and requirements!

Advance Level Courses

Nurse Anesthesia
— Common Diseases ....20 hrs
— Common Procedures ....21 hrs
— Drugs...17 hrs
Obstetric and Gynecologic Emergencies
— Obstetric ....22 hrs
— Gynecologic ....22 hrs
Practical Guide to Moderate Sedation/Analgesia...31 hrs
Geropsychiatric and Mental Health Nursing ....40 hrs
Palliative Practices: An Interdisciplinary Approach
— Issues Specific to Palliative Care ....20 hrs
— Specific Disease States and Symptom
    Management ....24 hrs
— The Dying Process, Grief, and Bereavement...22 hrs
Practice Guidelines for Pediatric Nurse Practitioners.46 hrs
The 12-Lead ECG in Acute Coronary Syndromes 42 hrs

Clinical Conditions/Nursing Practice

A Nurse's Guide to Weight Control
    for Healthy Living...25 hrs
Airway Management with a Tracheal Tube ....1 hr
Asthma: Nursing Care Across the Lifespan ....28 hrs
Auscultation Skills: Breath and Heart Sounds ......12 hrs
Cardiovascular Nursing: A Comprehensive
    Overview ....32 hrs
Care at the End of Life...3 hrs
Chest Tube Management ....2 hrs
Death, Dying & Bereavement ....30 hrs
Healing Nutrition ....24 hrs
Hepatitis C: The Silent Killer ....2 hrs
Holistic & Complementary Therapies ....18 hrs
Humor in Healthcare: The Laughter Prescription..20 hrs
Managing Obesity and Eating Disorders ....30 hrs
Orthopedic Nursing: Caring for Patients with
    Musculoskeletal Disorders ....30 hrs
Pain Management: Principles and Practice............30 hrs
Seizures: A Basic Overview ....1 hr
The Neurological Exam...1 hr
Wound Management and Healing...........................30 hrs

Critical Care/ER/OR

Ambulatory Surgical Care ....20 hrs
Case Studies in Critical Care Nursing: A Guide for
    Application and Review ....46 hrs
Principles of Basic Trauma Nursing (2nd ed.) ......30 hrs

Geriatrics

Alzheimer's Disease: A Complete Guide for Nurses ..25 hrs
Home Health Nursing ....30 hrs
Nursing Care of the Older Adult ....30 hrs
Psychosocial Issues Affecting Older Adults ....16 hrs

Infectious Diseases/Bioterrorism

Biological Weapons ....5 hrs
Bioterrorism & the Nurse's Response to WMD ......5 hrs
Bioterrorism Readiness: The Nurse's Critical Role .. 2 hrs
Infection Control Training for Healthcare Workers ..4 hrs
Influenza: A Vaccine-Preventable Disease ....1 hr
SARS: An Emerging Public Health Threat ....1 hr
Smallpox...2 hrs
West Nile Virus ....1 hr

Oncology

Cancer in Women..30 hrs
Cancer Nursing: A Solid Foundation for Practice ..30 hrs
Chemotherapy Essentials: Principles & Practice ..15 hrs

Pediatrics/Maternal-Child/Women's Health

Attention Deficit Hyperactivity Disorders
    Throughout the Lifespan..................................30 hrs
Diabetes in Children ....30 hrs
End-of-Life Care for Children and
    Their Families ....2 hrs
Manual of School Health ....30 hrs
Maternal-Newborn Nursing....................................30 hrs
Menopause: Nursing Care for Women
    Throughout Mid-Life ....25 hrs
Pediatric Nursing: Routine to Emergent Care........30 hrs
Pediatric Pharmacology ....10 hrs
Pediatric Physical Assessment...............................10 hrs
Women's Health: Contemporary
    Advances and Trends ....30 hrs

Professional Issues/Management/Law

Documentation for Nurses......................................24 hrs
Medical Error Prevention: Patient Safety ....2 hrs
Nursing and Malpractice Risks:
    Understanding the Law.....................................30 hrs
Ohio Law: Standards of Safe Nursing Practice ....1 hr
Supervisory Skills for Nurses ....30 hrs
Surviving and Thriving in Nursing ....30 hrs
Understanding Managed Care ....30 hrs

Psychiatric/Mental Health

Antidepressants ....1 hr
Antipsychotics ....1 hr
Anxiolytics and Mood Stabilizers............................1 hr
Basic Psychopharmacology......................................5 hrs
Depression: Prevention, Diagnosis, and Treatment...25 hrs
IPV (Intimate Partner Violence):
    A Domestic Violence Concern ....1 or 3 hrs
Psychiatric Principles & Applications for
    General Patient Care ....30 hrs
Psychiatric Nursing: Current Trends
    in Diagnosis and Treatment ....30 hrs
Substance Abuse ....30 hrs

Notes

Notes

Notes